THE *THIRD WAY* TRANSFORMATION
OF SOCIAL DEMOCRACY

For Sophie and Alissa

The *Third Way* Transformation of Social Democracy

Normative claims and policy initiatives in the 21st century

Edited by

OLIVER SCHMIDTKE
University of Victoria, Canada

ASHGATE

Published by
Ashgate Publishing Limited
Gower House
Croft Road
Aldershot
Hampshire GU11 3HR
England

Ashgate Publishing Company
Suite 420, 101 Cherry Street
Burlington, VT 05401-4405 USA

Ashgate website: http://www.ashgate.com

British Library Cataloguing in Publication Data
The third way transformation of social democracy :
  normative claims and policy initiatives in the 21st century
  1.Socialism - Europe 2.Europe - Social policy 3.Europe -
  Politics and government - 1989-
  I.Schmidtke, Oliver
  320.5'31'094

Library of Congress Cataloging-in-Publication Data
The third way transformation of social democracy : normative claims and policy initiatives in the 21st century / edited by Oliver Schmidtke.
     p. cm.
  Includes bibliographical references and index.
  ISBN 0-7546-3192-3
    1. Mixed economy--European Union countries. 2. European Union
countries--Economic conditions. 3. European Union countries--Economic policy. 4.
European Union countries--Politics and government. I. Schmidtke, Oliver.

  HC240 .T49 2002
  330.12'6--dc21   2002071691

ISBN 0 7546 3192 3

Printed and bound in Great Britain by MPG Books Ltd, Bodmin, Cornwall

Contents

List of Contributors

Vincent Della Sala received his doctorate at the University of Oxford and is currently an associate professor of political science at Carleton University. He specializes in comparative political economy in advanced industrialized states, European politics and the politics and government of the European Union. His articles on Italian politics, political economy and constitutionalism have appeared in journals such as *West European Politics* and *Journal of Common Market Studies*. Della Sala's current research focuses on the impact of greater economic interdependence on domestic state structures and the political economy of legalized gambling.

Stephen Driver received his B.A. from Sheffield and his M.A. and D.Phil. at Sussex. He teaches government and politics in the School of Sociology and Social Policy at the University of Surrey, Roehampton. He is currently the convenor for the Social Policy Degree Programme. He was previously lecturer in sociology at Sussex University. Apart from his work on New Labour, Driver has done research for the Economic and Social Research Council (ESRC) on the New Media in Britain and is presently working on a study of church support for families, funded by the Lord Chancellor's Department.

Michael Th. Greven received his doctoral degree at Bonn University and is currently a professor of political science at the University of Hamburg. His fields of expertise include modern political theory, theory of democracy, political sociology, and politics in Germany and the European Union. The present focus of Greven's research is on current problems and the future of democracy in 'political societies'. His most recent books are: *Die politische Gesellschaft* (1999); *Kontingenz und Dezision* (2000); and *Democracy Beyond the State* (ed. with Louis Pauly, 2000).

Peter A. Hall is Director of the Minda de Gunzburg Center for European Studies at Harvard University where he is also a Harvard College Professor and Frank G. Thomson Professor of Government. He holds a M.Phil. from Oxford University and M.A. and Ph.D. degrees from Harvard. He is the author of *Governing the Economy: The Politics of State Intervention in Britain and France* (1986), and has published over fifty articles in books and journals on European politics and policy making. He has edited or co-edited numerous books including *The Political Power of Economic Ideas: Keynesianism across Nations* (1989), *Developments in French*

Politics I (1990) and II (2001) and *Varieties of Capitalism: The Institutional Foundations of Comparative Advantage* (2001). Hall is currently working on a series of essays about the methodologies of political science that explores the processes of social and economic adjustment in Europe during the postwar era.

Thomas O. Hueglin is a professor of political science at Wilfrid Laurier University in Canada. His Ph.D. is from St. Gall University in Switzerland, and his Habilitation is from Konstanz University in Germany. His research focuses on the history of political thought, comparative federalism, globalization and the European Union. He is currently writing a book on comparative federal systems. Recent publications include *Early Modern Concepts for a Late Modern World* (1999) and 'From Constitutional to Treaty Federalism' (*Publius*, Fall 2000). 'Federalism at the Crossroads' is forthcoming in the *Canadian Journal of Political Science*. He also co-edited *Subsidiarität als rechtliches und politisches Ordungsprinzip in Kirche, Staat und Gesellschaft* (special issue 20 of *Rechtstheorie*, 2002). His home page can be visited at http://www.wlu.ca/~wwwpolsc/facpages/hueglin/index.htm.

Roger Keil received his Ph.D. in Political Science from the Johann Wolfgang Goethe-University, Frankfurt in 1992. He is an associate professor of Environmental Studies at York University, Toronto. His main research interests are in urban politics and governance and urban ecology in major internationalized cities. Much of his work has been empirically based on world city formation and urban governance restructuring in Frankfurt, Los Angeles and Toronto. Among his publications are *Los Angeles: Urbanization, Globalization and Social Struggles* (1998) and *Political Ecology* (ed. with D. Bell, P. Penz and L. Fawcett, 1998). He is currently completing a book on urban environmental policy making in Los Angeles and Toronto (with G. Desfor). Keil is a member of the International Network of Urban Research and Action (INURA). His website can be found at www.yorku.ca/keil.

Warren Magnusson is professor and chair of the Department of Political Science at the University of Victoria, Canada. A specialist in the political theory of local government and urban politics, he received his doctorate from Oxford in 1978. Among his publications are *The Search for Political Space: Globalization, Social Movements and the Urban Political Experience* (1996), and *A Political Space: Reading the Global through Clayoquot Sound* (with Karena Shaw, forthcoming).

Luke Martell is senior lecturer at the University of Sussex. He holds a Ph.D. from Birkbeck College, University of London. His main research interest is in the field of comparative party politics in Europe with a particular emphasis on New Labour, the Third Way and Social Democracy. Martell is author of *Ecology and Society* (1994), co-author of *New Labour: Politics after Thatcherism* (1998) and of *Blair's Britain: State, Social Democracy and Globalisation* (2002). He co-edited *The Sociology of Politics* (1998), *Social Democracy: Global and National Perspectives*

(2001) and *The Third Way and Beyond: criticisms, futures, alternatives* (forthcoming). He has published numerous articles on socialism, neoliberalism, New Labour and social movements.

Saskia Sassen is the Ralph Lewis Professor of Sociology at the University of Chicago, and Centennial Visiting Professor at the London School of Economics. Her forthcoming book is *Denationalization: Economy and Polity in a Global Digital Age* (Princeton University Press 2003) based on her five-year project on governance and accountability in a global economy. Her most recent books are *Guests and Aliens* (1999) and her edited volume *Global Networks/Linked Cities* (2002). *The Global City* is out in a new fully updated edition in 2001. Her books have been translated into twelve languages.

Oliver Schmidtke received a Ph.D. in Social and Political Science from the European University Institute in Florence. Currently he is an associate professor, a DAAD German Studies Lecturer, and acting director of the European Studies Program at the University of Victoria, Canada. Among his recent publications are *Politics of Identity. Ethnicity, Territory and the Political Opportunity Structure in Modern Italian Society* (1996), *Klasse und Klassifikation. Die symbolische Dimension sozialer Ungleichheit* (co-edited, 2001), and *Collective Identities in Action. A Sociological Approach to Ethnicity* (co-authored, 2002). Schmidtke's research interests lie in the field of comparative European politics, EU integration, and the political sociology of immigration and ethnic conflict.

Serenella Sferza is a political scientist whose primary interests are in long-term processes of political change, with particular emphasis on party formation and renewal. Her ongoing research focuses on the historical evolution of cleavage structures and party types. Her most recent publications are: 'Party Organization and Party Performance: The Case of the French Socialist Party', in R. Gunther, J. Linz, and R. Montero, eds, *The Future of Parties* (2002), 'What is Left of the Left? More Than One Would Think', *Daedalus*, Summer 1999. Sferza is coordinator of the MIT-Italy programme and visiting assistant professor at the MIT Political Science Department.

Frank Unger received his doctoral degree from the Free University of Berlin, and is a professor in political science at the Institute for European Studies, University of British Columbia, Canada. His areas of expertise comprise international political economy, comparative political cultures, and contemporary European history. Unger's current research project focuses on a political-economic and cultural history of the seventies as the 'crucial decade' for the understanding of the changes in the international economy that took place in Europe and North America more recently. Among his recent publications are *New Democrats—New Labour—Neue Sozialdemokraten* (co-edited, 1998) and *Reflections on Some Nations and Their Myths* (co-edited with S. Godfrey, forthcoming).

Acknowledgements

The idea for this book goes back to a conference on Third Way politics organized in the context of the European Studies Program at the University of Victoria in Canada. Geographically far removed from the main protagonists in Europe who are at the centre of interest of this book, the West Coast of Canada provided an ideal location for a passionate scholarly debate on the transformation of the social democratic left. The two days of intense discussion gave evidence of how profoundly the Third Way transformation of social democracy has changed our established way of thinking about the left-right distinction in (party-)politics and the challenges the moderate left has to face.

A book is mostly the result of a long process to which many contribute in substantive ways. I am particularly grateful for the generous financial support that I received from the German Academic Exchange Service (DAAD). Without DAAD's commitment neither the conference nor the book would have been possible. I would also like to express my appreciation to the University of Victoria for supporting the conference and providing a fruitful academic environment for establishing the field of European Studies.

With respect to editing the book I am deeply indebted to Lloy Wylie and my wife Beate whose extremely competent and diligent assistance was of invaluable help to me. I am also thankful for the patience of our daughter Alissa who was born two days after the completion of the manuscript. This book is dedicated to our daughters Sophie and Alissa.

Oliver Schmidtke

INTRODUCTION

Introduction

Transforming the Social Democratic Left: the Challenges to Third Way Politics in the Age of Globalization

Oliver Schmidtke

Party politics in Western Europe is normally characterized by a surprising degree of continuity and stability. In the second half of the twentieth century the power of some major political parties has remained essentially unchallenged by new political actors and a remarkably low degree of voter volatility. In general, two parties or blocs whose opposing political identity has been defined by the left-right divide have dominated the party system. In postwar European politics the moderate left and right challenged each other on a set of core political ideas and value orientations that were rooted in a particular model on how to define a desirable balance between the economy, civil society and the role of the state. Yet, this fundamental logic according to which citizens' political preferences are formed and political issues framed in public debate might gradually lose its decisive grip. Sometimes far-reaching systemic political change does not come in the form of entirely new actors or revolutionary transformations but through gradual, albeit persistent modification of some of its constituent elements. The development of traditional social democratic parties into what has become known as New Labour or the *Neue Mitte* (new centre) can indeed be interpreted as a highly significant transformation of established ideological positions and political cleavages. The notion of Third Way politics with its claim to overcome the binary logic of postwar West European politics marks a threshold in the reformulation of political identities and party competition.

In this respect the astonishing victories of the recreated Labour Party in Great Britain, the French Socialist Party under Lionel Jospin in France, the reformed Communist Italian left led by Massimo D'Alema and the red-green coalition under Gerhard Schröder in Germany (just to name the most prominent examples of the late 1990s) point to more than the unanticipated revival of ideas – which in the 1980s were portrayed as hopelessly outdated and out of touch with the economic necessities of the time. The fact that the vast majority of the EU member states' governments are now led by some sort of moderate, social democratic left – reversing the neoliberal hegemony of the 1980s – goes beyond simply confirming the continued vitality of this political actor. Concepts such as the 'Third Way', 'politics of the centre' or a political approach 'beyond left and right' as omnipresent features in public discourse indicate a qualitatively new step in the political development of social democratic parties in Western politics. Third Way political parties have adopted political positions that were traditionally thought to be incompatible with a genuine social democratic approach to politics. 'Modernized' social democracy has drastically redefined the centre-left's understanding of the equilibrium between state intervention in the economy and the commitment to deregulated market forces. In their Third Way manifesto Blair and Schröder describe their political project as an innovative attempt to reconcile the requirements of a modern and successful capitalist economy on the one hand with the goal of securing social cohesion through a commitment to social justice on the other hand. Combining strong trust in the dynamics of a free market economy with the belief in providing the basis for a new form of communal identity marks a radically revised stand of the moderate left in European politics.

At first sight, the revival of the social democratic left as the dominant force in European politics and its transformation into New Labour or the Third Way approach, supposedly beyond left and right, seems paradoxical. On the one hand, this transformation has been characterized by astonishing electoral victories, challenging the neoliberal hegemony of the 1980s and early 1990s. Reformed social democracy has been successful in developing a new political strategy designed to widen its political constituency beyond traditional class allegiances. However, at the same time the moderate left in Europe and North America is struggling desperately for a new political identity after discrediting much of what social democratic or socialist positions traditionally stood for. We have been witnessing a radical revision of the very nature of social democratic politics, superseding its traditional political identity and essentially forming a new force in party politics. There is a set of policy initiatives and programmatic declarations that hint at an emerging core idea of Third Way social democracy. Yet, the considerable variance across Europe and the alleged lack of clear principles for key policy areas have triggered a debate on the nature of Third Way politics. Unfortunately, this discussion often simply reproduces the ideological self-perception of political actors. Instead of engaging in a political debate on the normative desirability of the Third Way, the primary aim of this book is to direct attention at the structural changes that led to the transformation of 'Old Labour' and define the political opportunities and constraints for Third Way parties.

The focal point of this volume is to investigate more cautiously the social and political environment in which Third Way social democracy has been formed and how its basic political claims translate into policy initiatives. In order to evaluate whether there is indeed a new and coherent social democratic approach for the 21st century, identifiable by a set of consistent programmatic goals and policy initiatives, this introduction first provides a historic contextualization of the current transformation of social democracy. This is followed by a brief account of how Third Way politics claims to differ from old style social democracy. In a third step, attention is paid to the underlying structural social and political changes that have helped to trigger this transformation of the moderate left. Lastly, the contributions that follow address the critical dilemmas faced by governments under the guidance of modernized social democracy.

The Cyclic Transformation of Social Democracy

The transformation of social democracy is everything but a new phenomenon in the 20th century. Looking back at the ongoing dramatic history of the left in European politics, this political actor has reinvented itself under the pressure of changing political and social realities several times (Berger, 2000; Ross, 1982; Sassoon, 1996). The crucial question around which the course of modern social democracy was formed concerns its relationship to a capitalist economy and parliamentary democracy. For the political identity of modern social democracy, a decisive step in this respect has been the gradual and often painful departure from a Marxist, class-based approach, accepting the fundamental realities of a capitalist economy. In its early stage social democratic parties were deeply divided as to whether the basic institutions of bourgeois society offer an appropriate environment for the emancipation of the working classes, whose interests this political force claimed to represent. The power structures in the economic sphere were seen as a genuine threat to formal political democracy. Nonetheless, the moderate left in European politics has continuously been engaged in reformulating, or more appropriately, distancing itself from the revolutionary spirit of Marxist thinking that inspired much of the early working class movement. In the first part of the century this reconciliation with the reality of a capitalist economy and parliamentary democracy often led to a division into a reformist and revolutionary Communist left, a split that in its most radical forms found its manifestation in violent clashes between the opposing factions (Schorske, 1983).

After the Second World War, in light of the evolving polar world of the Cold War and the astonishing success of economic recovery in the West, moderate leftist forces moved towards a definite reconciliation with a free market economy and the principle of private ownership of the means of production (Paterson, 1974). The vision of a more humane and just society was now conceived of as being realizable within the framework of a capitalist economy, even though a high degree of macro-economic planning and ideas of nationalizing key sectors of the economy were still quite prominent in the immediate postwar era. The 1959 *Bad Godesberg* Programme of the German social democrats clearly marked a threshold in the development of a new form of social democracy, increasingly skeptical about the chances of transforming capitalism in a revolutionary or structural sense (Braunthal, 1983). Shedding its traditional affiliation with the Marxist tradition, reformed social democracy sought to use the enormous productivity generated by the market economy for building 'capitalism with a human face'. In light of the flexibility and dynamism of capitalism, the notion of a revolutionary change and socialism became an obsolete, albeit often romanticized, concept for the social democratic left. A new form of compromise between the operation of the market on the one hand and a redistribution of resources and rights towards those less favoured by it became the guiding principle for social democrats in dealing with the 'economic question'.

During the second half of the 20th century social democratic politics has at times been characterized by an adversarial struggle searching for a balance between its central normative goal of the emancipation of the working class and the continuously changing social structural realities of a highly dynamic capitalist world (Przeworski, 1980). Given the political climate and economic prosperity of the first decades after the War, the moderate left in West European politics felt that it had found a sustainable path towards organizing the economy in accordance with the needs of its constituency. The Golden Age of social democracy seemed to promise a 'Third Way' between Communism and Capitalism, built on Keynesian-style market interventionism, the extension of citizenship rights (Levitas, 1999) and a welfare state with, at least in Northern Europe, a high degree of de-commodifying social relations (Milner, 1990). It was the genuine claim of social democratic regimes after the War that under their rule capitalist economies would be less crisis-ridden, produce higher productivity and generate a more socially balanced outcome for all classes (Esping-Andersen, 1985; Hicks, 1999). Demand-oriented state intervention and an elaborated social system seemed to provide the magic formula for overcoming the flaws of capitalism and making its dynamic an integral part of the goal to construct a more equal, just and democratic society. In this respect social democracy at the time seemed to have found the appropriate answer to what Claus Offe described so vividly as the insurmountable contradiction of the welfare state, namely the fragile compromise between social groups that is inherently called into question by the structural reproduction of social inequality as a result of a capitalist mode of production (Offe, 1984, 1985; Przeworski, 1985).

However, this ideal model of social democratic politics came under severe pressure in the 1980s when the irreversible end of the social democratic area was announced. The social democratic or socialist governments in Europe in the 1970s, with their trust in Keynesian economic policy and a strong role of the state, no longer seemed to dispose of the appropriate instruments to come to terms with the reality of an increasingly internationally-organized and competitive economy. The *laissez-faire* or neoliberal reasoning – as represented most radically by Ronald Reagan and Margaret Thatcher – had its ideological base in denouncing social democracy as representing an outdated state-centred model, out of touch with the necessities of modern economic and social life (Merkel, 1993). Yet with the social costs of the neoliberal hegemony of the 1980s and early 1990s becoming more apparent there has been a revival of a political force that traditionally embodies the normative ideas of social justice and equality.

The 'modernized' social democrats of the 1990s, however, have altered the notion of what these claims of social justice mean in politics (Kitschelt, 1994, Merkel 2001). At its core is a new and significant shift in how social democracy defines its political identity, namely the devaluation of the 'economic axis' as the determinant of the political. In this respect contemporary social democrats have not only eradicated from the political agenda the alternative between capitalism and socialism as the meta-narrative of the traditional left. They have also critically devalued the reference to struggles over rare resources, the conflict between poor and rich, labour and capital, as the defining mark for what it means to be left or right. The underlying conflict over the social distribution of resources and power in a society is no longer the reference point for the political cleavages that Third Way social democrats consider of primary importance. Genuine political concerns over social inequalities and power structures have been widely replaced by the question of how a market economy can be run more effectively and less crisis ridden. From a distinctly critical point of view Finlayson speaks of a 'de-politicization' of questions concerning how to organize the economy that becomes evident in the British version of Third Way politics: '... the critique of capitalism as such turned into the particular capitalism of Thatcherite neoliberalism. It ceased being a political claim and became a managerial one about how to run things better' (Finlayson, 1999, p.276).

The 'managerial' approach also dominates how political issues regarding the future of the welfare state (how to address the problem of an aging population, an increasingly costly health system, et cetera) simply no longer seem to fall into the logic of the left-right bipolarity. This has found its expression in public political debate: Issues framed according to class concerning social justice are gradually transposed into discussions among parties who have truly 'modern' or 'innovative' solutions for market dysfunction. 'Modernization' has become a catch phrase for all mainstream parties to depict their qualification to rule. Policy preference seems to have lost – following the philosophical hypothesis of postmodernism – an integrating meta-narrative that would make political parties distinguishable along the lines of disputes over fundamental normative or political questions.

Yet, as a critical element of their electoral appeal one can identify the notion of social justice as a key issue of their campaigns. As a counter-movement against a sheer market approach and as an answer to the insecurities of the globalization process Third Way social democracy promises a political project based on the assurance to effectively face growing inequality and social tensions. According to the self-perception of social democratic parties, their programme is designed to confront prevailing forms of social exclusion and the marginalization of social groups. Employing key concepts such as fairness, equality of opportunity, and justice have played a critical role in bringing the pragmatic left back into office.[1] Giving credibility to these concepts in practical politics can thus be seen as crucial in forming a viable new social democratic force in Western politics. This book addresses this central issue by analyzing the policy fields, normative orientations and political processes on which the notion of social justice materializes in current forms of Third Way politics.

---

[1] If one analyses the political programmes of Third Way social democratic parties and the speeches of their political leaders, the decisive weight still given to questions concerning social justice becomes apparent.

The Structural Challenges and the 'Need for Modernization'

Third Way politics has recurrently been interpreted as a strategic operation to attract the modern middle classes. Beyond sheer political opportunism, however, this reorientation reflects a social and economic reality that has undergone a process of rapid alteration. Often structural changes in contemporary economics and society are credited with invigorating the breadth and acceleration of transformation in social democracies. In particular, the protagonists of Third Way politics tend to describe it as a rejuvenated social democratic approach that, with its new 'economic realism', has been the only feasible way to successfully challenge neoliberal opponents and to provide a promising leftist platform for the economic and social realities of contemporary society.

Given the severe economic pressures from a globalizing market, new policy initiatives are conducted under strict restrictions on national fiscal and economic policy. In this context, the traditional Keynesian measures seem unfeasible. In Europe, the Maastricht criteria on convergence as well as growing international competition are only the most widely discussed pressures (among a host of others) under which European governments have to formulate their policy goals and strategic preferences. The claim to successfully tackle the problem of inequality in the name of social justice is significantly restrained by pressures originating from increasingly interdependent and crisis-driven economies. The challenges to the social democratic parties are at their core a reaction to fundamental changes in contemporary society's socio-economic environment. Denationalization (the growing international economic and financial interdependence, the direct competition beyond national boundaries and pressure on elaborated welfare state schemes) and the transformation of modern economies towards a highly flexible service and information-based structure shape this environment. These developments and the social changes they triggered have nourished severe doubts about the effectiveness and the feasibility of traditional forms of state intervention into the economy, sustained fiscal spending and the reliance of social democratic parties on the core of industrial workers (Geyer et al., 1999).

In this respect it seems that Mitterrand's dramatic failure in attempting to establish a strong Keynesian, state-monitored regime in 1981, already indicated the end of the social democratic consensus that characterized much of Europe's post war history (Ross et al., 1987). Along similar lines the British Labour Party's goal to impose an incomes policy in the second half of the 1970s proved to be another example for the limits of state interventionism in highly modern capitalist economies (Hall, 1986). One lesson that the moderate left seems to have learned from this experience is the need to radically question the effectiveness and feasibility of Keynesian macro-economic interventionism. In the age of globalization the authority and interests of financial markets and international corporations is said to undermine the rationale on which social democratic politics (until the 1970s) was built. In contrast to a Mitterrand-like project, the Third Way claims to reflect an innovative economic realism, characterized by an acute awareness of the contemporary quest for productivity and flexibility. It has widely accepted the core idea of neoliberalism that deregulating the economy and emphasizing market dynamics is, if not desirable, at least unavoidable in spurring economic success and international competitiveness.

These economic imperatives of politics in the age of globalization and their shaping impact on the emerging agenda of Third Way politics have been interpreted from two politically opposing viewpoints. One argues that these pressures simply exclude certain more radical political options. The pragmatism adopted by Third Way social democracy in dealing with organizing the economy is portrayed as the only feasible rational response to the unavoidable. As the former advisor of Clinton, Robert Reich frames it: 'We are all Third Wayers now' (Reich, 1999); similar structural problems in organizing the economy have led to a common policy model in the entire Western world. From a more skeptical perspective, reformed social democracy's attitude towards the economy is seen as a symbol of the total depletion of politics. Here, Third Way politics is basically portrayed as a capitulation in response to the imperatives of capitalist reproduction (Laxer, 1996; Nairn, 2000; Petras, 2000).

However it is not only the economy that has nourished the drive towards Third Way politics. It is not by accident that the ghostwriter of the Third Way, Anthony Giddens, has dedicated a considerable part of his interest to the transformation of modern society (Giddens, 1994). The basic claims of Third Way politics are based on a series of observations about how modern society has changed with respect to its socio-economic organization, modes of cultural identities and ways of communicative interaction. These structural changes are said to have altered the environment to a degree that a state-centred approach built on the collective interests and identity of blue-collar workers is no longer feasible.[2] These strategic considerations that form a viable alternative to liberal and conservative parties have been a guiding force for broadening and altering the agenda of the moderate left (Piven, 1992).

Taking account of the dynamics and speed with which modern societies transform old social structures, the notion of the 'new individualism' (Beck, 1992, 2000) has become one of the key figures in the debate of new social democrats. It refers to a growing cultural and social diversification of society with significant consequences for the political sphere. People's interest in concerns regarding the political community is no longer primarily conditioned by those classical cleavages that Lipset and Rokkan (1967) described as the structuring principles for political conflicts in modern society. Concerns for the environment, human rights, sexual freedom, and 'lifestyle' issues no longer neatly fit into the framework of the ideological dispute that has characterized much of the 20th century. The plurality of political preferences and agendas is an important indicator of the constraints that

---

[2] Borrowing from Inglehart (1977), this change is often described as a radical shift in the value structure of modern society forcing traditional political actors to adapt to a new cultural environment.

social democracy as a 'people's party' is likely to feel more severely than its conservative counterpart, namely the eroding base for collectivist ideas and political projects.

Aside from pressures resulting from the global economy and the individualization of modern society, the end of the pre-1989 bipolar world is an important factor responsible for stimulating the transformation of what the moderate left in the Western world stands for. The seemingly definite end of an imaginable communist alternative to a capitalist system has altered the political setting of contemporary politics decisively. In most general terms, it has radically devaluated the range of political and economic alternatives to the present system; 'left' and 'right' simply can no longer be defined in terms of two radically opposed options for a social and political order. With the depletion of the bipolarity that has defined politics in the 20th century established parties cannot avoid redefining their political identity. Habermas coined the phrase the 'new perplexity' in politics, referring to a state in which the very notion of political cleavages and adversaries has become blurred (Habermas, 1985).

Transformation of Social Democracy: Central Features of its New Political Identity

Since the political project referred to as Third Way politics is a phenomenon in the making and shows substantial variation in different national contexts, it is probably too early to speak of a coherent programme. Still, beyond single policy initiatives there are some political core ideas and policy initiatives that can be identified as constituting the political identity of what modernized social democracy stands for politically. The critical ideas and differences to Old Labour have been summarized and discussed extensively so that the following schematic portrayal of the political cornerstones of Third Way politics is meant as a brief review.

Beyond 'Class Politics'

The project of 'modernizing' social democracy is critically motivated by acknowledging the threat that in the 1980s and early 1990s the established moderate left was on the verge of being permanently excluded from government in many European countries. Mainly because of the rapidly changing social com-position of its (potential) constituency and supporters, traditional social democratic parties had to deal with fading electoral support. Traditionally social democratic parties had their main support among blue-collar workers with a rather homogenous social background and subsequent political preferences (Kitschelt, 1993). In recent times however, the service and knowledge-based industry has become the main source of occupation. New, flexible forms of employment have spread considerably and the clear dividing line between blue and white collar has become blurred. The collective interest of labour, the fight for better wages, improved social security and, in broader terms, a more equal society dominated the agenda for the social democrats reflecting the class base of their political course.[3] Already in the 1970s and 1980s new issues and social movements significantly challenged this primary orientation of social democratic politics. As the social base of society became more diverse and new issues entered the political scene, the decision of many political campaigns to focus almost exclusively on questions concerning distributive justice turned out to be increasingly problematic. The life experiences and expectations of citizens simply have become far more diversified than presupposed in the social democratic emphasis on collective interest of the average worker.

This finds its expression in the gradual move of new social democrats away from their formerly firm links with the unions. In order to boost their attractiveness among those who do not belong to the shrinking blue-collar working class, and to gain more solid support among middle class voters, Third Way parties were keen on loosening their close ties to organized labour. This was also perceived as unavoidable in order to allow new political issues to enter the agenda of social democratic parties. Environmental issues are a good illustration of how the moderate left is trying to include concerns of growing importance especially for younger people and the middle class while simultaneously having to deal with the resistance of unions to this new agenda.

Towards a New Role of the State: Endorsing the Dynamic of a Free Market Economy

One of the most dramatic changes in social democracy of the Third Way type – and the focal point of harsh critique – is its adoption of a highly business-friendly approach as a core policy principle. Reducing tax benefits for enterprises while simultaneously substantially cutting public spending, social expenditure and deregulating labour-market provisions reflects the new notion that the labour-capital conflict is no longer seen as crucial for today's political life (on this point, see Hall's detailed discussion in this volume). Fiscal retrenchment, monetary stability and a reduced role for political authorities in organizing the economy are principles that have been widely accepted by modernized social democratic governments. In the field of economic and monetary governance much of the neoliberal supply-side-oriented, anti-inflationary reasoning has prevailed over formerly dominant social democratic policy principles.

In more general terms, the major thrust of the social democratic move is towards a new form of social consensus that is not primarily built on a strong and patronizing state. The aspired general goal for remodelling the relationship between individual citizens and the state is the reduction of pervasive state

---

[3] This holds regardless of the fact that social democrats gradually opened up for other social groups and issues; Willy Brandt with his 'daring more democracy' in the 1970s is a good illustration of this.

involvement in economic and social life. Contemporary social democracy is said to reflect the strong demand for individual choice and opportunities as dominant principles of contemporary society. The Third Way is designed as a political idea that distances itself on the one hand from an 'excessive' involvement of state institutions in civil society, and from a neoliberal agenda of minimal government and unlimited trust in the market mechanism on the other hand. The core idea is to shift the emphasis from the extended transfer of welfare provisions and re-distributive policies to empowering individuals to compete more successfully in the market themselves. Individual achievement and the general principle of meritocracy have replaced the traditional notion of the collective interest demanding innovative ideas about how to generate a social consensus beyond state interventionism.

Accordingly the priorities in defining the focus of welfare state provisions have changed. There is recurrent reference of Third Way proponents to overcome the threat to social cohesion, allegedly caused by the absolute trust of neoliberalism in market solutions and to find a new balance between individual responsibility and state interventionism. The core idea here is focused on empowering people to fully use their own resources and skills before allowing the state to provide needed services. The emphasis has shifted from protecting people from the market to establishing programmes that facilitate them to successfully compete in the market. Resources have been redirected from transfer payments and means-tested entitlements to those that aim at reintegrating people into the labour market (through education, training, et cetera). The term 'responsibility' is not by accident omnipresent in Tony Blair's speeches. The integrating idea of the Third Way involves taking account of the highly individualized nature of society and redesigning political programmes accordingly. Social security and tax systems are remodelled in a way that allows more room for individual initiative, as unemployment is believed to be addressed most effectively by boosting the entrepreneurial spirit of individuals. Accordingly, New Labour reinterprets the meaning of social equality on meritocratic grounds, emphasizing equal opportunities rather than equal outcomes.

Although not entirely without precedents in the history of social democratic policy initiatives, New Labour's 'welfare into work' programme radically alters the dominant focus and regulative idea of earlier policy making. The primary goal is no longer to maximize the process of de-commodifying social relationships (Esping-Anderson, 1990) and adjusting market generated inequalities. The new key phrase here is 'inclusion', which is intended to ameliorate the opportunities for all citizens to actively participate in the wealth created by a dynamic economy. Particularly in the British case of New Labour, there is an unaccustomed sense of enthusiasm for market mechanisms resulting in policy guidelines that are designed to create a favourable environment for private initiatives, entrepreneurship and the opportunities supposedly provided by the new information economy.[4] The underlying idea is that if the government creates the appropriate environment then the 'market is harnessed to serve the public interest' (Blair, 1998).

This principle also refers to reconfiguring macro-economic policies based on Keynesian reasoning as well as for a comprehensive welfare state, which is said to have overprotected and thus deprived citizens of their ability to take responsibility. However proponents of the reformed social democrats claim that it is not about simply reducing or even eliminating state involvement but in redefining it according to the principle of empowering individuals.[5] What is said to be at stake is the effectiveness and desirability of certain state interventions into economic and social life, not the responsibility for the public good as such. As Giddens puts it, it 'is a Third Way in the sense that it is an attempt to transcend both old style social democracy and neoliberalism' (Giddens, 1998, p.26).

The Plea for a Revitalized Civil Society: Redefining the Sites of the Political

As the focus of Third Way politics has shifted from a critical approach to market outcomes, new fields of political initiatives are described as contributing to a new political identity. One way of conceptualizing the transformation of social democracy is to describe it in terms of widening the leftist agenda and a repossession of political goals that over the last decades have been neglected due to an almost exclusive focus on the economy. One of the crucial programmatic points of Third Way politics is the claim to stand for political emancipation and a more meaningful form of democracy in terms of involving citizens in the political process. Rhetorically this is often framed as providing the grounds for a revitalized civil society in which, analogous to dealing with economic life, the individual is supposed to be given a more authentic opportunity to engage as a full citizen. More broadly they are confronted with new demands for individual autonomy and a more active citizenry. What Third Way politics claims to represent is a form of civic liberalism that is aimed at redefining to whom, and in what form, citizens are obligated to the political community and the state.

As for other major parties in Western politics, one of the crucial challenges to social democracy is the loss of its support in civil society and its subjection to the deeply rooted feelings of suspicion towards 'official' party politics. If Third Way politics were really about introducing new issues into (social democratic) politics

---

[4] Less radical, but in the same direction, the German government under Schröder introduced as one of its first policy initiatives a reduction of corporate taxation and removal of capital gain taxes on firms' sale of shares in other firms.
[5] The strong emphasis on education and training are an indicator for this idea to stimulate individual initiative rather than state protectionism. An ideal example of this basic orientation would be the 'welfare to work' programme adopted by Blair's government; it is designed to overcome dependency on transfer payments from the state and to encourage (some are inclined to say 'force') unemployed back into the labour market.

and redefining the relationship between the individual and the political community, then an account of the transformation of centrist-left politics would be incomplete without considering the new sites and processes of this type of politics. Decentralization or – in the British context, devolution – are expressions of related initiatives forwarded by social democratic governments. They are meant to redirect political power to other, more decentralized levels of political life and thereby make credible the notion of a vivid civil society (local autonomy, bottom-up decision making). In Germany, the government under Schröder launched its first major policy initiatives in the field of the environment and citizenship, shifting the political emphasis of social democratic government into formerly far less prominent areas.

Challenges to Third Way Social Democracy

As unavoidable as the 'modernization' of the moderate left seemed to be, the new agents of Third Way politics in Europe and North America have to face a series of uncertainties in terms of how viable Third Way politics is as a basic strategy for social democrats in the 21st century. The underlying questions referring to these challenges to the new social democracy primarily concern the solidity of their popular base of support. Three of these challenges can be identified by shedding light on the structural difficulties that some of its core political claims must face. They refer to the following key issues in reformulating the political identity of the social democratic left: (a) the credibility of claims for social justice and equality, (b) the vague mobilizing normative ethical goal, and (c) social democratic politics in the age of globalization. From different perspectives these challenges are frequently discussed throughout the book, establishing a set of key questions that guide this volume's discussion of Third Way politics.

(a) Credibility of Claims for Social Justice and Equality

This point refers to the main target of the Third Way's leftist critics: How can the reality of a capitalist economy with its inherent tendency to produce inequality be reconciled with the genuine claim of social democratic parties to provide an approach towards a necessary degree of social justice and cohesion (see Giddens, 2000)? It is too early to judge the current policy initiatives from social democratic governments in this respect. Still there seems to be a persistent trend in Third Way politics to accept a degree of inequality that, for instance, exceeds what social democratic parties were willing to accept in the 1970s.[6] The critical question now

---

[6] Along these lines critics from the left describe Third Way politics as a political project that has adapted fundamental positions of the neoliberal right and betrayed the very principle of leftist politics of addressing inequalities and power resulting from the economic sphere. Petras represents this position when he speaks about Third Way politics being a

is: Does it have a major impact politically, to the extent that it alienates those who feel deprived of the affluence of the New Economy and those who fundamentally disagree with the prospect of an increasingly socially divided society? It will be of decisive weight whether the 'old social question' – the concern for distributive justice and issues related to the realm of work – will still be one of the most crucial determinants of politics (Rosanvallon, 2000). Pointing to the diversity of experiences that individuals are exposed to in this respect, many commentators seem to agree that the process of individualization has undermined the very idea of likelihood of a collective identity based on class, and a notion of collective exploitation.

One of the crucial questions for the political success of Third Way politics will be whether it will prove to be counterproductive, if not politically damaging, for a reformed social democracy to give up the essential claim of the left to remedy the social effects of a free market economy. The underlying reasoning for this argument is that the new social democracy threatens to destroy the very reason for the left's genuine claim; namely to counterbalance the power and inequality as the intrinsic dynamic of a capitalist society. Critics of Third Way politics argue that if the social democratic left is willing to shift its emphasis of conducting politics of protection from and intervention into market results, it may simply lose its *raison d'être* as a political force distinct from its liberal or conservative political opponents. Here, one has to be aware of the fact that the appeal of social democracy is still strongly based on its willingness to defend the welfare state, while its political agenda has widely moved away from this type of support for state intervention. From a more theoretical perspective Noberto Bobbio (1987, 1996) referred to the idea of social equality and justice as the key values that still define a critical reference point in demarcating the left from the right. Hence, one of the key questions for Third Way politics is how they can credibly claim to stand for these values while at the same time integrating new cross-cutting cleavages (such as those concerning ecological values, cultural identity, equality among the sexes, et cetera) that follow different normative codes.

One indication of this challenge to centrist social democrats is that there is surprising success among parties that stress their roots in a more radically socialist, class based political identity. Under different auspices the formation of the *Partito della Rifondazione Comunista* (Communist Refoundation Party) in Italy, the unexpected success of the PDS (Party of Democratic Socialism) in (Eastern) Germany, and the resilience of the Communist party in France and Spain, each suggest that the social democratic move to the centre and away from traditional

---

'legitimation for the right turn of social democracy' and a 'dramatic shift from reformist socialism and welfare capitalism to neoliberalism' (Petras, 2000, pp. 30–31). In general, critics on the left describe the reformed social democrats' platform as a failed attempt to generate a sufficient degree of adjustment to market processes, while having an unjustified trust in the dynamic of a market economy.

leftist position based on class is likely to create a political void.[7] Here it is important to be aware of the fact that Third Way proponents have been privileged thus far, in that they were able to launch their political project in a comparatively favourable environment. One critical challenge to current social democratic governments will be to balance the claim to stand for social justice and social cohesion on the one hand and on the other hand the reality of a society in which many might not fully participate in the blooming prospects of a post-fordist economy.[8] It is an empirically open and normatively controversial question whether the idea of 'equality as inclusion' (Giddens, 1998, p.105) will provide sufficient answers in this respect.

Indeed, there are further indications that the integrative power of social democracy is seriously challenged, and not only by those who belong to the more radical left. Many former supporters of social democrats who now feel left behind by the pace of economic modernization have opted in favour of right wing or other populist political organization. As New Labour no longer seems to be a voice primarily for the less privileged and since the socialist idea of an alternative to the existing order seems to have disappeared entirely from the political agenda, these social groups feel excluded from official politics altogether.[9] As much as a rejuvenated political conservatism challenges Third Way politics, political apathy and indifference threatens to undermine the electoral support that new social democrats currently enjoy. The salience of the conflict between the normative self perception of the new social democracy to represent the principle of social justice and the persistent patterns of social inequality and exclusion are taken up with some fervour in the case studies elaborated in Part II of this book.

(b) Lack of a Mobilizing Normative Goal of the Left

One of the critical challenges that Third Way social democrats face is the need to create a new political identity that proves strong enough to generate political loyalties and support. Here the pragmatism of the new social democracy appears to be a source of electoral success, but also presents a potential threat to its long-term

---

[7] Along the same line we can interpret the opposition within the party itself that the new leaders of the reformed social democrats have to face. Tony Blair's adversaries from the traditional left of the Labour Party or Oskar Lafontaine's dramatic departure from Schröder's government in 1999 are indications that the new social democratic approach of organizing the economy does not go unchallenged.

[8] Myles and Quadagno argue along the same lines: 'The main Achilles heel of the Third Way scenario is its silence on the fate of those most disadvantaged by a strategy that relies on the labor market as the primary source of welfare: working-age adults who have no labor to sell.' (Myles and Quadagno 2000: 166.)

[9] Surveys consistently indicate that young people are rather disillusioned with 'official politics' and are likely either to abstain from politics at all (by now often the biggest fraction of the electorate in elections throughout Europe) or to engage in forms of politics far remote from party politics (Beck 2000).

political accomplishment. Adopting a market-friendly approach and de-politicizing social and economic issues by asking for allowance for the necessary modernization of society turned out to be a thriving strategy in electoral terms. Such an approach allowed social groups to be won over to social democratic politics, groups that formerly may have been alienated by an emphasis on the welfare state and redistributive politics. Yet, on the other hand, this project of 'pragmatic modernization' runs the risk of depleting the normative core idea of social democracy to a degree that it becomes almost politically indistinguishable from its political opponents in the centrist or conservative camp. Finlayson speaks of the 'absence of a motivational ethical core' (Finlayson, 1999, p.274) that characterizes this pragmatic, or as the leftist critics of Third Way politics would put it, technocratic approach to politics. Reconfiguring questions of distributive justice almost exclusively within the logic of a competitive market economy leaves a void in Third Way politics.[10] The presumption here is that it is more than doubtful that the Third Way left could firmly establish itself as a leading political force if it is deprived of a normative core idea that provides an integrative political framework for decisions in different political fields. To supersede their old ideological base in distributive justice without providing convincing alternative normative principles runs the risk of alienating the old constituency without providing strong incentives to new social groups.

Beyond the need for an integrating normative idea that could give Third Way politics a coherent and, in electoral terms, convincing political identity, there is another important dilemma inherent in the very nature of the social democrats' new course. This more far-reaching hypothesis would suggest that the very form of modernization endorsed by Third Way parties might further contribute to weakening and, in a long-term perspective, even undermining the loyalties that tie citizens to this political force. Every political project – and, given their core political values, social democratic ones in particular – is critically dependent on a form of social consensus that is strong enough to generate political solidarity and a genuine concern for a common good. In this respect social democrats of the Third Way type may have to pay a political price for wholeheartedly embracing the logic of market-oriented, individualistic approach to politics. Although, as Tony Blair recurrently emphasizes in his speeches, Third Way politics intends to apply market solutions to the sphere of the economy, not to society as a whole, it will prove to be of critical weight how successful this political force will be in bridging the gap

---

[10] It is against this background that challenging essential categories of the traditional identity of the left has spurred widespread skepticism towards the actual political project and goals of the 'Third Way' or 'New Labour'. From different political perspectives its political aspirations are often described as lacking clear and visionary ideas; its policy approach is accused of being pragmatic to the extent of simply continuing the policies of the preceding conservative or neoliberal governments. Third Way politics has been repeatedly criticized for lacking a guiding political idea or key projects of radical reform. Among many other critics from the left see the issue of *Dissent*, Spring 1999.

between pro-market policies and the claimed revitalization of civil society.

(c) Social Democratic Politics in the Age of Globalization

One of the driving forces of the transformation that social democratic parties undergo is the seemingly overwhelming weight of international economic realities. Some of its critics indeed interpret the Third Way as a form of replacement of genuine politics by an administration of sheer economic imperatives. One does not have to agree with this normative argument to realize that in setting the agenda for their political goals, social democratic governments are very well aware of the limits imposed on them by the logic of highly integrated economies. The dilemma that many social democratic parties find themselves in against this background is the following. On the one hand, they have accepted that there is no way of escaping the logic of international economic competition and to adapt domestically to these challenges in order to be successful. There does not seem to be a viable way back to the social democratic belief of the 1970s that it is left to the sovereign nation state and its government to 'manage' a national economy. Rather, globalization is seen as a promising economic and social tool for successful modernization. On the other hand, social democratic parties are painfully aware of the fact that for the foreseeable future the nation state remains the only level[11] on which some kind of regulation of sheer market outcomes seems to be viable and the aspired intact political community can be achieved. Wholeheartedly endorsing the promises of a deregulated free market economy at the international level at least runs the risk of depriving national governments of the ability to give meaning to principles of social justice. This development is one of the critical challenges to social democratic politics at the domestic and the European levels, as this political force has traditionally relied strongly on the nation states' capacity to intervene into the economy.

Along the same lines, the process of denationalization challenges the Third Way's promise to give more credibility to the idea of an intact and 'cohesive' society, a renewal of communal life. As traditional forms of communal life tend to disintegrate under the impact of globalization, a critical question is how the revitalized citizen society is to be achieved and which institutional arrangements are supposed to bring this about. Beyond the broad idea of strengthening local and regional levels of politics, it is one of those policy fields in which policy initiatives do not yet provide a clear picture of how key goals of the new social democracy will be applied in political practice.[12] A critical evaluation of new sites of the

---

[11] The EU does not seem to be ready to play this role in spite of the fact that a social and human rights Charter or even a comprehensive European citizenship status are being discussed.

[12] From conservative and liberal opponents this strong emphasis on communal life and civic responsibility has provoked a critique that accuses Third Way politics of illiberal, if not authoritarian tendencies (Dahrendorf 1999).

political and how Third Way parties seek to reanimate the alienating willingness of citizens to engage in politics will be the focal point of the third part of this volume.

The Contributions

Part I

The aim of Part I is to provide an account of the broader socio-economic and political environment in which Third Way initiatives are launched. What are the critical opportunities and constraints that a 'modernized' social democratic project has to face in the age of globalization? Does the economic sphere and the pressures resulting from an increasingly globalized market have a determining impact on political aspirations designed to moderate and regulate the social effects of a capitalist economic system? What impact does the Third Way's commitment to sustainable economic development have on national governments' ability to organize the economy and challenge the logic of market forces?

Peter Hall sets the agenda for the comparison of Third Way-style politics by providing a comprehensive framework of interpreting the transformation of the moderate left. His working hypothesis is that the search for Third Way politics beyond traditional political cleavages is mainly motivated, and structurally conditioned, by important changes in the political economy. Hall's contribution thus focuses on the opportunities and constraints that current leftist governments have to face due to the nature of the global economy and the fading possibility of sustaining genuine national policy regimes. Third Way politics is interpreted as an acknowledgement of economic realities that have undermined traditional social democratic accounts of organizing the economy. A highly competitive international economy and the emergence of a single European market have severely limited the room for manoeuvre when it comes to formulating national approaches to interventionist policies and fiscal spending.

Taking account of how different capitalist economies operate in national contexts and how distinct certain traditions of social policy regimes are, Hall develops an interpretative framework that helps to understand the variation of what Third Way politics means in practice. For instance, traditionally Great Britain, Germany and France show significantly different patterns in how the political economy is organized, welfare and unemployment programmes are institutionalized, and which interest groups have strong influence on policy decisions. Highlighting these structural variations, Hall develops his hypothesis about the range of policy options that are feasible for social democratic governments in each national context. According to his interpretation there is a certain 'path dependency', in that the specific character of the political economy conditions the direction of social democratic policy. The degree to which Third Way social democracy is willing and able to deregulate organized market economies and to introduce non-market co-ordination has to be understood with respect to vested interests and the way social systems are structured. On this basis

Hall shows that social democratic governments in conservative welfare states have to face far more severe policy problems in terms of dealing with the fiscal crisis and unemployment. He compares Britain, France and Germany in terms of how each of the reformed social democratic governments has to find a new equilibrium between market and non-market cooperation, and which opportunities and constraints they encounter resulting from the particular organization of their respective political economic systems.

From a different angle Saskia Sassen continues Hall's discussion of Third Way politics from a political economy perspective. She critically re-evaluates the claim that globalization has narrowed the scope of action for national governments to a degree that politics is basically determined by economic imperatives. Arguing that such an account would reproduce an oversimplified understanding of the effects of the global economy, Sassen develops her hypothesis regarding the role of the nation state as an actor in politics. National governments are described as still playing a pivotal role in providing the legal, social and political environment for market transaction. Sassen argues that in some areas the nation state might indeed be an even more decisive player in moderating economic processes.

Her contribution argues strongly that politics still matters and that Third Way politics cannot simply be described as the 'victim' of economic imperatives that are beyond its sphere of influence. The variation of national responses to economic globalization as well as the functional logic of modern markets to demand a pronounced regulatory intervention on behalf of political authorities (the nation state being still the most decisive agent) leads Sassen to conclude there is room for political priorities on the national level.

Part II

Part II seeks to shed light on the variety of Third Way politics that we can witness in contemporary Europe. In spite of increasingly similar international pressure on fiscal spending there is ample evidence for critical differences with regard to ideas, policy initiatives and outcomes in those countries where social democratic parties are in government. What are the most significant domestic factors that contribute to our understanding of the specific form Third Way politics takes in particular national contexts? Does the shift in the political landscape towards leftist governments in effect indicate a substantial change in politics and policy? Which normative goals and policy initiatives define the Third Way in these countries in light of the challenges resulting from a global economy? What have been the concrete achievements of these governments in selected crucial fields of policy formation?

The British case is most likely the most radical one when it comes to the transformation of the left into a pro-market political force. Yet, as Stephen Driver and Luke Martell argue, New Labour is more than simply a continuation of Thatcherite neoliberal policies. Describing in detail critical core principles of the policies of Third Way politics in Great Britain, they argue that the government under Blair indeed represents an attempt to transcend the traditional dichotomy between left and right. According to their interpretation, New Labour is still based on traditional social democratic values which however are reinterpreted in their policy implications responding to the challenges of a new socio-economic environment. In the first part of their chapter Driver and Martell develop an interpretative framework that shows how different forms of Third Way politics can be perceived in terms of the meaning that they attribute to its core normative principles: liberty, equality and community. In this perspective the Third Way is characterized as, far from being a coherent ideology, a pragmatic mix of values and policy approaches steered by a particular idea about the responsibility of the state.

In a second step this contribution shows that in spite of a common policy agenda among the moderate left in Europe there are notable differences among Third Way politics in practice. These variations can be accounted for by referring to the different varying cultures, institutions and economic regimes that characterize national contexts. In putting the British case into comparative perspective Driver and Martell argue that the political landscape in Britain has to be understood in light of the still critical divide between the Anglo-American and the European models of state interventionism. It is in this light that Blair's New Labour is portrayed as a vanguard of 'modernizing' social democracy taking advantage of the Thatcherite legacy to formulate innovative policy initiatives. Considering that the Third Way is far from being a coherent programme and that it reflects the political and socio-economic opportunities of a specific national context Driver and Martell assume that we can only speak about a plurality of third ways.

Italian politics constitutes, as Vincent Della Sala shows, a very particular context for the formation of Third Way politics. It was the opportunity for a left to get into government after almost fifty years of conservative hegemony by the *Democrazia Cristiana* in the First Republic. In Italy, with a distinct history of a radical, Communist left and a long tradition of class-based politics, the transformation into a Third Way type of party created severe problems for the new political identity of this political actor. With its transformation from the *Partito Communista d'Italia* (PCI) to the *Partito Demoractico della Sinistra* (PDS) in 1991, the newly formed party adopted a position that ten years earlier would not have been thinkable. With this it has developed into a credible alternative to the political right that seeks to reorganize after the political turmoil of the 1990s.

Della Sala argues that both the substantial economic pressure resulting from monetary integration in Europe and the deep political crisis of the First Republic in the early 1990s can explain the particular form and the rapidity of the transformation of the left. The neoliberal turn of the Italian moderate left is said to reflect a distinct Italian style of Third Way politics summarized by the slogan: 'democratization through markets and politics through markets'. The introduction of market principles by the center-left government is portrayed as more than simply a strategy of adapting to the realities of an increasingly competitive international economy. Against the background of the political scandals often related to funds in state dominated sectors of the economy, the endorsement of market principles is said to introduce democratic elements into a civil society that used to be paralyzed by oligarchic economic and political power groups. Third Way politics the Italian way is in Della Sala's perspective an effective instrument to dismantle entrenched networks of power and the grip that parties used to have on civil society in the First Republic.

The French case is, as Serenella Sferza argues, an indication of an emerging model for social democratic politics in the age globalization that is successful in translating the claim for social justice in meaningful policy initiatives. Interpreting the French left under Jospin in government, she suggests that downplaying the redistributive agenda should not simply be identified with a loss of a leftist identity as such. Rather, Sferza claims that the reformed socialists have found new ways of defining and implementing egalitarian principles and concerns for social justice. Their agenda has moved from the economic to the political field developing what may be an even fuller account of the emancipatory claims that the left stands for. This transformation regarding the ideological and social base of the socialist party can, as Sferza claims, be summarized in terms of a 'shift from a workers' to a citizens' party'.

In what Sferza labels a 'revitalization' of the left, is at its core a development away from a class-based party with a 'materialist ideology' towards a form of a 'citizen's party', based on a broader agenda than the conflict between labour and capital. Her argument stresses the role of new political issues and a highly diversified social constituency that made it inevitable for the left to broaden its agenda. Still, as she argues, abandoning a class-oriented approach does not mean that the French left has become politically almost indistinguishable from its political adversaries. In the field of immigration, European unification or the environment, the reformed socialist party is portrayed as redefining the left as the genuine advocate of individual freedom and social rights.

Part III

The third part offers an account and an interpretation of the changing political identity of the social democratic left. Here the focus lies on the ideational roots and the key political claims of Third Way politics. In which way does it transcend political core ideas and policies of traditional social democracy? In historic terms how radical is the break with the legacy of social democratic politics in the Twentieth Century? What are the main challenges to Third Way politics in a world whose socio-economic reality seems to have changed so fundamentally since the Golden Age of social democracy in the decades after the Second World War? This part is designed to shed light on the political debate about the reach and the meaning of the political change introduced by 'modernized' social democracy.

Putting Third Way politics into an historic perspective Michael Th. Greven provides a highly skeptical account of the intellectual and political endeavors underlying the contested notion of Third Way politics. He sees a growing gap between the intellectual criticism of leftist intellectuals and the realities of a capitalist order arguing that the discourse on a Third Way suggests alternatives to a global capitalism that are simply not feasible at this historic stage. According to his interpretation many of the critics of contemporary social democratic regimes are caught in the opaqueness of their anti-capitalist romanticism, out of touch with the realities of a globalized economy. The political consequence is said to be an astonishing lack of practical answers to the global mobilization of capital. The gap between an institutionalized intellectual anti-capitalism on the one hand and the void in meaningful political action to tackle most pressing social challenges on the other hand is described as presenting two closely related phenomena.

In his contribution on the cultural roots of Third Way politics, Frank Unger develops a hypothesis that focuses on the generational change in the postwar age cohort and the peculiar cultural environment created by the student revolt in the late 1960s. According to his interpretation the course of the Schröder government and the German social democrats can be traced back to an intellectual and political climate of the 1960s in which the leaders of today's Third Way proponents were socialized. With this perspective Unger seeks to formulate an explanation for why the German social democrats have so willingly abandoned much of the political identity of their heirs of the 1970s. The continuity of neoliberal policies by the Schröder government is for him an indication for a hedonistic, individualistic culture of the student left that from its very origins can be described as being at odds with classical social democratic concerns about class politics and social justice. His thesis points to the ambivalent long-term effects of the students' revolt on German politics: On the one hand, it is interpreted as a necessary, liberating force in the restorative climate of the Adenauer era. On the other hand, however, Unger claims that it paved the ground for a contemporary political culture, which, taking into account the radically left self-understanding of '68ers', shows a surprising affinity to individualistic and neoliberal ideologies.

Along the same lines a gradual professionalization of the party in terms of a dominance of academically trained personnel has undermined the worker-oriented tradition social democracy in its modern form after Godesberg in 1958 stood for in Germany. The very idea of what 'left' and 'right' are supposed to mean becomes blurred in an age dominated by neoliberal programmes and individualistic ideologies. On the basis of this interpretation Unger arrives at a rather pessimistic scenario for the new left-green government in Germany. The fading traditional political identity of the social democrats is not being replaced by a promising and politically viable approach. Old class cleavages and questions concerning social equality are likely to challenge the modernizers of the Third Way. Accordingly, Unger's account of Germany's Third Way indicates that it might alienate its traditional clientele and build its support on a media-staged platform, which is likely to prove too fluctuate to generate a solid social base for Third Way politics in Germany.

Warren Magnusson's reflection on the 'politics of nostalgia' completes this part on the political space for leftist emancipatory politics at the end of the twentieth century. The hypothesis that he develops departs from the observation that in the contemporary world any plausible leftist political project needs to be consistent with the unchallenged reality of a capitalist system and the lack of a credible socialist alternative. This poses the challenge to any leftist enterprise to re-imagine the very nature of politics and envision emancipatory approaches beyond the limits of a (nation-)centred approach. The nation state no longer seems to provide an adequate frame for progressive politics. In the heydays of traditional social democratic politics it might still have been possible to believe in the regulative power of national agencies and the idea of social progress in a nationally defined socio-political realm. To cling to this idea today, however, would be a sign of nostalgia that is out of touch with the realities of our contemporary world.

Part IV

Giddens, as one of the most prominent academic figures in discussing and shaping the notion of the Third Way spoke of a 'second wave of democratization' as a crucial element of this political project.[13] What are the dominant patterns of democratic reform we can observe? What are the likely outcomes and effects of the political reforms initiated by social democratic regimes and what are the possible agendas for such a democratic renewal? What roles do independent political actors who challenge Third Way proponents in an attempt to develop an agenda for progressive politics play? This part draws its attention to the political sites and processes that are said to set the agenda for Third Way politics in an age in which national politics can no longer claim to be the exclusive container of politics (Magnusson, 1996; Walker, 1993).[14]

Addressing the local level of politics, Roger Keil discusses the empirical and theoretical dimensions of urban governance restructuring in large North American and European cities during the 1990s. Taking account of the genuine claim of Third Way politics to remodel the relationship between the state and its citizens in terms of more meaningful forms of democracy, he comes to a surprising result. In a period when we saw the ascendance of Third Way policies in most Western countries urban politics seems to have taken another political path. It is argued that while some national or regional governments have moved to what is called the 'new middle', and while left-liberal governments seem to have experienced an upswing compared to the Thatcher-Reagan-Kohl era of the past decades, some governments of large cities have gone in the opposite direction. In fact, many big

---

[13] He also speaks about a 'deepening and widening of democracy' as being at the heart of Third Way politics (Giddens, 1998, p. 69ff.).

[14] As James Laxer concludes his search for a New Left: 'Today the real political opposition to right-wing policies is taking place almost exclusively outside the walls of Parliament' (Laxer, 1996, p. 205). It is part of the history of social democratic parties to be challenged by leftist and alternative forces in civil society. Be it in form of their own youth organization, be it in form of social movements, social democracy has to be understood in terms of its often problematic relationship to initiatives and protest originating beyond the limited realm of parliamentary life. Taking the claim of democratization seriously is dependent on initiatives emerging from civil society and bottom-up processes of changing institutions that cannot be induced by state-sponsored programmes.

city mayors (including those in New York, Los Angeles, Frankfurt, Berlin, and Toronto) are conservatives of all stripes that have turned their cities into testing grounds for a variety of socially authoritarian and economically neo-liberal policies.

Thomas Hueglin sheds light on another level at which the Third Way's claim to democratize civil society could be related, namely federalism or the decentralization of political power to subnational levels. Challenging the claim of Giddens and others (Gray 1998) that globalization – in conjunction with transformations of modern society – has rendered all previous political ideas irrelevant, he describes federalism as an important, albeit neglected arena for leftist politics. As Hueglin argues, the Left has generally ignored the traditions and practices of federalism as an organizing tool for democratic politics. As this contribution suggests, there are at least three reasons why a new democratic Left should rethink its historical aversion to federalism as a mere '*semblance* of feudal distinctions'. First, the processes of globalization and European integration entail a massive relocation of power to new political spaces. Second, the growing distance between civic consciousness and the structure of large political organizations leads to issue-specific politicization and a decline in political solidarity. Third, in such a world of integration and fragmentation parliamentary majority rule loses its legitimacy for the organization of the popular will.

If one takes seriously the aim of Third Way politics to encourage a new civic spirit then the question emerges in which social spaces and through which processes this is supposed to be achieved. New Labour's emphasis on devolution and decentralization is an indication that some sort of federalism could be at the very heart of the reformed social democrats' policy agenda. In this light, Hueglin's contribution discusses various federal options for a New Left, including plural forms of spatial and functional representation in bicameral legislative settings, a new division of powers based on criteria of particular and universal interest, and a spatially differentiated charter of social and economic rights.

The breadth of the approaches and empirical reference points employed in this book is designed to highlight both the nature of the transformation of contemporary social democracy and its varying manifestation in several national contexts. From different perspectives the authors emphasize how far-reaching the process of change is that established patterns of party politics have been undergoing. The traditional interpretative framework of a left-right divide defined primarily by positions on the question of distributive justice in national contexts is highly limited to capture the dynamic currently at work. The Third Way transformation of social democracy is an indication of a comprehensive change in the structure of cleavages shaping contemporary societies as it is itself a driving force in redefining the substance and sites of the political.

References

Bartolini, S. and Mair, P. (1990), *Identity, Competition, and Electoral Availability: The Stability of European Electorates 1885–1985*, Cambridge University Press, Cambridge.

Beck, U. (1992), *Risk Society: Towards a New Modernity*, Sage Publications, London, Newbury Park, Calif.

Beck, U. (2000), *The Risk Society and Beyond: Critical Issues for Social Theory*, Sage, London.

Berger, S. (2000), *Social Democracy and The Working Class In the Nineteenth and Twentieth Century Germany*, Longman, New York, Harlow (England).

Blair, T. (1998), *The Third Way: New Politics for the New Century*, Fabian Society, London.

Blair, T. and Schröder, G. (1999), *Europe: The Third Way/Die Neue Mitte*, Labour Party, London.

Bobbio, N. (1987), *The Future of Democracy. A Defense of the Rules of the Game*, Polity Press, Cambridge.

Bobbio, N. (1996), *Left and Right: The Significance of a Political Distinction*, Polity Press, Cambridge.

Braunthal, G. (1983), *The West German Social Democrats, 1969–1982. Profile of a Party in Power*, Westview Press, Boulder, Colo.

Dahrendorf, R. (1999), 'Whatever happened to liberty?', *New Statesman*, 6 September.

Esping-Andersen, G. (1985), *Politics Against Markets. The Social Democratic Road to Power*, Princeton University Press, Princeton, NJ.

Esping-Andersen, G. (1990), *The Three World of Welfare Capitalism*, Princeton University Press, Princeton, NJ.

Esping-Andersen, G. and Kersbergen, K. van (1992), 'Contemporary Research on Social Democracy', *Annual Review of Sociology*, Vol. 18, pp. 187–208.

Finlayson, A. (1999), 'Third Way Theory', *The Political Quarterly*, Vol. 1, pp. 271-79.

Gamble, A. and Wright, T. (1999), *The New Social Democracy*, Blackwell Publishers, Malden, MA.

Geyer, R., Moses, J.W. and Ingebritsen, C. (1999), *Globalization, Europeanization and the End of Scandinavian Social Democracy?*, Martin's Press, London.

Giddens, A. (1994), *Beyond Left and Right. The Future of Radical Politics*, Stanford University Press, Stanford.

Giddens, A. (1998), *The Third Way: the Renewal of Social Democracy*, Polity Press, Cambridge.

Giddens, A. (2000), *The Third Way and Its Critics*, Polity Press, Cambridge.

Gray, J. (1998), *False Dawn: the Delusions of Global Capitalism*, Granta Books, London.

Habermas, J. (1985), *Die neue Unübersichtlichkeit: kleine politische Schriften*, Suhrkamp, Frankfurt am Main.

Hall, P.A. (1986), *Governing the Economy: the Politics of State Intervention in Britain and France*, Oxford University Press, Oxford, New York.

Hicks, A.M. (1999), *Social Democracy and Welfare Capitalism: a Century of Income Security Politics*, Cornell University Press, Ithaca, NY.

Inglehart, R. (1977), *The Silent Revolution. Changing Values and Political Styles Among Western Publics*, Princeton University Press, Princeton, NJ.

Kitschelt, H. (1993), 'Class Structure and Social Democratic Party Strategy', *British Journal of Political Science*, Vol. 23, pp. 299–337.

Kitschelt, H. (1994), *The Transformation of European Social Democracy*, Cambridge University Press, Cambridge.

Laxer, J. (1996), *In Search of a New Left. Canadian Politics After the Neoconservative Assault*, Viking Penguin, Toronto.

Levitas, R. (1999), *The Inclusive Society? Social Exclusion and New Labour*, Macmillan, Basingstoke.

Lipset, S.M. and Rokkan, S. (eds.) (1967), *Party Systems and Voter Alignments*, Free Press, New York.

Magnusson, W. (1996), *The Search for Political Space: Globalization, Social Movements, and the Urban Political Experience*, University of Toronto Press, Toronto, Buffalo.

Merkel, W. (1993), *Ende der Sozialdemokratie? Wählerentwicklung, Machtressourcen und Regierungspolitik im westeuropäischen Vergleich*, Campus, Frankfurt.

Merkel, W. (2001), 'The Third Ways of Social Democracy', in R. Cuperus, K. Duffek and J. Kandel (eds.), *Multiple Third Ways. European Social Democracy Facing the Twin Revolution of Globalisation and the Knowledge Society*, Friedrich-Ebert-Stiftung/ Wiardi Beckmann Stichting/Renner-Institut, Amsterdam/Berlin/Wien, pp. 27-62.

Milner, H. (1990), *Sweden: Social Democracy in Practice*, Oxford University Press, Oxford.

Myles, J., and Quadagno, J. (2000), 'Envisioning a Third Way: The Welfare State in the Twenty-first Century', *Contemporary Sociology*, Vol. 29(1), pp. 156–67.

Nairn, T. (2000), 'Ukania under Blair', *New Left Review*, Vol. 1, pp. 69–103.

Offe, C. (1984), *Contradictions of the Welfare State*, Hutchinson, London.

Offe, C. (1985), *Disorganized Capitalism. Contemporary Transformations of Work and Politics*, Polity Press, Cambridge.

Paterson, W. (1974), *Social Democracy in Post-War Europe*, Macmillan, London.

Petras, J. (2000), 'The Third Way: Myth and Reality', *Monthly Review*, Vol. 51(10), pp. 19–35.

Piven, F.P. (ed.) (1992), *Labor Parties in Post-industrialist Societies*, Oxford University Press, New York.

Przeworski, A. (1980), 'Social Democracy as a Historical Phenomenon', *New Left Review*, Vol. 122, pp. 27–58.

Przeworski, A. (1985), *Capitalism and Social Democracy*, Cambridge University, Cambridge, MA.

Reich, R. (1999), 'We Are All Third Wayers Now', *The American Prospect*, Vol. 10(43), March–April 1999, pp. 46–51.

Rosanvallon, P. (2000), *The New Social Question: Rethinking the Welfare State*, Princeton University Press, Princeton, NJ.

Ross, G. (1982). *Workers and Communists in France: from Popular Front to Eurocommunism*, University of California Press, Berkeley.

Ross, G., Hoffmann, S. and Malzacher, S. (eds.) (1987), *The Mitterrand Experiment*, Oxford University Press, New York.

Sassoon, D. (1996), *One Hundred Years of Socialism: the Western European Left in the 20th Century*, I.B. Taurus, London.

Schorske, C.E. (1983), *German Social Democracy, Nineteen Hundred Five to Nineteen Eighteen: The Development of the Great Schism*, Harvard University Press, Cambridge, MA.

Walker, R.B.J (1993), *Inside/Outside: International Relations As Political Theory*, Cambridge University Press, Cambridge.

PART I

ORGANIZING THE ECONOMY IN THE AGE OF GLOBALIZATION – THE INSURMOUNTABLE CHALLENGE FOR THE SOCIAL DEMOCRATIC LEFT?

Chapter 1

The Comparative Political Economy of the 'Third Way'

Peter A. Hall

Introduction

One of the most prominent features of turn-of-the-century politics is the search for a 'Third Way', launched by social democratic parties seeking a new set of policies distinctive from those traditionally pursued by the political left and right. There are multiple dimensions to this quest. In some measure, it is an electoral gambit designed to lend a patina of coherence to policies that might otherwise seem disparate by grouping them under a single slogan. It can also be seen as an effort to define a new public philosophy marked by the integration of market and communitarian principles, analogous to the 'new liberalism' developed in Britain at the turn of the last century (cf. White, 1998; Giddens, 1998; Beer, 1978; Weiler, 1982). These features of the process are far from inimical: after all, it is through such trial-and-error efforts to associate novel policies with a coherent moral vision that political parties construct new images and coalitions for themselves.

In this chapter, I explore another dimension of the search for a third way, namely, its close relationship to developments in the political economy. While far from entirely economic enterprises, the platforms of contemporary social democracy have been deeply conditioned by recent socio-economic developments. In the following sections, I argue that recent changes in the policies of social democratic governments in Europe are similar enough to describe them as a common movement toward something like a 'Third Way' and explore the relationship of these changes to transnational economic developments. I then consider the principal differences in the political economies and social policy regimes of the European nations and argue that these differences will condition the opportunities and constraints facing social democrats in each nation. My principal contention is that the origins and fate of the political projects associated with a 'Third Way' are dependent on the character of contemporary political economies. I review the recent history of policy making by the social democratic governments of Britain, Germany and France with a view to establishing whether we find the differences in policy this perspective would lead us to expect and conclude that there are substantial differences in the recent trajectories of policy. My overarching point is that the British policies most often associated with the 'Third Way' are well suited to its liberal market economy but that social democrats will have to pursue somewhat different policies if they are to succeed elsewhere in Europe.

The Commonalities of the Third Way

The rhetoric of social democracy varies across Europe. Tony Blair, the Labour Prime Minister of Britain, has been a vocal exponent of the 'Third Way'. Gerhard Schröder, the Social Democratic Chancellor of Germany, accepted the idea but preferred to describe his policies as those of the *Neue Mitte* or 'new middle'. Lionel Jospin, when Socialist Prime Minister of France, explicitly disavowed the term in favour of a rhetoric that described his goals as ones of modernization and republicanism. Nevertheless, there are enough similarities in the break these three governments have made with previous socialist policy to justify the contention that they moved towards a 'Third Way'. Four commonalities characterize this movement.

The first is a new-found appreciation for the profitability of business. For over a century, the ideology of social democracy emphasized the conflicts of interest between capital and labour. The tension between the interest of workers in wages and of capital in profits was seen as central to this conflict, and social democrats long defined themselves as the defenders of labour. Accordingly, social democratic parties rarely presented themselves as the defenders of business interests, expressed frequent suspicion about the level of profits, and usually gave greater priority to increasing wages than profits.

The late twentieth century brought a sea-change in such views. After three years in which it had raised wages and substituted public for private investment, the socialist government of France made an abrupt turn in 1983. It expressed concern for the low levels of profitability of French business, began to reduce corporate taxes, and put new limits on wage increases in order to enhance the rate of return to French firms. Subsequent socialist governments followed suit, using a variety of measures to improve profit levels in France (cf. Hall, 1987, 1990, 2001). Some of the first steps taken by the German social democrats after their election in 1999 were to reduce the basic rate of tax on corporations and to eliminate capital gains tax on sales of corporate shareholdings. In each case, the object was to improve the profitability of German business. Even before its election in 1997, the British Labour party began to court the business community. Once in office, Blair appointed a leading industrialist as his minister for European affairs, and several initiatives to secure the profitability of British firms. Across Europe, social democratic governments have begun to evince real concern for corporate profitability.

After years of hostility, the social democratic governments of Europe have also begun to embrace market mechanisms. Inspired by Marx's biting critique of the 'cash nexus' and the alienating effects of market relations, social democratic parties have often seen their mission as one of limiting the role of markets in the allocation of resources and the impact of market relations on labour. Many of their social policies were designed to 'decommodify' labour, and their economic policies have sought to rectify the inefficiencies of market mechanisms by expanding the role of the state in the economy (cf. Esping-Andersen, 1990; Foote, 1986).

By the end of the 1980s, however, most of the social democratic parties of Europe were celebrating the value of market mechanisms for allocating resources. This was one of the central themes of the joint declaration that Blair and Schröder (1999, p.3) issued to promote the Third Way, announcing that 'the essential function of markets must be complemented and improved by political action, not hampered by it'. Shortly thereafter, Schröder endorsed the deregulation of shop hours in Germany, took measures to sharpen commercial competition, and expressed sympathy for deregulatory measures in several spheres of the economy. The socialist government of France made even greater efforts during the 1980s to deregulate financial markets, to increase the influence of public enterprises to market forces, and to expose the French economy to more extensive competition in a single European market (cf. Streeck, 1996). In Britain, the Blair government accepted most of the measures taken by its Conservative predecessors to enhance market competition in the economy; and it has embraced the use of market mechanisms inside the public sector itself with a view to improving the efficiency with which education, health and social services are delivered. A new 'welfare to work' scheme undercuts the capacity of individuals to use social benefits as a means of reducing their dependence on the labour market.

The social democratic governments of Europe have also significantly softened their emphasis on the value of addressing socioeconomic problems by expanding public spending in favour of a new emphasis on policies that are essentially regulatory in character, seeking improvements in social life without corresponding increases in social spending. Again, this represents a significant break with the past. For years, social democratic parties were associated with higher levels of public spending. They have been the most prominent proponents of large welfare states and industrial spending.

During the 1990s, however, the social democratic governments of Britain and Germany, and to a lesser extent France, all put strict limits on the growth of public expenditure. They balanced additions to spending in some spheres with cuts in others; and all have made a point of reducing various kinds of taxation. None made public spending the centrepiece of their programmes. Instead, the social democratic governments of the 1990s put increasing emphasis on what might be termed 'moral issues' of the sort associated with civil liberties, citizenship, and crime. It is surely far from coincidental that such issues can be addressed without spending large sums of money. The Jospin government liberalized the regulations governing civil marriage to improve the position of gay couples and others living together and took well-publicized measures to improve the rights of immigrants. The German government has implemented major reforms allowing immigrants freer access to German citizenship. In Britain, the government committed itself to a major series of constitutional reforms, including reform of the House of Lords, the establishment of regional assemblies for Scotland and Wales, and liberalizing access to government information, all in the name of improving the quality of British democracy. In each of these cases, a social democratic government sought to retain its mantle as the defender of 'social justice' without committing itself to extensive new spending, by redefining social justice in terms that emphasize regulatory reform rather than social benefits. Emblematic of this movement is the new attention Blair devoted to fighting crime, a dimension of social protection long seen as the preserve of the right.

Finally, all of these governments have reversed their traditional stance toward unemployment, moving away from Keynesian approaches in which deficit spending is used to stimulate demand toward ones that see unemployment as a supply-side problem to be addressed by manpower policy and changes in labour-market arrangements. The British Labour party was one of the first to adopt a Keynesian approach to unemployment during the 1950s, but reflation was also central to the initiatives of the German social democrats during the 1960s and of the French socialists in the early 1980s. One by one, these parties have backed away from such positions toward ones that stress the importance of active manpower policies and of improving the qualifications of the workforce.

During the 1980s, the French socialists embarked on a successful programme to provide all workers with at least two years of schooling beyond the *baccalauréat*. In the 1990s, the Jospin government implemented supply-side measures based on the creation of new kinds of positions in the public sector and extensive subsidies for hiring or training the unemployed, as well as a legislated movement to the 35-hour work week. The Blair government adopted a 'New Deal' for labour designed partly to strengthen vocational training by offering access to new forms of formal education. Although German initiatives have remained more tentative, they too concentrate on the supply-side of the economy. Schröder used tax reductions and the renegotiation of skill categories in vocational training schemes to address unemployment and called on business and labour organizations to negotiate more far-reaching supply-side solutions. All these governments moved away from activist macroeconomic management, pledging reductions in public sector deficits and accepting central banks that are independent from the political authorities.

In sum, the social democratic parties of Britain, France and Germany have all moved away from some of the positions long considered most central to social democracy. And, despite some differences in national paths, there are substantial enough similarities in them to support the contention that there is a transnational movement in European social democracy toward something like a 'Third Way'.

The Genesis of the Third Way

Behind this ideological transformation, of course, lies a struggle for electoral advantage. In democratic polities, most shifts in a major party's programme will be based on a calculation about how it can secure office, given the attitudes of the electorate and the placement of other parties vis-à-vis those attitudes (cf. Kitschelt, 1994). In this respect, the turn toward neoliberalism, taken to varying degrees by mainstream parties of the right during the 1980s, was an important precondition for these movements by their socialist competitors. By pushing the views of the electorate toward the right on some issues, neoliberal politicians helped push social democratic parties in that direction as well. It is implausible that the British Labour party would be taking many of its current positions if it had not been forced to react to the neoliberalism of Margaret Thatcher (Notermans, 1993).

However, there are good reasons for looking beyond electoral currents to explain these shifts in the platforms of social democratic parties. They occurred in France and Germany where neoliberal ideology was never as popular as it was in Britain during the 1980s. Even there, the views of the electorate did not shift as far to the right as did those of the Thatcher government: if the Labour party were simply chasing the attitudes of the electorate, it need not have moved so far on many issues (cf. Norris, 1999). Moreover, neoliberal ideology itself was partly a response to international economic developments, and it is notable that social democratic leaders have tended to justify their new positions by reference to such developments. In short, the recent transformation of European social democracy has some roots in fundamental shifts in the political economy, to which governments have believed they must respond. Three such developments are of prime importance.

The most prominent of these developments are increasing levels of international interdependence associated with the process of 'globalization' (cf. Giddens, 1998). Trade integration has been increasing since the 1950s; but the exponential increase in international financial transactions during the 1980s, the removal of exchange controls, the creation of a single European market, and the availability of new foreign markets created when Communism collapsed and liberal regulatory regimes were adopted in many nations fundamentally altered the set of opportunities and constraints facing the developed economies. There are many respects in which these developments militate against traditional socialist policies.

In more open economies, it is difficult for governments to reduce unemployment by increasing public spending, as the Mitterrand government discovered in 1982–83, because a significant portion of the consumer demand that is created leaks into imports, and the deficit spending that such policies entail puts downward pressure on exchange rates and can accelerate inflation. Movements toward floating exchange rates and higher levels of capital mobility of the sort that occurred in the 1970s and 1980s exacerbate such constraints. If they cannot limit flows of funds out of their economies, governments must adopt deflationary monetary policies if they want to defend their exchange rate; and interventionist industrial policies that depend on a government's capacity to ration domestic capital become less powerful once domestic firms have access to international capital markets (cf. Hall, 1987; Frieden, 1991; Notermans, 1993). The liberalization of international regimes for trade and finance rendered the activist macroeconomic and interventionist industrial policies on which some social democratic governments long relied much less potent than they might once have been.

Of course, social democratic governments could have withdrawn from these liberal international regimes to practice 'socialism in one country'. However, it is not difficult to understand why the European governments did not take that route. The new international economic order did not simply impose new constraints on governments. It also opened up new opportunities for national producers that even social democratic governments were loath to forego. The establishment of a single European market offered the firms of France, Germany and Britain an opportunity to produce for new markets that would be closed to nations not participating in the liberal regulatory regimes that govern it. Could any government refuse the employment opportunities this new continental market seemed to offer? Precisely such opportunities drew the social democratic governments of Sweden and Austria into the European Union (EU), notwithstanding the policy changes entry might entail. In recent years, significant portions of business and organized labour have been strong proponents of international integration.

The impact of such developments on the thinking of social democrats is evident in the words Tony Blair chose to justify his search for a Third Way:

> We live in a world of global capital and rapid knowledge transfer…We cannot as governments guarantee prosperity for our people by putting up barriers that protect them against the rigors of the new competitive challenge. But what we can do is equip people with the capabilities to meet that challenge (Blair, 1999, p. 2).

In short, the new social democracy is conditioned by globalization and deeply committed to it. International economic integration of the sort Europe has recently experienced encourages precisely the type of policy shifts associated with the Third Way. Because public sector deficits put greater pressure on exchange rates and inflation in a more open economic context, the latter engenders caution about public spending. Liberal trade regimes tend to interpret traditional industrial subsidies as unfair trade practices and militate against subsidies that inhibit firms from developing the competitive practices that guarantee survival amidst intense international competition. Therefore, increases in international economic integration encourage the replacement of industrial subsidies with manpower policies designed to improve the skills of the workforce, so as to enhance the comparative advantage of developed nations vis-à-vis developing ones and to facilitate the productivity gains that justify wage increases even in the face of international price competition. As Giddens (1998) has observed, the Third Way can be seen as an effort to adapt social democracy to more intense international integration.

However, globalization is not the only important economic development of the current era. Although it is given less attention, the shift from an industrial to increasingly post-industrial economies may be just as consequential for social democracy (cf. Esping-Andersen, 1999; Cusak and Iversen, 2000). Traditional social democratic policies built on efforts to strengthen trade unions and increase wages were suited to industrial economies where high rates of productivity growth could be used to sustain high wages, and wage growth could be relied upon to expand demand. Because the industrial sector is a propitious site for productivity growth, in an economy that is largely industrial, wages, profits and social spending can grow in tandem. The social stability of the post-war years depended on the virtuous circles associated with increases in industrial productivity that brought high rates of economic growth and made it possible for the public and private sectors to expand simultaneously (cf. Boyer, 1990; Appelbaum and Schettkatt, 1994).

In recent decades, as industrial employment has moved to the developing world and consumer tastes have shifted, however, employment in the industrial sector has been shrinking and employment in the service sector expanding throughout most of the developed world. A significant portion of economic activity today takes place in services, whether in retailing, tourism, personal services, health and education, or business and financial services, and, if jobs are to be created in the coming years, they are likely to have to be created in the service sector (Esping-Andersen, 1999). But productivity in services has tended to increase at rates lower than those of industry. As a result, the growth of employment in many parts of the service sector depends on the tolerance of an economy for lower levels of wages and lower rates of wage increase there (Iversen and Wren, 1998).

The implications for social democracy are substantial. These developments call into question policies designed to strengthen the trade unions, to equalize wages by raising the compensation of the low paid, and to provide social protection via policies that raise the reservation wage or impose high non-wage costs on employers. Those policies militate against the development of a low wage sector on which job creation in some spheres of services may depend. But social democratic parties remain committed to full employment and find themselves in a bind: should they encourage the development of low wage, service sector jobs or resign themselves to relatively high rates of unemployment, as the high wage industrial sector declines?

This tension is reflected in new divisions within the labour movement. A core labour force composed of 'insiders' with high skills and high wages tends to resist measures to lower labour costs or deregulate labour markets, lest it encounter more intense wage competition without adequate social protection. Against it are arrayed groups of 'outsiders' composed of those who are unemployed or on the margins of the labour force seeking measures to expand employment even if that entails the development of a low wage service sector. In many nations, the natural constituency for social democratic parties is divided along such lines.

Thus, the rise of the service sector is putting pressure on social democratic parties to move beyond traditional efforts to equalize wages and strengthen trade unions. The growing importance of the service sector to the employment prospects of a nation has encouraged many of these parties to consider forms of labour market deregulation they would never have countenanced in previous eras, including the relaxation of restrictions on hiring and firing, measures to encourage part-time employment, and provisions for more flexible labour contracts. Despite strong resistance from the trade unions, the German government has expanded the opening hours of retail shops. The French government has made strenuous efforts to expand part-time employment. And both governments are trying to drive down health and social security benefits so as to reduce the social charges that drive up the cost of labour. Much of the fiscal pressure on the governments of continental Europe today stems from taxation systems that pay for social security with social charges on employers and employees that militate against the expansion of employment by driving up the non-wage cost of labour, while demographic pressures demand expansion of the labour force in order to support an aging population that will generate many more pensioners in twenty years' time. Rightly or wrongly, most European governments in the 1990s believed that the expansion of employment will depend on reductions in labour costs; and this is driving many social democratic parties in new directions.

Finally, many of Europe's social democratic parties have been influenced by profound disillusionment with the effectiveness of the economic measures they took when they were in government during the 1970s or early 1980s. Although many factors produced high rates of unemployment and inflation across the developed world in those years, the decade from 1974 to 1984 was a watershed for European socialism. Many social democratic governments pursued traditional policies in that period only to find that they failed to stem the rising tide of unemployment and inflation (cf. Lindberg and Maier, 1985; Goldthorpe, 1984; Berger, 1982). As much as anything else, this experienced inspired a search for new types of policies.

The strenuous efforts of the 1974–79 Labour government to impose an incomes policy and cut public spending resulted in an industrial relations crisis and electoral defeat that left a deep mark on the electorate and those who would later lead the party. It convinced many that an incomes policies could not be made to work in Britain and that other means would have to be found to tackle inflation. In France, the failure of attempts in 1980–83 to expand investment via redistributive reflation and activist industrial policies that channeled vast sums into industry left many leaders of the Socialist party convinced that investment and employment would grow only if the profitability of French business was improved. It led them to turn away from *dirigiste* policies based on state intervention toward strategies of selective deregulation in labour and capital markets designed to improve the capacity of the economy to reallocate resources across endeavours.

In short, the search for a Third Way is not simply an electoral tactic designed to steal the clothes of the political right while preserving a base on the left. It must also be seen as a response to fundamental economic changes that called into question traditional socialist policies and demanded new responses. There are many respects in which traditional social democracy was well-designed for an 'industrial age', when high rates of growth and rapid increases in productivity allowed the public and private sectors to expand in tandem, and when powerful trade unions could be seen as the social agents for a virtuous circle in which rising wages fed aggregate demand. Today, European social democracy is adapting to an era in which international integration has rendered many of its traditional instruments less effective and the rise of the service sector has driven a wedge through its traditional constituency. Whether or not it is successful, the search for a Third Way is the latest stage in a long learning process linked to the transformation of capitalism itself.

National Variation in Political Economies and Welfare States

The history of policy debate within the social democratic movement is a long and distinguished one stretching back to the nineteenth century. For the most part, it is a debate that treats capitalism as a monolithic form, subject to variation over time, but relatively homogenous across the developed world. Most contributors to that debate have sought policies that would work across all the developed democracies, much as proponents of the Third Way do today (cf. Przeworski, 1985).

However, the field of comparative political economy draws our attention to systematic differences in the operation of capitalism across nations (cf. Shonfield, 1969; Hall, 1986; Esping-Andersen, 1990). It suggests that nations may face distinctive economic challenges that demand quite different policy regimes. Of course, the relationship between the organization of the political economy and the national set of policy regimes is also symbiotic: each influences the development of the other. The clear implication is that, despite the commonalities I have outlined, the paths taken by social democratic parties in Europe should diverge. I now turn to this variation.

To characterize political economies, I will employ a 'varieties of capitalism' perspective that is elaborated more fully elsewhere.[1] It begins from the contention

---

[1] For an extended discussion of this approach, see Hall and Soskice 2001. I am indebted to David Soskice and the contributors to this volume for collaborative work that informs this account.

that individual firms are key actors in any capitalist economy. It is their response to economic developments that aggregates into overall economic performance. Firms develop core competencies that turn on the quality of the relationships they form with other actors to cope with the challenges they face in five arenas, those of industrial relations, finance, skill acquisition, inter-firm relations, and employer-employee relations. To meet these challenges, the firm must coordinate its strategies with the actions of others in each of these arenas, and economic performance will depend on the effectiveness of this coordination.

Accordingly, national political economies can be compared with reference to the ways in which firms coordinate their endeavours. The principal difference lies between *liberal market economies*, where firms rely for coordination primarily on the arm's length relations and formal-contracting characteristic of competitive markets, and *coordinated market economies*, where firms put greater reliance on non-market forms of coordination that entail strategic interaction with other actors, underpinned by facilities for the exchange of information, monitoring, sanctioning and deliberation of the sort that effective strategic coordination demands. Within each of these two types, there is variation, but many political economies can be described by how they combine these types of coordination.

The kind of coordination in which the firms of a nation will engage depends on the presence of institutional support for that type of coordination in the national political economy. Coordinated market economies typically contain dense inter-corporate networks based on cross-shareholding, powerful business associations and trade unions capable of providing the network monitoring that strategic coordination demands. Liberal market economies provide the legal systems and regulatory regimes that render markets more competitive and generate the effective price signals important to coordination there. Thus, the organization of the political economy gives rise to systematic variations in corporate strategy across nations and comparative national advantages for undertaking certain kinds of economic endeavours. Firms in liberal market economies, for instance, find it easier to engage in radical innovation, while coordinated market economies provide more support for incremental innovation and high levels of quality control (cf. Soskice, 1994; Hall and Soskice, 2001).

Among the OECD nations, six can be classified as liberal market economies (the U.S., Britain, Australia, Canada, New Zealand, Ireland) and ten as coordinated market economies (Germany, Japan, Switzerland, the Netherlands, Belgium, Sweden, Norway, Denmark, Finland, and Austria), leaving six others in a cluster around the Mediterranean (France, Italy, Spain, Portugal, Greece, and Turkey) which do not conform completely to either model and where the role of the state in the economy still remains prominent (cf. Rhodes, 1997).

The social policy regimes of these nations also display systematic differences related to the variety of capitalism in place there. The influential typology of Esping-Andersen (1990) provides a nice characterization of these regimes. In general, liberal market economies have a *liberal welfare state* characterized by relatively low levels of social benefits, a restrictive approach to eligibility for benefits that emphasizes means testing, and benefit periods of relatively short duration. Britain provides the paradigmatic case of such a regime. Coordinated market economies are more likely to have *social democratic welfare states* or *conservative welfare states*. The former offer generous levels of benefits available for substantial periods of time and on a universalistic basis that bases access to benefits on a general social citizenship. The latter also offer high levels of benefits that can be drawn for significant periods of time, but benefits levels and access to particular types of benefits varies more substantially by occupational status. In conservative welfare states there is typically a mosaic of benefit systems, administered partly by producer groups, with the most generous benefits assigned to public employees and skilled workers employed in the core economy. France and Germany both have conservative welfare states, while the social democratic variant is commonly found in the Nordic nations.

These social policy regimes are relatively resilient features of the national political economy. As Pierson (1996) has noted, it is difficult to change the structure of a nation's benefit programmes because strong constituencies for those programmes arise among the electorate and the groups that administer them. Recent scholarship shows that firms also develop strong interests in particular types of social policies that increase political resistance to proposals to shift from one social policy regime to another (Mares, 1998; Estevez, 1999; Swenson, 1999).

Social policy regimes connect to varieties of capitalism primarily through the support they provide for particular kinds of corporate strategy. By forcing people into the workforce, the low benefit levels and strict eligibility criteria of a liberal welfare state, for instance, help sustain the highly fluid labour markets on which firms in liberal market economy tend to depend. They complement the low-wage, cost-conscious strategies characteristic of many firms in such economies by depressing the reservation wage. In contrast, by assuring workers of generous benefits should they become unemployed, the high benefit levels and prolonged benefit periods available to skilled workers in conservative welfare states encourage individuals to develop the industry-specific skills central to the production strategies of many firms in coordinated market economies; and they encourage firms to make use of such skills by assuring them that skilled labour will remain available through a recession (cf. Estevez et al., 1999). Firms in coordinated market economies use the generous early retirement programmes of these welfare states to renew their labour force without violating the spirit of the long-term labor contracts that firms in these economies typically employ (Mares, 1998).

The Implications of Variation for the Third Way

Systematic variations in the organization of the political economy and social policy regimes of the sort I have just described conditions both the direction taken by social democratic parties as they search for new policies and the likely success with which any particular type of policy can be implemented in a nation. The character of the political economy affects both the complexion of the problems it faces and the feasibility of specific solutions. This perspective contains a number of implications for the contemporary efforts of European social democrats to identify and pursue a Third Way.

This analysis implies that many of the new policies associated with the Third Way as it has developed in Britain may not work as well in the continental nations. The *leitmotif* of Britain's Third Way is its emphasis on the market. Compared to the manifestos of previous Labour governments, the most striking feature of the Blair government's platform is its insistence on retaining and sharpening market mechanisms. Few of the deregulatory measures of the Thatcher era have been reversed. The government continues to expand the role of markets for allocating resources even within the spheres traditionally reserved to the government. The position of the trade unions has been improved only marginally. The significant social reforms associated with Blair's 'welfare to work' programme have been designed to reinforce, rather than undercut, the incentives associated with competitive labour markets.

As a result, the government's programme is congruent with the demands of a liberal market economy for highly fluid labour markets, readily available labour at low cost, and general, rather than firm- or industry-specific, skills. The Blair government has sharpened the operation of market mechanisms in an economy whose firms depend on such mechanisms to coordinate their endeavours. By contrast, most firms in the coordinated market economies of Europe rely more heavily on various forms of strategic coordination to accomplish the same tasks, and policies that sharpen market competition can undermine the institutions that sustain strategic coordination. Accordingly, a Third Way heavily oriented toward market mechanisms may threaten the corporate strategies on which economic success depends in coordinated market economies, such as that of Germany.

However, some of the policies associated with social democratic efforts to define a Third Way will be more difficult to implement in Britain than on the continent. Among these are efforts to improve the skill levels of the workforce, the centrepiece even of British efforts to expand employment. Vocational training designed to foster industry-specific skills is invariably difficult to accomplish in a liberal market economy because its firms typically lack the dense interconnections provided by powerful employers' associations and on which effective firm-based collaboration in vocational training depends (cf. Culpepper, 2001; Finegold and Soskice, 1988). Individuals have few incentives to acquire specialized or industry-specific skills in the contexts of high labour turnover where social benefit regimes force those who become unemployed to seek any job available. Instead, in liberal market economies, the government must rely primarily on improvements in formal education to raise general skill levels, as the British Labour government has done, and this can be a relatively blunt instrument.

By contrast, many of the continental nations are likely to find it easier to raise and maintain the skill-levels of their workforce. In Germany, dense inter-corporate networks and powerful employers' associations organized along industry lines support a vocational training scheme that can deliver high levels of industry-specific skills. The main problem here is to adjust skill categories and training systems to accommodate the changes demanded by new technology and, although the relevant negotiations take some time, the organizational vehicles for renegotiating skill categories exist in such an economy. Similarly, in coordinated market economies like that of Germany, it is easier for governments to mount the 'framework programmes' that diffuse new technology throughout a sector. Industry associations privy to the relevant private information that firms would be reluctant to share with governments can be used to administer such programmes (Katzenstein, 1987; Ziegler, 1997; Wood, 1997). In short, it may be easier for the social democratic governments of coordinated market economies to encourage strategies of industrial adaptation grounded on efforts to raise skill levels, increase the value-added of production, and improve quality control so as to capture important market niches in a more global economy.

Accordingly, we should expect to see systematic differences in the initiatives undertaken by social democratic governments across liberal (LME) and coordinated (CME) market economies. In LMEs, various forms of deregulation are likely to be a prominent component of government initiatives, because they are complementary to market modes of coordination and governments presiding over such economies lack the organized social partners required if they are to mount alternative strategies built around negotiation and framework policies. Conversely, it will be more difficult to secure deregulation in coordinated market economies because they face highly organized producer groups with strong interests in preserving the regulatory regimes that support strategic, rather than market, coordination.

Instead, the programmes of social democratic governments in coordinated market economies should be oriented somewhat differently, to capitalize on the distinctive strengths of such economies. Consider the sphere of labour market regulation. Many firms in coordinated market economies rely on long-term employment and high levels of employment security to pursue production strategies that demand the active cooperation of the workforce. Such firms will be loath to endorse labour market deregulation and more inclined to seek other ways of improving labour flexibility via negotiated changes to labour practices. Accordingly, the social democratic governments are more likely to encourage negotiation among the social partners about working conditions and the organization of work. Their efforts to increase employment are more likely to emphasize schemes for work-sharing and shorter working hours that do not threaten existing work practices, rather than relaxation of the regulations governing the hiring and firing of workers.

The policy problems facing social democratic governments that preside over conservative welfare states are also considerably more difficult than those facing British governments that superintend a liberal welfare state. All recent European governments have been preoccupied with public spending. But the British welfare state is in relatively good fiscal shape: the eligibility requirements for social benefits have encouraged high rates of labour force participation, and low benefit levels, while a problem in other respects, limit the fiscal pressure on the state. By contrast, because their conservative welfare regimes offer more generous benefits, the governments of France and Germany face more intense fiscal pressure as their workforce ages. Because many of the programmes characteristic of such welfare regimes, including substantial maternity benefits, expansive disability plans, and early retirement programmes privilege exit over entry into the labour force, overall rates of labour force participation are also low in these nations.[2] They face serious questions about how they will support the large number of retirees expected in the coming years with a relatively small labour force. As a result, the governments of France and Germany face a more substantial fiscal crisis and much greater pressure to expand the workforce than do the British.[3]

Adding to their woes is the structure of taxation. The conservative welfare states of France and Germany are financed largely by social charges paid by employers and employees, while the British fund their social benefits more fully from income taxes. In the context of an industrial era that provided full employment, these differences did not pose major problems. As the expansion of the service sector raises the importance of creating low-cost jobs, however, the substantial increment that social charges add to labour costs has become a major drawback. These economies are having difficulty creating jobs in many parts of the service sector (cf. Esping-Andersen, 1999; Scharpf and Schmidt, 2000).[4] Their governments face a fiscal squeeze because the imperatives of job creation make it impractical for them to increase social charges to support the growing proportion of the population that is retired; and efforts to bring the social security system back into fiscal balance entail major changes to the tax structure, a task that is fraught with political peril (cf. Levy, 1999).

---

[2] The labour force participation rate is currently almost 70 per cent in Britain, 64 per cent in Germany and barely 59 per cent in France.

[3] In the European Union as a whole, current estimates are that the active workforce will drop from 185 million today to 135 million in 2020, as an additional 50 million people move into retirement.

[4] It has been observed that, when non-wage costs are added to the minimum wage, the cost of employing a worker in France at the lowest feasible rate of pay is higher than that at which about 20 percent of the American workforce is employed.

Finally, the organization of the political economy conditions the *politics* of social reform. In Britain, the organization of trade unions and employers is relatively decentralized and power within the state itself is highly concentrated in the political executive. Accordingly, organized social interests have few capacities with which to resist the government's initiatives (cf. Wood, 1997). Vis-à-vis producer groups at least, the Labour government enjoys considerable room for manoeuvre. Where producer groups are more highly-organized and power is concentrated in a few peak organizations, however, as in Germany for instance, and power within the state itself relatively dispersed among legislative chambers and powerful Länder, it is much more difficult for any social democratic government to dictate the pace or direction of change (cf. Katzenstein, 1987). Here, a negotiated path toward reform is the only feasible one, and reform processes are bound to be slower, as the government attempts to mobilize consent from the many groups with substantial influence over policy.

The administration of the welfare state is also relevant to the politics of social reform. In Britain, social policy falls largely under the control of officials of the central government, rendering changes to social policy straightforward, if not without electoral risk. By contrast, many of the social policies of Germany and France, while funded from the public purse, are administered by para-public bodies in which professional or employer associations and trade unions are strongly represented. In these contexts, producer groups are better placed to resist changes to social policy, and the highly variegated benefit structures of conservative welfare states intensify the political problems by providing key groups of workers with distinctive sets of benefits that they will be inclined to mobilize to protect.

In sum, despite broad similarities in the challenges that social democratic governments face across Europe, it would be unreasonable to expect a monolithic response from them. Systematic differences in the political economies and welfare states of the developed nations generate distinctive problems in each that militate in favour of distinctive responses. The new social democrats do not face a *tabula rasa*. Comparative political economy specifies that what they can do will be conditioned by where they begin.

One Third Way or Many?

Are the predictions that this perspective generates about variation in the strategies of social democratic governments borne out by the evidence? Although we have only a few years of experience against which to test this perspective, I turn to that task, considering the cases of Britain, France and Germany.

Britain

The Labour governments under Tony Blair that Britain elected in 1997 and again in 2001 have taken great pains to emphasize their break with the traditional doctrines of social democracy and the importance of a search for a Third Way. The Blair governments have cultivated close relations with business and distant relations (at least in public) with the trade unions. While expressing distaste for a 'market society', Blair (1999) has endorsed the 'market economy'. Pledged to preserve the welfare state, the government has nonetheless made substantial reforms to it that tend to intensify, rather than offset, the impact of market incentives.

The Labour government's programme can best be seen as a highly-selective reaction to the eighteen years of Conservative governance that preceded it and to the deep imprint Margaret Thatcher left on the British polity. She took full advantage of the powerful British state to impose a forceful set of reforms (cf. Gamble, 1988; Riddell, 1990). On the one hand, the Blair government has reacted against the *political* agenda of the Thatcher years and its authoritarian tinge, by initiating constitutional reforms designed to strengthen civil liberties, devolve power to the regions, and reform the House of Lords. On the other hand, the government has accepted much of the *economic* agenda of the Thatcher government, rolling back few of Thatcher's industrial relations reforms, accepting the privatization of nationalized enterprise, rendering the Bank of England more independent from the government, and pursuing efforts to introduce market competition into public services.

It is in the realm of social services that the government has been most innovative and most inclined to describe its policies as harbingers of a Third Way. The centrepiece of these efforts is a 'welfare to work' scheme, based on the American model of 'workfare', that requires large numbers of people who formerly received social benefits to take up subsidized positions in firms or training schemes, including most of those under the age of 25 or over 55, single parents, and some of the disabled (cf. King and Wickham-Jones, 1999). Coupled to this is a 'New Deal' for labour designed to tackle the problems of unemployment and national competitiveness by increasing the skills of the workforce. For this purpose, the New Deal relies heavily on incentives for the young to continue their formal education and it provides some new vehicles for them to do so.

In general, as I have noted, these measures are designed to serve the needs of firms in a liberal market economy, and they conform closely to the orientations of a liberal welfare state. The Blair government has avoided major initiatives to develop apprenticeship programmes delivering industry-specific skills in favour of alternative schemes that raise general skill levels through the extension of formal education.[5] This type of initiative speaks to the high demand from firms in liberal market economies for general skills and the limited organizational capabilities of employers in such an economy for mounting effective apprenticeship programmes. The 'welfare to work' scheme is congruent with an economy in which firms make extensive use of low-wage labour. Not only does it avoid more generous social benefits that might raise the reservation wage (the wage below which the unemployed will not seek work), it actively pushes those on social benefit into the labour force, further reducing upward pressure on wages.

The enthusiasm that the British Labour government has shown for market mechanisms is striking. Many social democrats have argued that the central mission of social democracy is to reduce the dependence of individuals on markets (cf. Polanyi, 1944; Esping-Andersen, 1990). In many cases, the Blair government has not simply accepted the role of market mechanisms in the allocation of resources but reinforced their bite. It is apparent that the character of the British economy has influenced the government. In a liberal market economy, where firms use markets to coordinate their endeavours, the government's initiatives conform well to the existing corporate strategies of British firms.

Germany

The social democratic coalition elected in Germany in 1999 under Gerhard Schröder has moved more slowly, and it is difficult to associate it with a clear pattern of policy. However, like Blair, Schröder declared himself anxious to break with tradition in search of a 'new middle'. He argued that Germany must change in directions that give greater prominence to market competition and followed through with significant reductions in social spending and corporate taxation. One of his boldest moves has been to remove the capital gains taxes on a firm's sale of shares in other firms, paving the way for German companies to divest themselves of the extensive cross-shareholdings that have long been one of the pillars of close inter-corporate relations there.

From the perspective of comparative political economy, this last move is somewhat perplexing. The access to patient capital, upon which many German firms rely, has long been dependent on the presence of dense inter-corporate networks that allow suppliers of finance to monitor developments inside the firms they are funding; and cross-shareholding is central to such networks. If the practice of cross-shareholding declines significantly in the wake of this initiative, German firms may find it more difficult to secure access to this kind of capital; and the

---

[5] General skills are those that are portable across firms or industries as compared to the firm- or industry-specific skills that may entail greater technical proficiency and efficiency at some tasks but that cannot readily be used beyond the firms or industries for which they were developed (cf. Estevez et al., 1999).

effects of being exposed to more stringent demands to sustain shareholder value could be far-reaching, ultimately affecting the labour practices of many German firms as well (cf. Hall and Soskice, 2001). How much cross-shareholding will decline and whether it will significantly damage the capacities of German firms for network monitoring remains to be seen. It is clear, however, that Schröder is responding to two demands, one from the large German banks seeking the freedom to become global enterprises, the other from firms seeking greater capacities to transfer resources into high-growth sectors (cf. Vogel, 1999; Ziegler, 2000).

The cuts the German social democrats have made in social spending are less surprising and can be explained by the dilemmas of a conservative welfare state in the contemporary era. The cutbacks emphasize pensions, where fiscal pressure is severe given the low rates of labour force participation that such a welfare state encourages combined with an aging population. It is notable that, unlike the British, the German government has not made extensive changes to its system of unemployment benefits. This acknowledges the key role those benefits play in securing the high levels of industry-specific skills important to a coordinated market economy (Estevez et al., 1999; Mares, 1998).

Equally noteworthy is the slow pace of deregulation in German labour markets. Schröder endorsed the lengthening of shop hours, despite opposition from the trade unions, and his government made efforts to expand part-time employment, with a view to increasing the labour force available to support social spending. But, even in the face of high levels of unemployment, there have been no efforts to make hiring and firing easier, despite suggestions that such measures would encourage new hires. Instead, Germany has continued to tackle its employment problems by finding novel forms of work sharing, often through sectoral agreements in which employers reduce working hours in exchange for greater flexibility in shift work and working practices.[6] Here, we see the influence of the longstanding practices of a coordinated market economy in which the production strategies of many firms depend on intensive cooperation with employees who have a long-term stake in the enterprise. To shift to a labour regime marked by high rates of labour turnover would disrupt many of the work practices on which German firms depend for their competitive advantages. Of course, an emphasis on work sharing also tends to preserve jobs in the industrial economy, where the core constituency of the trade union movement is concentrated. As such, it is politically feasible even though it tends to disadvantage those on the margins of the labour force who might prefer to see jobs created in other sectors, even at the cost of higher wage differentials and less employment security (cf. Manow and Seils, 2000).

---

[6] Significant agreements of this sort have been undertaken in both the automobile and chemical sectors.

In many respects, the dilemmas that the German social democrats have faced are more intense than those confronting the British. They have had to contend with demands from German business for greater flexibility to reallocate resources to cope with a rapidly changing international environment without damaging the capacities of the German economy for strategic coordination. This calls for a careful balancing act in which market competition is enhanced in some spheres without eroding the basis for cooperation in others. At the same time, the government has had to find ways of expanding employment in a capital-intensive economy in the face of a trade union movement that is disproportionately sensitive to the needs of a core industrial labour force. In a decentralized political system, virtually all reforms must be preceded by intensive negotiations. As a result, the pace of progress has naturally been slow.

France

The French socialists spent years in office during the 1980s, well before the election of the Jospin government in the spring of 1997. By the end of the 1980s, the French socialists had already decided to promote the profitability of French firms, confirmed the deregulation of French financial markets, and added two years to the formal education of most workers. In some respects, their initiatives anticipated those that would later be taken by Blair and Schröder. Rather than associate himself with a 'Third Way', however, Jospin turned to traditional French themes to characterize his government's approach, emphasizing the importance of 'modernizing' the French economy to cope with 'globalization' and associating himself with the promotion of 'republican' values that assign social solidarity a privileged position in the national mission.

In keeping with these themes, Jospin walked a tightrope, sometimes promoting market measures to enhance the market competitiveness of the French economy, at other times increasing spending to provide social protection in the face of market forces. Although, early in his term, Jospin reacted strongly against the efforts of a Belgian subsidiary of a French firm to layoff workers without a proper social plan, he encouraged the deregulation of markets for corporate governance and allowed foreign investors to purchase large holdings in French firms. His government asserted more control over the health and social security systems, imposing incremental efficiencies on each despite resistance from the associated professional groups, but, in the face of public protests, he stopped short of making major cuts in the generous pension benefits accorded public-sector workers. As a result, levels of public spending as a share of GDP are higher in France than in all but two other western European nations.

In the social sphere, Jospin's strategy was ingeniously suited to the problems and possibilities inherent in a conservative welfare state (cf. Levy, 2000). He cut back the benefits once available to the middle class in favour of concentrating resources on the most needy, veiling each cutback with an extension of means-tested programmes; and, following the precedents set by the social democratic governments of the 1980s, he gradually reduced the social charges that add to labour costs and increased taxes on incomes in order to put social spending on a new fiscal basis. In the social sphere, the 1997–2002 Jospin government proceeded, in some respects by stealth, to reinforce the means-testing of benefits, to shift spending toward active manpower policy, and to enhance the incentives individuals face to enter the labour force.

Jospin's employment strategy was more radical and distinctive. If the British strategy was to minimize regulations on hiring and firing and to push those on welfare into work, while the German strategy stressed work sharing negotiated voluntarily between employers and trade unions, the French strategy depended heavily on the expansion of public sector employment and the provision of subsidies to firms willing to take on the unemployed. Shortly after taking office, Jospin created over 100,000 new jobs in the public sector, often by creating 'new' positions, for instance, ensuring security on public transit, and his government continues to provide substantial incentives to firms to hire and train new workers, giving priority to the 'long-term unemployed'. Shortly thereafter, over the strenuous objections of employers, the government legislated a 35-hour week to be accomplished over five years and on terms to be negotiated at the local level. The calculation was that, if wage increases were kept to low levels over this period, this measure need not increase the labour costs facing French firms.

In the French strategy, we can see the residual impact of the state's prominent role in the economy. Unlike Blair or Schröder, Jospin did not hesitate to use public resources to expand employment or to dictate the terms under which firms could hire labour. Facing a relatively weak set of employers' associations, his government found it easier to implement reforms that were much more difficult to secure in Germany; and a tradition of state intervention rendered forceful measures more palatable in electoral terms than they would have been in Britain.

Like its counterparts elsewhere, however, the Jospin government also took great pains to emphasize its moral vision and progressive legal stance. In the face of the National Front, it took more liberal positions toward immigrants than its conservative opponents, and it liberalized regulations regarding civil marriage despite the opposition of the church. The touchstone for such measures was the commitment to 'republican' values that stress the openness of France to immigration, provided that immigrants assimilate to a French culture, and that prize the secular character of the law. With these measures, the government was appealing beyond the traditional socialist constituency toward a broader 'republican' coalition.

Conclusion

It should be apparent that European social democracy is reinventing itself, much as it did in the 1950s and early 1960s when Gaitskell campaigned against clause four of the Labour party constitution and the German social democrats passed the *Bad Godesberg* Programme (cf. Crosland, 1956). Then as now, a prolonged period of poor electoral results provided the immediate impetus for reform and the broader economic context conditioned much of its content. During the 1950s, the social democratic parties of Europe accepted the basic organization of a capitalist economy but argued that such an economy could be rendered more efficient and humane with limited state intervention built on Keynesian principles and more extensive social benefits. In the 1960s, social democracy became the midwife for the development of a Keynesian welfare state, one of the most striking political developments of the twentieth century (cf. Offe, 1984).

Today, the context for change is different. Although much of the electoral appeal of European social democracy is still based on its defence of the welfare state, the principal problem it faces is how to reconfigure, rather than how to expand, the social programmes that now account for about a quarter of national income in most European nations. After making an uneasy truce with market principles forty years ago, social democratic parties are now being asked to reconcile themselves to more integrated international markets. Most have not rejected the value of state intervention, but all are more cautious about that than they once were, and the modalities of intervention have shifted away from industrial subsidies towards supply-side measures focused on the skill levels of the workforce and the flexibility with which labour and capital are allocated. In this respect, the large countries of Europe are following a path already blazed by its smaller, open economies (Katzenstein, 1985a, b).

In my view, there are enough similarities in the directions that social democracy is taking across Europe to describe the relevant changes as a common movement toward what might be termed a 'Third Way'. However, I have argued that the precise complexion of that Third Way is likely to vary across nations because of national differences in both political economy and political context; and there are significant differences in what the recent social democratic governments of Britain, France and Germany have done that correspond to these variations in context.

All of these governments have taken steps to improve the flexibility of their markets but the Germans have put more emphasis on negotiated adjustment and the French on the power of public intervention. Like the Americans, the British Labour government has embraced a set of social reforms that reinforce the pressure of labour markets on individuals, while the French and Germans have concentrated on incremental reforms to social spending and taxation systems designed to relieve the fiscal pressure threatening continental welfare states (cf. Esping-Andersen, 1996). Although all have tried to improve the skill levels of the workforce, the

French and British social democrats have focused resources on the extension of formal education to improve general skills, while the Germans have been fine-tuning a para-public vocational training system that delivers industry-specific skills. All have sought to expand employment, partly to fund social programmes for an aging population, but the Germans have stressed the value of work sharing as a means to this end, while the French rely more heavily on public employment, and the British on new restrictions governing social benefits. I have suggested that these differences flow not only from national political traditions but from differences in the way in which each political economy is organized.

It remains to be seen how successful each of these programmes will be. They can be assessed along several dimensions. In *electoral* terms, the three social democratic parties considered here all benefited from disarray on the political right, much of it inspired by conflicts over the desirability of international integration. One of the striking features of contemporary political realignment has been the tendency of Europe's social democratic parties to support more extensive international integration, even though the cost is some loss of traditional working-class support to those on the political right who mobilize economic resentment against globalization and the European Union.

In *economic* terms, the success of each nation's strategy will depend heavily on the overall rate of growth in Europe. Any government finds it easier to improve the flexibility of the national economy while simultaneously providing social protection to those who suffer from adjustment in a context where real incomes are rising. After some years of broad, if uneven, prosperity, the recession of 2001 sharply increased the dilemmas of social democrats in France and Germany, threatening both with electoral defeat. Until then, the social democratic governments of Britain, France and Germany elected in the 1990s could be said to be doing well if success were measured by modest rates of economic growth and gradual declines in levels of unemployment. In broader terms, however, the balance sheet that could be drawn up for each government reflects the distinctiveness of its strategy. Although the British Labour government presided over the most sustained prosperity, its failure to invest even more heavily in public services, after two decades of prior neglect, has left many dissatisfied with the transport, health and cultural systems that dominate collective life. In France, the Jospin government managed to create jobs and enhance the international competitiveness of French firms without significant sacrifices in the sphere of social protection, but at the cost of raising levels of taxation and public spending to unprecedented levels. The German social democrats have had the most difficulty securing substantial reforms, as one might expect in a context where every initiative must be negotiated among a set of entrenched, and often partisan, interests.

For many, however, the most pressing question is whether social democracy in its new guise remains an effective force for *social justice*. These parties can no longer claim, as they once did, to be harnessing the power of the modern state to the ends of the working class. Their leaders are more skeptical about the effectiveness of the state and many of their followers now come from the middle class (cf. Przeworski and Sprague, 1986). Their electoral appeal is based on a cross-class politics that is more cautious and less triumphalist than it once was.[7] Nevertheless, the claim of these parties to the mantle of social democracy rests on the priority they still give, in rhetorical terms at least, to social justice. Do their new platforms still justify this claim?

Although it is too early to come to a judgement that is not open to dispute, there are at least four grounds on which these parties can still found a claim to be the defenders of social justice. First, all are committed to providing jobs for those who want one, in line with the longstanding commitment of the left to full employment; and each has made the expansion of employment its foremost priority. Second, all have devoted substantial resources to improving the educational levels of the populace, thereby emphasizing the element that Marshall (1949) considered most crucial to social rights and equality of opportunity. Third, all have been attentive to legal rights, including the rights of those, such as immigrants, whose position might otherwise be precarious. Finally, despite the efforts to trim social spending in France and Germany and the new work requirements associated with social assistance in Britain, these parties remain committed to extensive social security systems. They devote more of their resources to the working poor and fewer to those living entirely on social assistance than they once did, and their social initiatives are less generous than those of yesteryear; but these parties are redesigning, rather than dismantling, the welfare state. On each of these dimensions, there remain discernible differences between the social democratic parties of Europe and their conservative counterparts, which, if less marked than they were forty years ago, are nonetheless palpable (cf. Boix, 1998).

Today, as in the past, the development of social democracy is conditioned by the development of capitalism. Having accepted a market economy some decades ago, the social democratic parties of Europe now find themselves coping with more deeply integrated international markets. And many of the differences found in their policies correspond to national variations in the character of capitalism. Social democracy remains an effort to master the economy rather than simply to conform to it, but we can only understand that effort if we acknowledge that there is a comparative political economy to the search for a Third Way.

---

[7] Of course, even in the past, socialist parties usually reached office only on the basis of cross-class coalitions, such as the farmer-labour alliances of the inter-war years, but these were often simpler than the coalitions that must be built today, composed of groups with a more coherent internal identity, and rooted in stronger partisan identities (cf. Gourevitch, 1986; Przeworski and Sprague, 1986; Panitch, 1975).

References

Aoki, M. (1994), 'The Japanese Firm as a System of Attributes: A Survey and Research Agenda', in M. Aoki and R. Dore (eds.), *The Japanese Firm: Sources of Competitive Strength*, Clarendon Press, Oxford.

Appelbaum, E. and Schettkat, R. (1994), 'The End of Full Employment? Economic Development in Industrialized Economies', *Intereconomics*, Vol. 57, pp. 120–30.

Beer, S.H. (1978), 'The New Public Philosophy', *American Political Science Review*, Vol. 72, pp. 9–21.

Beer, S.H. (1982), *Modern British Politics*, Norton, New York.

Beer, S.H. (1997), 'Britain after Blair', *Political Quarterly*, Vol. 68(4), pp. 317–25.

Beer, S.H. (1999), 'Strong Government and Democratic Accountability', *Political Quarterly*, Vol. 70(2), pp. 146–51.

Berger, S. (1982) (ed.), *Organizing Interests in Western Europe*, Cambridge University Press, New York.

Berger, S. and Ronald D. (1996) (eds.), *National Diversity and Global Capitalism*, Cornell University Press, Ithaca.

Blair, T. (1998), *The Third Way: New Politics for the New Century*, The Fabian Society, London.

Blair, T. (1999), *Europe: The Third Way, Die Neue Mitte*, Speech delivered on June 8, 1999.

Blair, T. and Schröder, G (1999), *Europe: The Third Way, Die Neue Mitte*, Joint Statement, June 8.

Boix, C. (1998), *Political Parties, Growth and Equality*, Cambridge University Press, New York.

Boyer R. (1990), *The Regulation School: A Critical Introduction*, Columbia University Press, New York.

Boyer, R. and Drache, D. (1996), *States Against Markets*, Routledge, London.

Crosland, A. (1956), *The Future of Socialism*, Strauss Farrar, London.

Culpepper, P. (2001), 'Employers Associations, Public Policy and the Politics of Decentralized Cooperation', in P.A. Hall and D. Soskice (eds.), *Varieties of Capitalism: The Institutional Foundations of Comparative Advantage*, Oxford University Press, Oxford.

Cusak, T. and Iversen T. (2000), 'The Causes of Welfare State Expansion: Deindustrialization or Globalization', *World Politics*, Vol. 52(3), pp. 313–37.

Deeg, R. and Lutz S. (1998), 'Internationalization and Financial Federalism: The United States and Germany at the Crossroads?', Discussion Paper of the Max Planck Institut für Gesellschaftsforschung, Köln.

Dettke, D. (1998), *The Challenge of Globalization for Germany's Social Democracy*, Berghahn, New York.

Driver, S. and Martell L. (1998), *New Labour: Politics after Thatcherism*, Polity Press, Cambridge.

Ebbinghaus, B. and Manow, P. (2001), 'Studying Welfare-State Regimes and Varieties of Capitalism: An Introduction', in B. Ebbinghaus and P. Manow (eds.), *Comparing Welfare Capitalism*, Routledge, London.

Esping-Andersen, G. (1986), *Politics Against Markets*, Princeton University Press, Princeton.

Esping-Andersen, G. (1990), *Three Worlds of Welfare Capitalism*, Princeton University Press, Princeton.

Esping-Andersen, G. (1996), 'Workers without Work', in G. Esping-Andersen (ed.), *Welfare States in Transition: National Adaptations in Global Economies*, Sage, London.

Esping-Andersen, G. (1999), *Social Foundations of Post-Industrial Economies*, University Press, Oxford.

Estevez, M. (1999), *Welfare and Capitalism in Post-War Japan*, Ph.D. Dissertation, Harvard University.

Estevez, M., Iversen T. and Soskice D. (1999), 'Social Protection and the Formation of Skills: A Reinterpretation of the Welfare State', Paper presented to the American Political Science Association.

Finegold, D. and Soskice D. (1988), 'Britain's Failure to Train: Explanations and Some Possible Strategies', *Oxford Review of Economic Policy*, Vol. 4(3), November, pp. 21–53.

Foote, G. (1986), *The Labour Party's Political Thought*, Croom Helm, London.

Forsythe, D. and Notermans T. (eds.) (1997), *Regime Changes*, Berghahn, New York.

Freeden, M. (1999), 'The Ideology of New Labour', *Political Quarterly*, Vol. 70 (1), pp. 42–51.

Frieden, J.A. (1991), 'Invested Interests: The Politics of National Economic Policies in a World of Global Finance', *International Organization* 45 (4), pp. 425–51.

Gamble, A. (1988), *The Free Economy and the Strong State*, Duke University Press, Durham.

Giddens, A. (1998), *The Third Way*, Polity Press, Cambridge.

Goldthorpe, J.A. (ed.) (1984), *Order and Conflict in Contemporary Capitalism*, Oxford University Press, New York.

Gourevitch, P.A. (1986), *Politics in Hard Times*, Cornell University Press, Ithaca.

Granovetter, M. (1985), 'Economic Action and Social Structure: The Problem of Embeddedness', *American Journal of Sociology*, Vol. 91, pp. 481–510.

Hall, P.A. (1986), *Governing the Economy*, Oxford University Press, New York.

Hall, P.A. (1987), 'The Evolution of Economic Policy under Mitterrand', in G. Ross, S. Hoffmann and S. Malzacher (eds.), *The Mitterrand Experiment*, Oxford University Press, New York.

Hall, P.A. (1990), 'The Evolution of Economic Policy', in P.A. Hall, J. Hayward and H. Machin (eds.), *Developments in French Politics*, Macmillan, London.

Hall, P.A. (1997), 'The Political Economy of Adjustment in Germany', in F. Naschold et al. (eds.), *Ökonomische Leistungsfähigkeit und Institutionelle Innovation*, Sigma, Berlin.

Hall, P.A. (1998), 'The Political Economy of Europe in an Era of Interdependence', in H. Kitschelt et al. (eds.), *Continuity and Change in Contemporary Capitalism*, Cambridge University Press, New York.

Hall, P.A. (2000), 'Organized Market Economies and Unemployment in Europe: Is it Finally Time to Accept Liberal Orthodoxy', in N. Bermeo (ed.), *Context and Consequence: The Effects of Unemployment in the New Europe*, Cambridge University Press, New York.

Hall, P.A. (2001), 'The Evolution of Economic Policy-Making', in H. Machin, A. Guyomarch, J. Hayward and P.A. Hall (eds.), *Developments in French Politics 2*, Macmillan, London.

Hall, P.A., Franzese, Jr. and Robert J. (1998), 'Mixed Signals: Central Bank Independence, Coordinated Wage Bargaining and European Monetary Union', *International Organization*, Vol. 52(3), pp. 505–35.

Hall, P.A. and Soskice, D. (2001), 'An Introduction to Varieties of Capitalism', in P.A. Hall and D. Soskice (eds.), *Varieties of Capitalism: The Institutional Foundation of Comparative Economic Advantage*, Oxford University Press, Oxford.

Hayward, J. (1996), *The State and the Market Economy*, Wheatsheaf, Brighton.

Hemerijck, A. and Jelle, V. (1998), 'The Dutch Miracle: An Obvious Candidate for the "Third Way"?', Paper presented to a conference on 'Labour in Government: The "Third Way" and the Future of Social Democracy', Harvard University.

Huber, E. and Stephens, J.D. (1999), 'Welfare State and Production Regimes in the Era of Retrenchment', Occasional Papers, School of Social Science, Institute for Advanced Study, Princeton.

Iversen, T. and Wren, A. (1998), 'Equality, Employment and Budgetary Restraint: the Trilemma of the Service Economy', *World Politics*, Vol. 50(4), pp. 507–46.

Johnson, P. (1998), 'New Labour: A Distinctive Vision of Welfare Policy?', Paper presented to a conference on 'Labour in Government: The "Third Way" and the Future of Social Democracy', Harvard University.

Katzenstein, P. (1985a), *Small States in World Markets*, Cornell University Press, Ithaca.

Katzenstein, P. (1985b), *Corporatism and Change*, Cornell University Press, Ithaca.

Katzenstein, P. (1987) *Politics and Policy-Making in West Germany*, Temple University Press, Philadelphia.

King, D. and Wickham-Jones M. (1999), 'From Clinton to Blair: The Democratic (Party) Origins of Welfare to Work', *Political Quarterly*, Vol. 70(1), pp. 62–74.

Kitschelt, H. (1994), *The Transformation of European Social Democracy*, Cambridge University Press, New York.

Krieger, J. (1999), *British Politics in the Global Age*, Polity Press, Cambridge.

Lehrer, M. (1997), *Comparative Institutional Advantage in Corporate Governance and Managerial Hierarchies: The Case of European Airlines*, Ph.D. Thesis, INSEAD, Fontainbleau.

Levy, J. (1998), *Tocqueville's Revenge*, Harvard University Press, Cambridge.

Levy, J. (1999), 'Vice into Virtue: Progressive Politics and Welfare Reform in Continental Europe', *Politics and Society*, Vol. 27(2), pp. 239–74.

Levy, J. (2000), 'France: Directing Adjustment?', in F. Scharpf and V. Schmidt (eds.), *From Vulnerability to Competitiveness: Welfare and Work in the Open Economy*, Oxford University Press, Oxford.

Lindberg, L. and Maier, C.S. (eds.) (1985), *The Politics of Inflation and Economic Stagnation*, Brookings, Washington.

Manow, P. and Seils, E. (2000), 'Adjusting Badly: The German Welfare State, Structural Change and the Open Economy', in F. Scharpf and V. Schmidt (eds.), *From Vulnerability to Competitiveness: Welfare and Work in the Open Economy*, Oxford University Press, Oxford.

Mares, I. (1998), *Negotiated Risks: Employers' Role in Social Policy Development*, Ph.D. Dissertation, Harvard University.

Mares, I. (2001), 'Business and Social Policy: A Theoretical Framework for the Understanding of Firms' Roles in the Process of Social Policy Develoment', in P.A. Hall and D. Soskice (eds.), *Varieties of Capitalism: The Institutional Foundation of Comparative Economic Advantage*, Oxford University Press, Oxford, pp. 184–212.

Marshall, T.H. (1949), 'Citizenship and Social Class', *Class, Citizenship and Social Development*, Beacon Press, Boston.

Martin, A. (1979), 'The Dynamics of Change in a Keynesian Political Economy: The Swedish Case and its Implications', in C. Crouch (ed.), *State and Economy in Contemporary Capitalism*, Croom Helm, London.

Milgrom, P. and Roberts, J. (1992), *Economics, Organisation and Management*, Prentice-Hall, Englewood Cliffs, N.J.

Milgrom, P. and Roberts, J. (1995), 'Complementarities and Fit: Strategy, Structure and Organizational Change in Manufacturing', *Journal of Accounting and Economics*, Vol. 19, pp. 511–28.

Norris, P. (1999), *Critical Citizens: Global Support for Democratic Government*, Oxford University Press, New York.

Notermans, T. (1993), 'The Abdication from National Policy Autonomy: Why the Macroeconomic Policy Regime has Become so Unfavorable to Labor', *Politics and Society*, Vol. 21 (2), pp. 133–68.

Offe, C. (1984), *The Contradictions of the Welfare State*, MIT Press, Cambridge, Ma.

Oppenheim, C. (1998), 'Welfare Reform and the Labour Market: A "Third Way"?', Paper presented to a conference on 'Labour in Government: The "Third Way" and the Future of Social Democracy', Harvard University.

Panitch, L. (1975), *Social Democracy and Industrial Militancy*, Cambridge University Press, Cambridge.

Perez, S. (1999), 'The Resurgence of National Social Bargaining in Europe: Explaining the Italian and Spanish Experiences', *Estudios Working Papers* No. 1999/130, Instituto Juan March, Madrid.

Pierson, P. (1994), *Dismantling the Welfare State?*, Cambridge University Press, New York.

Pierson, P. (1996), 'The New Politics of the Welfare State', *World Politics*, Vol. 48(2), pp. 143–79.

Polanyi, K. (1944), *The Great Transformation*, Beacon, Boston.

Pontusson, J. and Swenson P. (1995), 'Labor Markets, Production Strategies and Wage-Bargaining Institutions', *Comparative Political Studies*, Vol. 29, pp. 223–50.

Przeworski, A. (1985), *Capitalism and Social Democracy*, Cambridge University Press, Cambridge.

Przeworski, A. and Sprague, J. (1986), *Paper Stones*, University of Chicago Press, Chicago.

Rhodes, M. (1997), 'Globalization, Labour Markets and Welfare States: A Future of Competitive Corporatism?', in M. Rhodes and Y. Meny (eds), *The Future of European Welfare*, Macmillan, London.

Riddell, P. (1990), *The Thatcher Decade*, Blackwell, Oxford.

Roman, J. (1999), 'The Search for a French Way', *Dissent*, Spring, pp. 85–86.

Ryan, A. (1999), 'Recycling the Third Way', *Dissent*, Spring, pp. 77–80.

Sandel, M. (1982), *Liberalism and the Limits of Justice*, Cambridge University Press: New York.

Scharpf, F. (1990), *Crisis and Choice in European Social Democracy*, Cornell University Press, Ithaca.

Scharpf, F. (1997), 'Employment and the Welfare State: A Continental Dilemma', Paper presented to the Center for European Studies, Harvard University.

Scharpf, F. (1998), 'The Institutional Capacity for Effective Policy Responses', Paper prepared for a project on The Adjustment of National Employment Policy and Social Policy to Internationalization.

Scharpf, F. and Schmidt, V. (eds.) (2000), *From Vulnerability to Competitiveness: Welfare and Work in the Open Economy*, Oxford University Press, Oxford.

Schettkat, R. (1992), *The Labor Market Dynamics of Economic Restructuring*, Praeger, New York.

Schludi, M., Seils, E. and Ganghof, S. (1999), *An Adjustment Data Base*, Max Planck Institut for the Study of Societies, Cologne.

Sferza, S. (1999), 'What is Left of the Left? More than One Would Think', *Daedalus*, Vol. 128(2), Spring, pp. 101–26.

Shonfield, A. (1969), *Modern Capitalism*, Oxford University Press, Oxford.

Soskice, D. (1990), 'Wage Determination: The Changing Role of Institutions in Advanced Industrialised Countries', *Oxford Review of Economic Policy*, Vol. 6(4), pp. 1–23.

Soskice, D. (1991), 'The Institutional Infrastructure for International Competitiveness: A Comparative Analysis of the U.K. and Germany', in A.B. Atkinson and R. Brunetta (eds.), *The Economies of the New Europe*, Macmillan, London.

Soskice, D. (1994), 'Innovation Strategies of Companies: A Comparative Institutional Analysis of Some Cross-Country Differences', in W. Zapf (ed.), *Institutionenvergleich und Institutionendynamik*, Sigma, Berlin.

Soskice, D. (1998), 'Divergent Production Regimes: Coordinated and Uncoordinated Market Economies in the 1980s and 1990s', in H. Kitschelt et al. (eds.), *Continuity and Change in Contemporary Capitalism*, Cambridge University Press, New York.

Streeck, W. (1992), *Social Institutions and Economic Performance*, Sage, Beverly Hills.

Streeck, W. (1996), 'Public Power Beyond the Nation-State: The Case of the European Community', in R. Boyer and D. Drache (eds.), *States Against Markets*, Routledge, New York.

Streeck, W. (1997), 'German Capitalism: Does it Exist? Can it Survive?', in C. Crouch and W. Streeck (eds.), *The Political Economy of Modern Capitalism*, Routledge, London.

Swenson, P. (1999), 'Varieties of Capitalism and Illusions of Labor Power: Employers in the Making of the Swedish and American Welfare States', Paper presented to a Conference on Distribution and Democracy, Yale University.

Van Kersbergen, K. (1995), *Social Capitalism: A Study of Christian Democracy and the Welfare State*, Routledge, London.

Vogel, S. (1999), 'The Crisis of German Capitalism: Stalled on the Road to the Market Model?', Paper presented to the Max-Planck Institute for the Study of Societies, Cologne.

Weiler, P. (1982), *The New Liberalism: Liberal Social Theory in Britain 1889–1914*, Ashgate, Brookfield.

White, S. (1998), 'Interpreting the "Third Way"', *Prospect*, Vol. 6(2), Spring, pp. 17–30.

Wood, A. (1994), *North–South Trade, Employment and Inequality*, Clarendon Press, Oxford.

Wood, S. (1997), *Capitalist Constitutions: Supply–Side Reform in Britain and Germany 1960–90*, Ph.D. Dissertation, Harvard University.

Wood, S. (1998), 'Education, Training and the British Third Way', Paper presented to a conference on 'Labour in Government: The "Third Way" and the Future of Social Democracy', Harvard University.

Wood, S. (2001), 'Business, Government and Patterns of Labor Market Policy in Britain and the Federal Republic of Germany', in P.A. Hall and D. Soskice (eds.), *Varieties of Capitalism: The Institutional Foundation of Comparative Economic Advantage*, Oxford University Press, Oxford, pp. 247–74.

Ziegler, N. (1997), *Governing Ideas: Strategies for Innovation in France and Germany*, Cornell University Press, Ithaca.

Ziegler, N. (2000), 'Corporate Governance and the Politics of Property Rights in Germany', *Politics and Societies*, Vol. 28, June, pp. 195–221.

Chapter 2

The State and Globalization[1]

Saskia Sassen

The global economic system requires the implementation of a broad range of standards. This has happened most visibly through supranational institutions, notably the WTO (World Trade Organization) and the IMF (International Monetary Fund). The focus in this chapter is on two less visible and less noted mechanisms that have played a crucial role are, on the one hand, a whole new world of private agents, such as financial firms and credit rating agencies. And on the other, a variety of legislative and judiciary measures executed inside national states to ensure guarantees and protections of global capital and markets. This participation of national states in the implementation of a global economic system is not new, but it has intensified enormously over the last decade. The rise of private authority in governance is receiving considerable attention (Biersteker et al., 2002; Cutler et al., 1999, Ferguson and Mansbach, 1996); with important exceptions (Cerny, 2000), the role of the national state is not.

National states have had to accommodate foreign firms and markets in their territory and in their legal systems. The global economic system partly inhabits national territories and national institutions. One overall effect is what I call an incipient 'denationalizing' of several highly specialized national institutional orders (Sassen, 1996, and forthcoming). One of the reasons this has not received more attention, and study, is the presence of very powerful assumptions in the general understanding of economic globalization. One of these is the zero-sum game: whatever the global economy gains, the national state loses, and vice-versa. The other is the assumption that if an event takes place in a national territory it is a national event, whether a business transaction or a judiciary decision. The result has been that much of the scholarship on globalization has left the role of national states in the implementation of a global economy under-examined or reduced to

[1] This is based on a longer research project on governance in the global economy. A first part of this project was published as *Losing Control? Sovereignty in an Age of Globalization.* I thank the Schoff Memorial Fund for its support. The current text is a revised and updated edition of a paper first published in Smith, D., Solinger, D. and Topik, S. (ed) (1999), *States and Sovereignty in the Global Economy*, Routledge, London.

the condition of pure victim of the forces of globalization. Yet it is not simply the push by global firms and markets that is shaping the dynamics of interaction as is implied in much of the literature on the declining significance of the national state under globalization. States are also shaping the dynamics of interaction. They are doing so in the form of resistance and in the form of accommodation. (See, e.g. various chapters in Mittelman, 1996; Picciotto and Mayne, 1999; Ferleger and Mandle, 2000; Calabrese and Burgelman, 1999, Aspen Institute 1998.) In doing so, however, national states themselves are transformed (Jessop, 1999; Sassen, 1996; Rosenau, 1997). My central argument is that while many sectors of the national state lose influence and resources due to globalization, some gain power because of globalization.

The encounter of a global actor – firm or market – with one or another instantiation of the national state can be thought of as a new frontier zone. It is not merely a dividing line between the national economy and the global economy. It is a zone of politico-economic interactions that produce new institutional forms and alter some of the old ones. Nor is it just a matter of reducing regulations or shrinking the role of government generally. For instance, in many countries, the necessity for autonomous central banks in the current global economic system has required a thickening of regulations in order to delink central banks from the influence of the executive branch of governments.

Neglected Elements in Explanations of Globalization

We cannot understand globalization by focusing merely on international trade and investment and other cross-border flows, as if globalization came simply from the outside. Neither is it adequate simply to focus on the fact of the often minimal share of foreign inputs in national economies: in most countries the share of foreign in total investment, the share of international in total trade, the share of foreign in total stock market value, is very small. However, to infer from this that economic globalization is not really a significant issue, misses a crucial feature of this current phase of economic globalization: most global processes materialize in national territories and do so to a large extent through national institutional arrangements, from legislative acts to firms, and thereby are not necessarily counted as 'foreign'. Conversely, for that same reason we cannot simply assume that because a transaction takes place in national territory and in a national institutional setting it is ipso facto national. In my reading, the imbrications of global actors and national institutions are far more ambiguous. We need to decode what is national in the national.

One key implication is that economic globalization has actually strengthened certain components of national states, notably those linked to international banking functions, such as ministries of finance, even as it has weakened many others. A second important implication is that insofar as certain components of national states are engaged in the implementation and governing of the global economy, there is a bridge for citizens to exercise some of their powers vis-à-vis the global economy. Clearly, this would require significant innovation and initiative. But it does mean that we, still largely confined to national institutions for the excercise of our powers as citizens, can enact a politics that demands accountability of global actors through our national state institutions and do not need to wait for a 'world state' to come about.

The internal transformation of the national state is shaped both by trends towards standardization, as is the growing convergence in the role of central banks, and by national particularities. The tension between the weight of national specificity and the weight of the new global rules of the game is well illustrated by some aspects of the 1997–98 Asian financial crisis. We saw responses by the Asian countries involved in IMF 'rescue packages', signalling the weight of specific domestic institutional arrangements and leadership. At the same time, the emergent consensus in the community of states to further globalization has created a set of specific obligations on participating states, no matter how reluctant some of these states might be.

State and Non-state Centred Mechanisms for Globalization

Implementing today's global economic system in the context of national territorial sovereignty requires multiple policy negotiations. One of the roles of the state vis-à-vis today's global economy, unlike earlier forms of the world economy, has been to negotiate the intersection of national law and foreign actors – whether firms, markets or supranational organizations. What makes the current phase distinctive is, on the one hand, the existence of an enormously elaborate body of law which secures the exclusive authority of national states over their territory to an extent not seen in the 19th century, and on the other, the considerable institutionalizing of the 'rights' of non-national firms, the 'legalizing' of a growing array of cross-border transactions, and the growing, and increasingly institutionalized, participation by supranational organizations in national matters.[2] This sets up the conditions for a necessary engagement of national states in the process of globalization.

We generally use terms such as 'deregulation', financial and trade liberalization, and privatization to describe the outcome of this negotiation. The

---

[2] There is a parallel here between the institutionalizing of the rights of non-national economic actors with that of immigrants who have also gained rights – even though now they experience an attempt to shrink those rights (Sassen, 1998, chapter 2). Further, there is a parallel with the fact that subjects other than the national state are emerging as objects of international law and as subjects in international relations, notably Non-Governmental Organizations (NGOs). I have explored this in terms of various struggles by women (Sassen, 1998, chapter 5).

problem with such terms is that they only capture the withdrawal of the state from regulating its economy. They do not register all the ways in which the state participates in setting up the new frameworks through which globalization is furthered, nor do they capture the associated transformations inside the state, even though these changes are happening and are being documented (e.g. Picciotto and Mayne, 1999; Shapiro, 1993; Aman, 1998; Indiana Journal of Global Legal Studies, 1999). One way of putting it then, would be to say that certain components of the national state operate as necessary instrumentalities for the implementation of a global economic system.

There is much more going on in these negotiations than the concept 'deregulation' captures. 'Deregulation' actually refers to an extremely complex set of intersections and negotiations, which, while they may preserve the integrity of national territory as a geographic condition, do transform the exclusive territoriality of the state, i.e. the national and international frameworks through which national territory has assumed an institutional form over the last seventy years. National territory and exclusive territoriality have corresponded tightly for much of the recent history of the developed nation states (for critical accounts see, for example, Walker, 1993; Jessop, 1999, Kratochwil, 1986; Latham, 1997). Today, globalization may be contributing to an incipient slippage in that correspondence. Much deregulation has had the effect of promoting that slippage and giving it a legitimate form in national legal frameworks (Aman, 1998). The reconfiguring of the institutional encasement of national territory also brings with it the ascendance of subnational spaces (e.g. Magnusson, 1996; Taylor, 1995; Knox and Taylor, 1995; Isin, 2000).[3]

The fact that we cannot simply reduce these negotiations to the notion of deregulation is also illustrated by the privatization of public sector firms. Such privatization is not just a change in ownership status, but also a shift of regulatory functions to the private sector where they re-emerge under other forms, most notably, private corporate legal and accounting services (Sassen, 2001, chapter 5).

Recognizing the importance of place and of production – in this case the production of a system of power – helps us refocus our thinking about the global economy along these lines. The global economy needs to be implemented, reproduced, serviced, financed. It cannot be taken simply as a given, or a set of markets, or merely as a function of the power of multinational corporations and financial markets. There is a vast array of highly specialized functions that need to be executed and infrastructures that need to be secured. These have become so specialized that they can no longer be subsumed under general corporate headquarter functions. Global cities, with their complex networks of highly specialized service firms and labour markets are strategic sites for the production of these specialized functions. In this sense, global cities are one form of this

---

[3] One illustration is the concept of global cities (Sassen, 2001).

embeddedness of global processes in national territories and in national institutional arrangements.[4] The role played by these strategic places in the organization and management of the global economy, along with the fact that much investment and all financial markets – no matter how deregulated – are located somewhere, shows us that the global economy to a large extent materializes in national territories.[5]

It means, in turn, that various instantiations of the national state are inevitably involved. The result is a particular set of negotiations which have the effect of leaving the geographic condition of the nation state's territory unaltered, but do transform the institutional encasements of that geographic fact, that is, the state's territorial jurisdiction or, more abstractly, the state's exclusive territoriality.[6]

My argument is that precisely because global processes materialize to a large extent in national territories, many national states have had to become involved, even if at times peripherally, in the implementation of the global economic system and have, in this process, experienced transformations of various aspects of their institutional structure.[7]

---

[4] The global city is a function of a network, and in this sense different from the old capitals of empires or the more general concept of the world city (Sassen, 2001, chapters 1 and 7). The network of global cities today constitutes a strategic geography of centrality for the coordination and servicing of the global economy. It is a geography that cuts across the old North-South divide (it includes Sao Paulo and Bombay, for instance) and strengthens the territorial unevenness, both inside developed and less developed countries. The corporate world of Sao Paulo and of New York gain strength, power and wealth. The world of the middle class and of the working class loses in both cities (see also Friedmann, 1995, for an overview).

[5] A key aspect of the spatialization of global economic processes which I cannot develop here (but see Sassen, 1998, chapter 9) is digital space (see also Aspen Institute, 1998). The topography for economic activities such as finance and specialized services, moves in and out of digital space. However at this time there is no purely and exclusively digital topography in any firm and in any sector. One of the interesting features about finance is that though it is one of the most digitalized and dematerialized industries, when it hits the ground it does so in some of the largest and densest concentrations of infrastructure, structures and markets for resources.

[6] In this regard, I see the cross-border network of global cities as concentrating a significant share of institutional orders that are partially denationalized, and hence see this network as a partially denationalized – rather than internationalized – strategic geography (Sassen, 1998, chapters 1, 9 and 10).

[7] I cannot develop this subject here at length (see Sassen, 1996 and Sassen, 1998, chapters 2 and 10).

Implementing the New Norms Through National Institutions

On a fairly abstract level we can see the ambiguity of the distinction between 'national' and 'global' in the normative weight gained by the logic of the global capital market in setting criteria for key national economic policies. I discuss this more fully elsewhere (Sassen, 1996, chapter 2). The multiple negotiations between national states and global economic actors signal that the logic of the global capital market is succeeding in imposing itself on important aspects of national economic policy making. Autonomy of the central bank, anti-inflation policies, parity in exchange rates, and the variety of other items usually included under so-called 'IMF conditionality', have all become a set of norms.

This new normativity can be seen at work in the design of the 'solution' to the Mexican economic crisis of December 1994. This crisis was described as a consequence of the global financial markets having 'lost confidence' in the government's leadership of the Mexican economy and the 'solution' was explicitly aimed at restoring that confidence.[8] In 1997–98 we saw the (attempted) imposition of that same set of norms on several countries in Asia, no matter how different the underlying conditions from those of Mexico and in each of the Asian countries involved.[9] The actual architecture of the crisis, and most recently that in Argentina, may well have had more to do with the aggressive attempts to globalize these economies from the outside than with their governments' leadership of these economies. Corruption, favouritism and weak banking systems were features of these economies long before these financial crisis and throughout their period of growth, when they were much admired and put up as models for Latin America, the Caribbean and Africa.

In this context I read the financial crisis as a dynamic that has the effect of destabilizing national monopoly control of these economies, and IMF conditionality as facilitating a massive transfer to foreign ownership. The outcome is further globalization and further imposition of the new normativity attached to the logic of the global capital market. However the actual materialization of these conditions will go through specific institutional channels and assume distinct forms in each country, with various levels of resistance and consent – hence my notion of this dynamic as having the features of a frontier zone. It is worth noting that all the Latin American countries that deregulated their financial markets had a banking

---

[8] The fact that this 'solution' brought with it the bankruptcy of middle sectors of the economy and of households, who suddenly confronted interest rates that guaranteed their bankruptcy, was not factored in the equation. The key was to secure the confidence of 'investors', that is to guarantee them a profitable return – and today 'profitable' has come to mean very high returns.

[9] The data used in this and the next section come from a data set that is part of the author's project *Governance and Accountability in the Global Economy* (Department of Sociology, University of Chicago).

system crisis. More generally, foreign direct investment (FDI) in emerging markets went from US$ 24 billion in 1990 to US$ 90 billion in 1995. It does suggest that the 'financial crises' experienced by many of these emerging markets cannot only be a function of inadequate government performance. The globalization of their financial markets has something to do with it: there have been over one hundred financial crises in the world since the late 1970s (Sassen, 2001, chapter 4). And this globalization follows the logic of the global capital market.

Let me elaborate on this. After the Mexican crisis, there was a general collapse in emerging markets. But a mere six months later there was a sharp recovery. The trade literature describes this as a partly engineered result: international investors got together with the most creative talent in financial institutions and banks to design some of the most creative and never before seen deals. The US$ 40 billion emergency loan package from the IMF and the US government, along with the hiring of Wall Street's top firms to refurbish its image and find ways to bring it back into the market, helped Mexico 'solve' its financial crisis. With J.P. Morgan as its financial advisor, the Mexican government worked with Goldman Sachs and Chemical Bank to come up with several innovative deals. The trade literature noted, at the time, that these innovations could change the face of other emerging markets – words that now ring with foresight.[10] The aim was to produce assets of emerging markets attractive to the scared-off investors.

There are also more subtle ways in which globalization operates through national institutions and in national terrains. This can be illustrated with a key feature of globalization: privatization. What matters for my purposes here is that this enormous transfer of firms from the public to the private sector is not simply a change in ownership regime. It is also a privatizing of coordination and governance functions which shift from the public to the private corporate sector. In some particular geographic situations, these developments can be captured in the image of a shift of functions and authority from Washington's government world to New York City's corporate world, from New Delhi to Bombay, from Brazilia to Sao Paulo. In most countries the national capital is also the leading financial and business centre, so this geographic image does not hold even though the institutional transfer may take place.

The key issue is this transfer of what were regulatory functions embedded in government bureaucracies to the corporate world where they re-emerge as corporate management functions or specialized corporate services. Insofar as

---

[10] Goldman organized a US$ 1.75 billion Mexican sovereign deal in which the firm was able to persuade investors in May 1996 to swap Mexican Brady bonds collateralized with US Treasury bonds (Mexican Bradys were a component of almost any emerging market portfolio until the 1994 crisis) for a 30-year naked Mexican risk. This is in my reading quite a testimony to the aggressive innovations that characterize the financial markets and to the importance of a whole new subculture in international finance that facilitates the circulation, i.e. sale, of these instruments.

foreign investors and foreign firms are increasingly part of this privatization of public sector firms – and indeed, in many cases, are the main investors – we could argue that this represents not only a privatizing of economic governance functions but also an incipient denationalizing of such functions. Thus, while central, the role of the state in producing the legal encasements for economic activity is no longer what it was in earlier periods. There is a growing world of privatized governance of global economic operations. At the same time, it is crucial for the purposes of my analysis here, to recognize that national states had to participate in the organizing and 'legalizing' of this transfer. The depth and transformative character of this transfer has been underlined by World Bank documents recently (March 2002) publicized – without permission of the institution, but neither disavowed by it – about its agreements with Argentina and the systematic nature of the imposed obligation on the government to sell off everything of value in the public sector to private investors, thereby relinquishing state control over many of these sectors.

The New Intermediaries

Economic globalization has also been accompanied by the creation of new legal regimes and legal practices, and the expansion and renovation of some older forms that have the effect of replacing public regulation and law with private mechanisms, which sometimes even bypass national legal systems (e.g. Biersteker et al., 2002). The importance of private oversight institutions, such as credit rating agencies, has increased with the deregulation and globalization of the financial markets. These agencies are now key institutions in the creation of order and transparency in the global capital market and have considerable power over sovereign states through their authority in rating government debt. Also the rise of international commercial arbitration as the main mechanism for resolving cross-border business disputes entails a declining importance of national courts in these matters – a privatizing of this kind of justice (e.g. Salacuse, 1991; Dezalay and Bryant, 1996; Maxfield, 1997). Further, the new international rules for financial reporting and accounting largely implemented by the late 1990s also relocate some national functions to a privatized international system.

All of these begin to amount to a privatized system of governance ensuring order, respect for contracts, transparency, and accountability in the world of cross-border business transactions. To some extent this privatized world of governance has replaced various functions of national states in ensuring the protection of the rights of firms. This privatization contributes to a change in the dynamics and a fuelling of new dynamics in the zone of interaction between national institutions and global actors (Biersteker et al., 2002; Calabrese and Burgelman, 1999; for a more historical perspective see Davis, 1999). The state continues to play a crucial, but no longer exclusive, role in the production of 'legality' around new forms of economic activity.

There is a new intermediary world of strategic agents that contribute to the management and coordination of the global economy. These agents are largely, though not exclusively, private. And they have absorbed some of the international functions that used to be carried out by states in the recent past, as was the case, for instance, with international trade under the predominantly protectionist regimes in the post-World War II decades. Their role is dramatically illustrated by the case of China: When the Chinese government in 1996 issued a 100 year bond to be sold, not in Shanghai, but mostly in New York, it did not have to deal with Washington, it dealt with J.P. Morgan. This type of transaction can be seen repeatedly in a broad range of countries. Private firms in international finance, accounting and law, the new private standards for international accounting and financial reporting, and supra-national organizations such as WTO, all play strategic non-government centred governance functions. But they do so to a great extent inside the territory of nation states.

Many of these rather abstract issues are well illustrated by the work being done to create new private international standards for accounting and financial reporting. And they can be illustrated with the aggressively innovative deals launched by the major financial services firms in the last few years to sell what had often been considered unsaleable (or at least not gradable debt), and to ensure the continuing expansion of the financial markets.

(a) The New Accounting Standards

The International Accounting Standards Committee (IASC) is an independent private sector body which has been working intensely to create uniform standards to be used by business and government. In 1995 the International Organization of Securities Commission agreed to endorse the IASC's standards. While this is a world of private actors and private standards, national states have a crucial presence in the whole operation. It is worth noting that by early 1997, IASC standards had been accepted by all stock exchanges except Japan, Canada and the US – though these eventually also joined.[11]

This evolution was not without incidents that made clear the extent to which national governments and firms resisted or had difficulty accepting the concept of standards acceptable in other countries, let alone uniform international standards as pursued by the IASC. For instance, Japan resisted changing its national accounting system, one lacking the standards of 'transparency' that have become the norm in international transactions. It was indeed Japan's reluctance to implement such

---

[11] One of the issues for the U.S. has been that it considers its own standards more stringent than the new standards being proposed. It is also the case that Anglo-American standards have emerged as de facto international standards over the last few years, thereby greatly expanding the market for Anglo-American firms.

standards of transparency in a wide range of business activities in conjunction with its reluctance to continue deregulating its financial sector which, it seems to me, aborted Tokyo's rise as a major international financial centre. Tokyo, one might say with some irony, remained too Japanese. Japan's Ministry of Finance is now gradually implementing a whole set of measures aimed at deregulation and transparency. The sharpest pressure for change is coming from Japan's increasing dependence on international markets and trade. Indeed, the only Japanese financial institution listed on the NY Stock Exchange, The Bank of Tokyo-Mitsubishi Bank, conformed to US accounting standards long before the Japanese government's decision to adopt international standards.

The case of Japan is interesting because it is one of the powerful countries in the world. It has resisted implementing the IASC standards, but finally had to accept them under pressure from its own firms. The US stock exchange, another powerful actor, resisted even longer and insisted on having its own standards (or something approaching them) as the international norm, but eventually accepted those of the IASC. These are instances that illustrate the degree of contestation in the new frontier zone where the encounter of global actors and national institutions is enacted. The dominance first of Anglo-American standards and now of the new international standards is one component of the new normativity derived from the logic of the global capital market.

(b) Working to 'Solve' Financial Crises

The role of the new intermediaries is also revealed in the strategic work done by leading financial services firms in the wake of the Mexican financial crisis. It might be interesting to speculate the extent to which this kind of 'activism' towards ensuring growth in their industry will also be deployed in the case of the Asian countries now involved.

The events following the Mexican crisis provide us with some interesting insights about these firms' role in changing the conditions for financial operation, about the ways in which national states participated, and the formation of a new institutionalized intermediary space. J.P. Morgan worked with Goldman Sachs and Chemical Bank to develop several innovative deals that brought back investors to Mexico's markets, as discussed in the note above. Further, in July 1996, an enormous US$ 6 billion five year deal that offered investors a Mexican floating rate note or syndicated loan – backed by oil receivables from the state oil monopoly PEMEX – was twice oversubscribed. It became somewhat of a model for asset-backed deals from Latin America, especially oil rich Venezuela and Ecuador. Key to the high demand was that the structure had been designed to capture investment grade ratings from S&P and Moody's. This was the first Mexican deal with an investment grade. The intermediaries worked with the Mexican government, but on their terms – this was not a government to government deal – to secure acceptability in the new institutionalized privatized domain for global economic transactions. Acceptance by investors allowed the financial markets to grow on what had been a crisis.

After the Mexican crisis and before the first signs of the Asian crisis, we see a large number of very innovative deals that contribute to further expanding the volumes in the financial markets and incorporating new sources of profit, that is, debts for sale, even as a major emerging market (Mexico) had just gone through a devastating crisis for investors (and, of course, for major sectors of the workforce and Mexican small and medium enterprises). Typically these deals involved novel concepts of how to sell debt and what could be a saleable debt. Often the financial services firms structuring these deals also implemented minor changes in depository systems to bring them more in line with international standards; this continuing practice represents, in my reading, a significant microintervention on the part of private firms in the national legal, administrative and/or institutional frameworks of these countries – a partial and highly specialized denationalizing of particular features of these frameworks (Sassen, and forthcoming). The aggressive innovating and selling on the world market of what had hitherto been considered too illiquid and too risky for such a sale further contributed to expand and strengthen the institutionalization of this privatized domain for global transactions operating partly outside the inter-state system.

In sum, these types of developments have consequences for certain features of the state and the interstate system, and in this regard, perhaps inevitably for representative democracy as well as for international law and the modes of accountability therein contained (see, e.g. Chicago Journal of International Law 2000; Gill, 1992). Firstly, growth in cross-border activities and global actors operating outside the formal inter-state system affects the competence and scope of states and of international law, as these have been constituted historically. Secondly, the fact that this domain is increasingly institutionalized and subjected to the development of private governance mechanisms, affects the exclusivity of state authority and the (albeit always partial) exclusivity of international law. Thirdly, growing normative powers in this private domain affects the normative power of international law. To some extent, though with considerable variability from one state to another, national states have accommodated these transformations.

Conclusion

A central effort in this paper was the identification of the ways in which the state participates in governing the global economy in a context increasingly dominated by deregulation, privatization and the growing authority of non-state actors. In many of these new dynamics and conditions, the state continues to play an important role, often as provider of the institutional home for the enactment of the new policy regimes we associate with globalization.

This participation by the state in the implementation of a global economic system stems in good part from the embeddedness of globalization in national territory and hence the need to negotiate the elaborate legal framework within which this territory is encased. The new geography of global economic processes – the strategic spaces for economic globalization – had to be produced, in terms of the practices of corporate actors and the requisite technical and institutional infrastructure (i.e. global cities), and in terms of the work of the state in producing or legitimating new legal regimes. This signals a necessary participation by the state, including in the regulation of its own withdrawal. The mode in which this participation of the state has evolved has been towards strengthening the advantages of certain types of economic and political actors, and weakening those of others. The claims of global capital on the state have been given legitimacy, while those of disadvantaged workers, the unemployed, state institutions linked to the social wage and so on, have not.

The question then becomes one of understanding: a) the specific type of authority/power this participation gives to the state, and b) whether this authority can also be used to address broader issues of a social democratic agenda rather than just those linked to economic globalization as is the case now. My emphasis on the multiple, including very minor, ways in which the new regime for the implementation of the global economy is constituted partly through the work of states, aims at understanding the possibilities for constructing new forms of state authority aimed at enhancing the role of states, and geared towards a broader agenda of the public good. Can we push our states to also participate in activities that aim at instituting measures to enhance social democracy, rather than simply enhancing the market, which is what is happening today.

References

Aman, A.C. Jr. (1998), 'The Globalizing State: A Future-Oriented Perspective on the Public/Private Distinction, Federalism, and Democracy', *Vanderbilt Journal of Transnational Law*, Vol. 31(4), pp. 769–870.

Aspen Institute (1998), *The Global Advance of Electronic Commerce. Reinventing Markets, Management and National Sovereignty. A Report of The Sixth Annual Aspen Institute Roundtable on Information Technology*, Aspen, Colorado, August 21–23, 1997, David Bollier, Rapporteur, Washington, D.C.: The Aspen Institute, Communications and Society Program.

Biersteker, Th.J., Hall, R.B. and Murphy, C.N. (eds.) (2002), *Private Authority and Global Governance*, Cambridge University Press, Cambridge.

Calabrese, A. and Burgelman, J.-C. (eds.) (1999), *Communication, Citizenship and Social Policy*, Rowman & Littlefield, New York.

Cerny, P.G. (2000), 'Structuring the Political Arena: Public Goods, States and Governance in a Globalizing World', in R. Palan (ed.), *Global Political Economy: Contemporary Theories*, Routledge, London, pp. 21–35.

Chicago Journal of International Law Special Issue (2000), *What's Wrong with International Law Scholarship?*, Vol. 1(1), Spring.

Cutler, C.A., Haufler, V. and Porter, T. (eds) (1999), *Private Authority in International Affairs*, SUNY Press, Sarasota Springs, NY.

Davis, D.E. (ed.) (1999), 'Chaos and Governance', *Political Power and Social Theory*, Vol. 13(IV), Scholarly Controversy, JAI Press, Stamford, CT.

Dezalay, Y. and Bryant, G. (1996), *Dealing in Virtue. International Commercial Arbitration and the Construction of a Transnational Legal Order*, The University of Chicago Press, Chicago.

Ferguson, Y.H. and Mansbach, R.W. (1996), *Polities, Authority, Identities and Change*, Columbia University Press, New York.

Ferleger, L. and Mandle, J.R. (eds.) (2000), 'Dimensions of Globalization. Special Millenial Issue', *The Annals*, Vol. 570, July, American Academy of Political and Social Science, Boston.

Friedmann, J. (1995), 'Where We Stand: A Decade of World City Research', in P.J. Knox and P.J. Taylor (eds.), *World Cities in a World-System*, Cambridge University Press, Cambridge, UK.

Gill, S. (1992), 'The Emerging World Order and European Change', in R. Milliband and L. Panitch (eds.), *New World Order? The Socialist Register 1992*, Merlin, London, pp.157–96.

Indiana Journal of Global Legal Studies (1999), *Special Issue: The Internet and Sovereignty*, Spring.

Isin, E.F. (ed.) (2000), *Democracy, Citizenship and the Global City*, Routledge, London, New York.

Jessop, R. (1999), 'Reflections on Globalization and its Illogics', in K. Olds et al. (eds.), *Globalization and the Asian Pacific: Contested Territories*, Routledge, London.

Knox P.J. and Taylor, P.J. (eds.) (1995), *World Cities in a World-System*, Cambridge University Press, Cambridge, UK.

Kratochwil, F. (1986), 'Of Systems, Boundaries and Territoriality', *World Politics*, Vol. 34, October, pp. 27–52.

Latham, R. (1997), *The Liberal Moment: Modernity, Security, and the Making of Postwar International Order*, Columbia University Press, New York.

Magnusson, W. (1996), *The Search for Political Space*, University of Toronto Press, Toronto.

Maxfield, S. (1997), *Gatekeepers of Growth*, Princeton University Press, Princeton.

Mittelman, J. (ed.) (1996), Globalization: Critical Reflections, *International Political Economy Yearbook* IX, Lynne Rienner Publishers, Boulder, Co.

Picciotto, S. and Mayne, R. (1999), *Regulating International Business: Beyond Liberalization*, Macmillan, in association with OXFAM, London.

Rosenau, J.N. (1997), *Along the Domestic-Foreign Frontier: Exploring Governance in a Turbulent World*, Cambridge University Press, Cambridge.

Salacuse, J. (1991), *Making Global Deals: Negotiating in the International Marketplace*, Houghton Mifflin, Boston.

Sassen, S. (1996), *Losing Control? Sovereignty in an Age of Globalization. The 1995 Columbia University Leonard Hastings Schoff Memorial Lectures*, Columbia University Press, New York.

Sassen, S. (1998), *Globalization and its Discontents. Essays on the Mobility of People and Money*, New Press, New York.

Sassen, S. (2001), *The Global City: New York, London, Tokyo* (New Updated Edition), Princeton University Press, Princeton, NJ.

Sassen, S. (forthcoming), *Denationalization: Economy and Polity in a Global Digital Age*, Princeton University Press, Princeton, NJ.

Shapiro, M. (1993), 'The Globalization of Law', *Indiana Journal of Global Legal Studies 1*, Fall, pp. 37–64.

Smith, D., Solinger, D. and Topik, S. (ed.) (1999), *States and Sovereignty in the Global Economy*, Routledge, London.

Taylor, P.J. (1995), 'World Cities and Territorial States: the Rise and Fall of Their Mutuality', in P.J. Knox and P.J. Taylor (eds.), *World Cities in a World-System*, Cambridge University Press, Cambridge, UK, pp. 48–62.

Walker, R.B.J. (1993), *Inside/Outside: International Relations as Political Theory*, Cambridge University Press, Cambridge.

PART II

WHAT IS THE THIRD WAY?
THE ROLE OF SOCIAL
DEMOCRATIC REGIMES IN
COMPARATIVE PERSPECTIVES

Chapter 3

Third Ways in Britain and Europe

Stephen Driver and Luke Martell

Contemporary Third Way thinking in Britain emerged out of the worldwide reform of the centre-left that began in the early 1980s (see Sassoon, 1996). In Britain and the United States, New Labour and the New Democrats, faced with the hegemony of radical conservative governments espousing economic liberalization, were concerned with finding a politics that would mark a break with their own parties' past and with conservative governments in office. It is also seen as having had wider reverberations – from like-minded reforms in Dutch and Swedish social democracy and amongst the Italian ex-communists and German social democrats to interest from the Spanish conservatives on the Right. Beyond Europe, one of the Third Way's most prominent exponents has been the sociologist and Brazilian President Cardoso and it has attracted sympathizers in the Labour parties of Australia and New Zealand. The 'Third Way' is an attractive label for British Labour modernizers because it challenges conventional notions of left and right – and thus reinforces the 'newness' of New Labour. It allows them to distance themselves from the alternatives of both Thatcherism and Old Labour.

The First and Second Ways

Within New Labour politics, the Third Way is defined as 'beyond old left and new right' (see, for example, Blair, 1998; Blair and Schröder, 1999). By 'old left', Labour modernizers have in mind the social democratic Labour politics of the postwar period – in particular, of a post-Sixties liberal hue. Labour modernizers mean the Keynesian, egalitarian social democrats who tended to favour state and corporatist forms of economic and welfare governance within the context of a mixed economy. They accuse this 'old left' of being too statist; too concerned with the redistribution (and tax-and-spend policies) and not the creation of wealth; too willing to grant rights but not demand responsibilities; and of being too liberal and individualist in terms of social behaviour and social relationships such as the family. So, if the 'old left' are all of these, then New Labour's Third Way is concerned to find alternatives to state provision and government control; to promote wealth creation by accepting inequalities and being fiscally 'prudent'; to match rights with responsibilities; and to foster a culture of duty within 'strong communities'.

By 'new right', Labour modernizers mean Thatcherite conservatism. New Labour accuses successive Conservative governments – and here they echo significant voices on the right (Gilmour, 1992; Gray, 1993; Scruton, 1996) – of being the slave to neoliberal dogma by favouring market solutions in all cases; by having a *laissez-faire* view of the state; by promoting an asocial view of society; and by championing economic individualism that places the value of individual gain above wider social values. When New Labour opposes the 'new right', as well as the 'old left', they argue for a Third Way that will promote wealth creation *and* social justice, the market *and* the community; embrace private enterprise but not automatically favour market solutions; it can endorse a positive role for the state – for example, welfare to work – while not assuming that governments provide public services directly: these might be done by the voluntary or private sectors; and it can offer a communitarian rather than individualist view of society in which individuals are embedded in social relations which give structure and meaning to people's lives – and that it is the role of governments to promote 'the community' as a way of enriching individual lives.

There are obvious problems with defining the Third Way simply in terms of what it is not. It can appear negative, lacking substance. As Stewart Wood suggests, it is 'product differentiation without really knowing what the product is' (Halpern and Mikosz, 1998, p. 7; see also Dahrendorf, 1999). There is also the tendency to create caricatures of the alternatives. New Labour's view of the 'old left', for example, is a catholic one (Shaw, 1996; Hirst, 1999). It combines disparate political positions under one label – from the social democracy of Tony Crosland in the 1950s and 1960s (itself a 'middle way') to the state socialism of the Alternative Economic Strategy in the late 1970s and early 1980s. New Labour's view of the 'new right' has similar faults. In particular, it suffers from an exaggeration of the neoliberal influence on Conservative governments in the 1980s and 1990s – any government that continues to spend over 40 per cent of GDP can hardly be described as *laissez-faire* – at the expense of acknowledging their conservative social interventions, the growth in economic regulations and the centralization of government.

The advantage to Labour modernizers of this negative or relational approach is to highlight – and exaggerate – the novelty of New Labour. Continuities with the 'old left' can be downplayed (except where, before a Labour audience, it is opportune to claim inheritance of traditional Left values). Discontinuities with Conservative policy making in the 1980s and 1990s can also be drawn (except where it suits New Labour to appear 'tough', on inflation or trade unions, for example). This is not to suggest that New Labour is simply a more up-to-date version of a postwar Labour government – there are too many important discontinuities – and nor is New Labour simply a continuation of Thatcherism. But if a Third Way is neither 'old left' nor 'new right', then it – or the political territory where it might be found – can cross the centre ground of politics from Left to Right, and a Third Way politics might embrace not just the centre-left but include more traditional 'one nation' strands of Toryism, as well, perhaps, as notions of 'compassionate conservatism' (Dionne, 1999).

Blair's position is that the Third Way represents a 'modernized social democracy', in other words a path on the *centre-left* of modern politics (see also Giddens, 2001). While it retains progression – the Third Way is at a better point further on – there are strong connections with the past. So, Blair argues, the Third Way offers an opportunity to advance traditional centre-left values using new policies that reflect the changing circumstances of the modern world. Blair's attempt to substantiate a Third Way falls into three parts: first, the general conditions or bases for the Third Way; second, its values; and third, the new means required to achieve these ends taking into account the new conditions.

'New Times': Globalization, Information, Individualism

The general conditions for Third Way politics rest on the argument that late 20th century society is undergoing profound and irreversible changes, and that these 'new times' call into question established political and policy making frameworks. A central theme here is 'globalization'. In a speech in South Africa in January 1999, Tony Blair suggested:

> The driving force behind the ideas associated with the Third Way is globalization because no country is immune from the massive change that globalization brings... what globalization is doing is bringing in its wake profound economic and social change, economic change rendering all jobs in industry, sometimes even new jobs in new industries, redundant overnight and social change that is a change to culture, to lifestyle, to the family, to established patterns of community life (Blair, 1999).

A Third Way, then, is required to cope with these 'new times'. For Blair, the 'old left' – postwar social democracy – 'proved steadily less viable' (1999, p. 5) as economic conditions changed as a result of globalization. In particular, Keynesian economic management to achieve full employment, partially repudiated by James Callaghan in the mid-1970s and again under question during Labour's Policy Review in the late 1980s, is seen as redundant in the context of a global economy.

Third Way thinking supports the view that globalization brings with it greater risk and insecurity, and that it is the role of policy making not to shield individuals from these but to provide the 'social capital' and 'proactive' welfare states that enable them to respond to such changes and prosper in the global age. And where globalization is bound up with the new digital information and communication technologies and the 'knowledge economy', individuals need the education and training appropriate to these conditions. Public policy should support business in the creation of 'knowledge-rich products and services' which will be the source of future economic growth (Leadbeater 1998, 1999). As a result, it is suggested, the competing goals of economic success and social justice/cohesion can be squared. Government promotes economic growth by creating stable macro-economic conditions; and its supply-side social interventions enhance individual opportunity (social justice) and increase non-inflationary growth, which together bring greater social cohesion by reducing social exclusion, enhancing choice and protecting from risk.

But within and beyond Third Way thinking there are divergences over the significance of globalization and how a Third Way politics might or should respond to it. There are different views on the extent to which governments can or should control, regulate and respond to the global free markets at the heart of economic globalization. There are different interpretations of globalization, the extent and nature of change involved in it, and consequently the sorts of politics implied. For some, nation states retain significant powers as shown by national differences in, for instance, welfare policies and regimes. For others the era of the nation state is coming to an end (Held et al., 1999; Hirst and Thompson, 1996; Dearlove, 2000, and chapter 5 for the variety of interpretations). Even if the extent or nature of globalization is agreed upon, commentators like Hay (1999) argue that the response to it is contingent. For him the Third Way is sociologically deterministic, portraying as economically fixed what is actually a matter for political choice. Anthony Giddens may be particularly vulnerable to this criticism, frequently seeing Third Way values as an issue of social necessity in a global age.

New Times but Old Values

If these, then, are general conditions for a Third Way, what about the values that Third Way politics promotes? There have been a number of attempts to pin these values down and we shall focus on the four identified by Tony Blair in his Third Way pamphlet for the Fabian Society: 'equal worth', 'opportunity for all', 'responsibility' and 'community' (see also LeGrand, 1998; Giddens, 1998; Hargreaves and Christie, 1998; White, 1998; Latham, 2001).

Blair's first value, 'equal worth', is the old liberal nostrum that all human beings are equal and should be treated as such and not discriminated against. It should be noted here that equal worth is not the same as equality of *outcome* – having equal worth with others does not itself mean you are entitled to the same income or wealth if, for instance, you work harder than them. Equal worth itself also does not necessarily imply equal *opportunities* – it is consistent for someone who is of equal worth as another to not necessarily get the same opportunities as them, if there is a right to private education, for instance, or if one person works harder to earn greater opportunities or has greater luck. Nevertheless it does seem to imply that in New Labour hands everyone should have some *minimum* opportunities or some basic fair chance in life and that no-one should be excluded from this, even if beyond these basic opportunities there isn't necessarily equality of opportunities or of social and economic outcomes.

The second value, 'opportunity for all', reflects the New Liberalism in New Labour's Third Way: that substantive (or positive) freedom requires that individuals have the resources to develop their talents and exercise their liberty – rather than being concerned solely with the legal conditions which support individuals to lead free lives (negative freedom). In this case those resources include things like educational opportunities and access to the labour market. Equal opportunities do not only go beyond the New Right, though. Blair attempts to make a distinction crucial to the Third Way: that 'opportunity for all' is principally concerned with opportunities and not outcomes: 'The Left...has in the past too readily downplayed its duty to promote a wide range of opportunities for individuals to advance themselves and their families. At worst, it has stifled opportunity in the name of abstract equality' (Blair, 1998, p. 3; see also Brown, 1997). By 'abstract equality' Blair means equality of outcome.

While he goes on to suggest that 'the progressive Left must robustly tackle the obstacles to true equality of opportunity', and that these might include 'gross inequalities...handed down from generation to generation', Blair offers what has widely been interpreted as a meritocratic understanding of equality. Inequality is a necessary part of a market economy, an important incentive and often deserved. White and Giaimo argue that one reading of this is as a 'Left Thatcherism' – 'an ideology which says that we should try to ensure citizens roughly equal initial endowments of marketable assets and then let the free market rip' (White and Giaimo, 2001, p. 216). As Merkel puts it, the trend in social democracy under the British Third Way has been 'to the recognition of societal inequality as a legitimate and functional stratification pattern in highly developed market economies under the conditions of globalized economic transactions' (Merkel, 2001, p. 50). Supporters of the Third Way 'seem fully prepared to accept greater income inequality as a market and policy outcome. Their acceptance ends only at the point where this leads to voluntary and involuntary exclusion in the higher and lower strata of society' (ibid, p. 53). In Blair's case the focus may be more on involuntary exclusion at the bottom than voluntary exclusion at the top. Furthermore, Giddens (2002) argues that equal opportunities cannot be divorced from more equal outcomes because some commitment to redistributional equality, in which income and/or wealth is more equally spread, is a precursor to equal opportunities. Inequalities in economic outcomes are themselves a basis for unequal opportunities. For Callinicos (2001) New Labour's neoliberalism has led them to abandon the sort of redistributional egalitarianism that is necessary for equality of opportunity: here is a place where a tension between Labour's neoliberalism and their egalitarianism has had to be resolved and it has been done so in favour of the former over the latter.

So New Labour's focus is more on opportunities than greater equal outcomes.

As far as opportunity goes their focus is as much on greater chances for those excluded from basic, minimum opportunities as on equalizing opportunities. This leads, to some extent, to greater equality of opportunities as those excluded from fair chances get better access to them and, consequently, more equal opportunities relative to others than before. But a key characteristic of this approach is an orientation to *inclusion* into the world of opportunities as much as *equality* of opportunity within it. On the basis of minimum opportunities for the socially excluded there can still be inequalities in opportunities. So speaking to a 1999 conference of Third Way politicians the political philosopher Ronald Dworkin warned that the Third Way had replaced 'equality' as an objective with 'sufficiency' in which 'once those minimal standards are met, government has no further obligation to make people equal in anything' (Dworkin, 2001, p. 172).

The third of Blair's four values is 'responsibility' and links closely with the fourth, 'community'. 'Responsibility' reflects Blair's ethical turn spelt out in his 1995 Spectator Lecture that 'we do not live by economics alone': 'a society which is fragmented and divided, where people feel no sense of shared purpose, is unlikely to produce well-adjusted and responsible citizens' (Blair, 1995). In a decent society, individuals should not simply claim rights from the state but should also accept their individual responsibilities and duties as citizens, parents and members of communities. A Third Way should promote the value of 'community' by supporting the structures and institutions of civil society – such as the family and voluntary organizations – which promote individual opportunity and which ground 'responsibility' in meaningful social relationships.

It is notable that New Labour's discourse of community differs in emphasis from more traditional social democratic ideas of social and economic community based on greater equality and universal experience of services such as welfare, health and education and with a stress on the obligations of business to the community (even if this was not always followed in practice as effectively as it could have been). The Third Way is based more on opportunities than greater equality of outcomes. It retains an emphasis on universal, collective services such as health and education but some of its social policies make welfare more selective and targeted. The Third Way has a more business-friendly tone that stresses, rhetorically at least, moral as well as socio-economic community and work. Responsibility of the citizen to the community is emphasized relatively more than corporate obligations. Community is less linked to class than moral cohesion and social inclusion. (We discuss New Labour's communitarianism in greater depth in Driver and Martell, 1997.)

Old Values but New Means

Blair's claim to a pragmatic view of means is indicative of much Third Way thinking: 'These are the values of the Third Way. Without them, we are adrift. But in giving them practical effect, a large measure of pragmatism is essential. As I say continually, what matters is what works to give effect to our values' (Blair, 1998, p. 4). For Blair, as times change, so must the means to achieve centre-left values; and it is these values, not the policies in themselves, which matter. To be pragmatic rather than ideological about the choice of means is central to New Labour's case for a Third Way between 'old left' and 'new right' – and to aspire to continuity in values is central to Blair's assertion that the Third Way is a centre-left political project.

The Third Way debate about public policy reflects the Left's long preoccupation with the appropriate role for government in a market society. Bill Clinton and the New Democrats argued that the Third Way offered a new role for government between the Left's 'big government' and the Right's attempts to dismantle it; and this, in part, can be seen as a debate about the balance between the state and the market and the character of public policy instruments. What is common to the Third Way is the notion that there is an active role for government in contemporary market societies; and that this breaks with the state versus market approach which, it is suggested, typified the 'old left' and 'new right'. New Labour's Third Way pragmatism, Le Grand (1998) argues, lies in the fact that it has no automatic commitment to either the public sector (as 'old left' social democrats did) or the private sector (as 'new right' neoliberals do). New Labour's Third Way approach to public policy is said to break with the state/market approach by being more pragmatic and less ideological about them.

Put more concretely, a Third Way approach to public policy encompasses a number of features: the state working in 'partnership' with the private and voluntary sectors (e.g. the New Deal and public-private cooperation in health and education, such as hospital building or private sector school management); government regulating and acting as guarantor but not direct provider of public goods or of basic standards (e.g. of the minimum wage and local government services such as refuse collection); the reform or 'reinventing' of government and public administration (e.g. government departments and agencies working together to tackle complex social problems – so-called 'joined-up government'); the welfare state working 'proactively' to help individuals off social security and into work ('employment-centred social policy' or the 'social investment state') not leaving it to market forces or direct state provision of welfare or jobs; government working to provide public goods (such as childcare, education and training) to underpin greater equality of opportunity ('asset-based egalitarianism'); government targeting social policy on the socially excluded and at the same time encouraging greater individual responsibility for welfare provision (e.g. 'stakeholder pensions'); and government redrawing the 'social contract' – rights to welfare matched by responsibilities, especially regarding work. A Third Way government can, then, be distinguished from an 'old left' one by its willingness to find new forms of public intervention in the economy and society, in particular, by giving up its role as the direct provider of public goods; and from a 'new right' one by its willingness to embrace a wide definition of public goods, especially in social policy, and a more active and interventionist role for the state.

Such policies are not original or exclusive to the Third Way. Many of the public policy instruments and reforms, like public-private partnerships or 'reinventing government', now seen as being at the heart of New Labour's Third Way were features of previous Conservative administrations from which the Third Way is meant to be clearly distinguished. The fact that governments of the Right, whether at the state level in the USA or national governments like that of José María Aznar in Spain, are attracted to so-called Third Way public policy instruments, presents problems for any attempt to identify the Third Way as a uniquely centre-left political project.

There are further reasons to doubt whether Labour's new approach to means remains a centre-left or even pragmatic approach. One is that in situations where the government has been faced with decisions over the role of the public or private sectors in the provision of services they have tended to favour increasing the role of private sector money and management but have not done so with regard to extending the role of the public sector in private sector services. The government has controversially increased the role of the private sector in health and education while partly privatizing air traffic control and pursuing plans for part privatization of the London Underground. It could be argued that Labour's approach to public-private partnerships appears not to be entirely 'what works matters' but just as much an ideological commitment to an increased role for the private sector in provision of previously public services (Shaw, 2000).

For Plant (2001) New Labour fetishize means too much, stressing them as the arena in which change has happened and underplaying the extent to which the Third Way also involves shifts in ends. Changing means may affect the ends they are supposed to achieve. So a shift from policies of public ownership, Keynesian economics and tax redistribution affects whether centre-left ends such as equality can be pursued. Without such means the ends they were intended to achieve may become less realizable. A bias to private ownership and supply-side economics and inclusion strategies are less amenable to egalitarian redistribution and more to minimum opportunities within an inegalitarian market economy. Similarly a shift away from ideas of, for instance, a universal welfare state and the comprehensive ideal in education affects the goals of certain kinds of equality and community. Targeted welfare and a pluralistic education system, whatever their vices or virtues, undermine egalitarianism as a goal and take away some means for achieving community.

Is the Third Way Really *Beyond* Left and Right?

As we have seen, Third Way arguments claim that with changing economic and social circumstances a new politics is required that departs from the major political paradigms of the postwar years: namely social democracy ('old left') and Thatcherism ('new right'). But does the Third Way dispense with the traditional divide between left and right, and with the established political categories of liberal, conservative and social democrat? Does it, as Bobbio (1996) has asked, transcend and make such categories redundant? Or is it simply a cobbling together of different intellectual positions combining principles and practices which could cohere or be contradictory and mutually undermining?

There is a degree of ambiguity on these questions. Blair, for example, argues that 'the Third Way is not an attempt to split the difference between Right and Left', suggesting not a middle way but something more novel. He also states that the Third Way offers a new synthesis between liberal and socialist thinking: the Third Way 'marks a Third Way *within* the left' (Blair 1998, p. 1, italics in original). But some commentators have their doubts. Stuart White argues that the Third Way 'can all too easily be taken to imply that we need, not to modernise, but to exit the social democratic tradition in pursuit of something wholly new and distinctive' (White, 1998; see also Marquand, 1998).

John Gray is a leading advocate of the argument for a new politics that transcends established political frameworks: 'The place we occupy is not a halfway house between rival extremes. Our position is not a compromise between two discredited ideologies. It is a stand on a new common ground' (Gray, 1997). Elsewhere he argues for his 'conviction that the established traditions of British political thought: liberal, conservative and socialist, cannot meet the challenges posed by the technological and cultural environment of Britain in the late modern period. New thought is needed, in which 'debts to the past are light' (Gray, 1996, p. 7). The 'debts' Gray alludes to include, crucially, political values not just policy instruments – the dominant theme in New Labour thinking. He argues for a politics 'beyond the new right' (Gray, 1993) and '*after* social democracy' (Gray, 1996).

Anthony Giddens (1994 and 1998) argues that 'emancipatory politics' – concerned with questions of political economy; with the distribution of rights and resources – is giving way to 'life politics' – concerned with questions of identity and the quality of life. Giddens suggests that these shifts in contemporary political culture blur distinctions between left and right outside the domain of party politics:

> a whole range of other problems and possibilities have come to the fore that are not within the reach of the Left/Right scheme. These include ecological questions, but also issues to do with the changing nature of the family, work and personal and cultural identity' (Giddens, 1998, p. 44).

Left and right concerns cut across these areas and, it is argued, fail to encapsulate differences between points of view on life politics.

Giddens also argues that traditional attachment of left and right to radicalism and conservatism respectively were becoming less and less meaningful after a decade of Thatcherite neoliberal radicalism and in a cultural environment he calls 'post-traditional'. New Labour has since conformed to Giddens's thesis with a social conservative strand to their politics. For Giddens this makes it seem that old left-right associations do not work any more: particular views are no longer exclusively the property of one or the other. This is reinforced by the fact that popular attitudes do not so easily divide into consistently left or right positions as they used to. On many issues people divide into liberal or communitarian camps, for example, rather than Left and Right ones.

Such views suggest the moving of politics to areas beyond categories of left and right. But does this mean that left and right are transcended or synthesized or that they merely co-exist? We believe that the Third Way involves the combination rather than transcendence of these traditional foes. Principles such as equality, efficiency, autonomy and pluralism, over which the left and right have long been divided, get mixed together rather than left behind. The novelty of the Third Way lies in this combination: a mixture which is neither exclusively of the left or of the right. In this way, the Third Way offers a politics which is beyond the closed ideological systems of the past; but which still combines them and remains within the tradition of middle way politics that has been a feature of much of 20th century British politics – most notably New Liberalism, postwar social democracy and one nation conservatism.

Blair has argued that public policy 'should and will cross the boundaries between left and right, liberal and conservative' (Blair, 1995). In his Fabian pamphlet, he suggested that the Third Way offers 'a popular politics reconciling themes which in the past have wrongly been regarded as antagonistic' (Blair, 1998, p. 1). So, a Third Way stands for social justice *and* economy efficiency, rights *and* responsibilities, a successful market economy *and* social cohesion. It overcomes these bipolar divisions by suggesting that they are mutually supporting. Social justice, for instance, can be supported by ensuring everyone has the education and training needed to give them a fair chance in life; this also underpins economic efficiency by providing a skilled workforce which can attract investment and enhance productivity in the new global economy. You can have social justice and economic efficiency at the same time.

Blair offers practical examples of Third Way policy positions which he sees as crossing traditional political divides: cutting corporation tax *and* introducing a minimum wage; giving the Bank of England independence *and* developing a programme of welfare to work to promote social inclusion; reforming schools to give marginalized kids better chances *and* tough policies on juvenile crime; giving central government 'greater strategic capacity' *and* introducing devolution; more money for health and education *and* tight limits to the overall level of government spending or limits on income tax. For Blair, the distinctiveness of these policies in terms of a Third Way is the italicized '*and*' in each case: it is in the combinations that the originality of Third Way thinking lies. The New Deal illustrates how the principles of autonomy, opportunity and rights balanced with responsibilities might actually complement one another. The Third Way approach also allows the Labour government to have a more pluralistic approach to policy making, in the sense that certain principles operate in some spheres of policy making and not in others: for example, rights-based liberal individualism in constitutional reform but social conservatism in education and the criminal justice system.

This notion of a mix of values and approaches better encapsulates the Third Way than the more radical definition of it as a synthesis or as transcending left and right – finding some balance or *modus operandi* between the demands of competing political values. But such compromises come with price tags as principles and values have to be traded-off against one another. Blair's Third Way often appears to try to combine what are in the end contrary principles. New Labour's Third Way can at times appear as if, as Albert Hirschman (1996) puts it, all good things go together – when very often they do not. While reciprocity and mutual dependency between different values and policies is possible in particular circumstances, there are also different interests at work and tensions remain permanent features of the political and policy making landscape.

It follows that as a perspective that combines different principles the Third Way cannot be said to be a coherent ideology or philosophy. There is no systematic, consistent guide to action or to which principles should be favoured in circumstances where they clash. So the Third Way is more of a framework than a philosophy, more of a space between other alternatives within which policy can be developed than a guide to policy making (White, 2001; Giddens, 2001). What decisions and 'hard choices' should be made in adjudicating between contrary principles is left open. So, in criminal justice liberal and conservative views can co-exist but sometimes they come into conflict and choices have to be made between them. In economic policy the commitment to minimum opportunities may come into conflict with the success of a market economy and so choices have to be made between these two: in fact choosing the market economy is one key reason why the principle of egalitarian redistribution has been considerably downgraded in Labour's approach. Giddens (2001) expresses sympathy for egalitarian redistribution, the European social model and global economic regulation including policies such as taxes on currency speculation. Yet he also rejects demand management and a role for government in supporting ailing industries and enthuses about flexible labour markets. Where some commitments undermine others, and how choices might be made between them where they clash, is not considered.

Thatcherism Mark II?

Is this Third Way simply the mark of a new consensus between left and right – in particular, a consensus based on the Thatcherite reforms of the 1980s and 1990s which New Labour has adopted and which has replaced the postwar social democratic consensus on Keynesianism and the welfare state? For many critics the consolidation of Thatcherism is what New Labour amounts to and Blair is little more than the 'son of Margaret' (Hall, 1994; Hall and Jacques, 1997; Hall, 1998; Hay, 1999). In being more pragmatic about what works best the Third Way has opened the left up more to non-left inputs.

Certainly the political agenda shifted to the Right under Mrs Thatcher and the main political parties now are fighting on a similar post-Thatcherite terrain. This is not evidence for the 'beyond left and right' view. The new consensus consists of a shift from left to right, not one which goes beyond both to something new. The occupancy of positions has moved but the old divides on which they are based still remain. But the 'beyond left' view is also, on a factual level, too simple. The case for consensus is based on Labour's adoption of an orthodox macro-economic policy that has low inflation as its central policy objective and interest rates as the key policy instrument. While giving the Bank of England the power to set monetary policy marks a point of departure from previous Conservative governments, it is in other public policy areas – the labour market (the minimum wage, the Social Chapter), constitutional reform, public spending on health and education, the scale and scope of the New Deal – in which it is possible to identify imprints of the left. Those who advocate the Labour as Thatcherism view downplay or even ignore social democratic elements to the Third Way (as is the case, for instance, in Hay, 1999). Many of these differences involve a combination of small practical measures based in centre-left values and involve important symbolic differences from the right.

There is a mixture of left and right in between old left and new right, a mixture of ideology and pragmatism and of different responses to differently interpreted social changes. If there is one Third Way in that space, there may be room for others (see Dahrendorf, 1999; Freeden, 1999; White, 1998). Different Third Ways might be more or less centre-left in orientation: some social democratic, others not – and some to the right of the political divide. We wish to go on to argue in this chapter that there are different Third Ways, both in Britain and across Europe.

Third Way Values in Question: Equality and Community

On closer examination there are further ways in which there are differences within Third Way politics. Stuart White offers his definition of Third Way values (White, 1998). These, he suggests, are: 'real opportunity', 'civic responsibility' and 'community'. They tally more or less with those offered by the Labour leader we examined earlier. However, unlike Blair, White suggests that they are open to different interpretations, not all of which will fall on the centre-left. This leads him to suggest two lines of division within the Third Way. The first between 'leftists' and 'centrists' concerns the nature of equality. Like Bobbio (1996) he identifies equality as a crucial issue that divides those on the Left from those further on the Right. The second line is between liberals and communitarians and concerns the degree of individual freedom in relation to community enforced norms.

White's first line of division is between leftist-egalitarian and more centrist-meritocratic Third Ways (see also Holtham's distinction between the 'centre-left' and 'radical centre' in Halpern and Mikosz 1998, pp. 39–41). Leftists would like to see greater redistribution of income and wealth rather than of just asset-based opportunities; and critics such as Roy Hattersley (1997a and 1997b; see also Levitas, 1999) have condemned New Labour's shift from equality of outcome to meritocracy and inclusion as the principal aims of the Third Way. Giddens (1998, 2001, 2002) launches a stern attack on the inadequacy of meritocracy and equality of opportunity alone.

A second line of division identified by White is between communitarians and liberals: between those who have a broad understanding of the range of behaviour for which the individual may be held responsible to the community, and for which the state may legitimately intervene, and those who have a much more limited notion. White argues that any Third Way view must have some commitment to civic responsibility. And it is New Labour's communitarian understanding of civic responsibility – its apparent willingness to set public policy that challenges liberal notions of the private sphere – which is distinctive and which has drawn fire from, among others, the liberal Left for being too conservative, too prescriptive, even socially authoritarian (*Marxism Today*, 1998; see also, Dahrendorf, 1999; *The Economist*, 1999).

Table 3.1. Liberty, Equality and Community in Contemporary British Political Debates

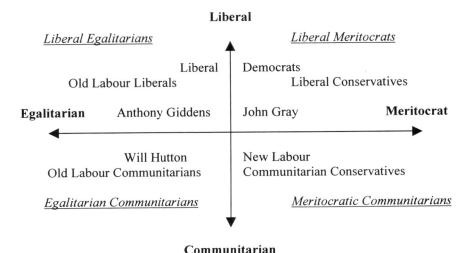

This liberal-communitarian distinction conceals further differences in Third Ways – among liberals and among communitarians. Some who are liberal on social matters, for example, may be left-egalitarian; less interventionist socially but in favour of greater economic interventionism and equality. It is conceivable that some who are liberal on social intervention could be more centrist-meritocrats, although this combination begins to move us to the Right rather than left of centre. Similarly those who are sympathetic to Labour's communitarian interventionism on social matters may be leftist-egalitarians or more centrist-meritocrats when it comes to questions of economic equality. So between liberal and communitarian Third Ways there may be differences and within each yet further Third Way approaches can be distinguished. Table 3.1 shows how such positions can be seen in the space between old left and new right.

These distinctions leave out a third axis to do with the nature of communitarianism along which there is space between old left and new right for Third Ways to differ. Different sorts of communitarianism can be progressive or conservative, voluntaristic or statist. As we have suggested, criticisms of Labour's communitarianism are often liberal and suspicious of prescriptive moralism. But another line of criticism could come within communitarianism from anyone at odds with its conservative content (again, see *Marxism Today*, 1998). This raises issues not of whether community should be promoted but of what sort of community – a 'progressive' community (which promotes modern teaching methods and support for non-nuclear family forms, for instance) or a more 'conservative' sort of community (which emphasizes more traditional norms for education and the family). Alternatives here may concur over the idea that it is the role of government to have a moral agenda about what kind of community is desirable, but disagree over the sort of community prescribed.

Also glossed over by the liberal-communitarian distinction is a difference between voluntaristic and top-down communitarians. Again, the difference is not over whether greater community or shared moral norms are needed but, in this case, where these come from – state action or more organically. Those who stress the latter can include one-nation or 'compassionate' conservatives or leftist communitarians of more voluntaristic, civil society and social movement traditions, in search of more community but not through state action. Those, like New Labour, who stress the former see governments – through exhortation, symbolic action and legislation – taking the lead in fostering community in society, even if they are also open to some forms of community action from below, a New Deal in the Community programmes, for instance.

Table 3.2. Progressive and Conservative Community

Progressive Labour/Liberal Democrats   Conservative Labour/Moral Conservatives

←—————————————————————————————————————→

Progressive community   Conservative community

This is one example of where Third Ways diverge on means. The Third Way can involve the initiative of civil society or state in delivery of, for instance, welfare by the state or by greater delegation to the private and voluntary sectors. The question here is whether a government committed to strong social objectives can deliver on them without the old levers of power (see Coote, 1999). There might be divisions over whether welfare is universal or more targeted, with any implications this may have for impinging upon social democratic values. There can be Third Ways pursued via global governance or national or local action, or through cooperation between state and other actors, whether governmental or non-governmental. In this way, the Third Way can diverge on means – and the choice of means in each of these cases will affect the character of the ends reached.

In identifying Third Ways old political labels continue to be useful. Versions of the Third Way are more left or right, more or less social democratic, more liberal or conservative; and criticisms and defences of Blair's Third Way often break down along such lines. This casts doubts on Blair's oft-repeated claim that the Third Way is necessarily a centre-left project. A social democratic Third Way, whether it is actually called that or not, is discernible (see Gamble and Wright, 1999 and the 'new social democracy'). Equally apparent are Third Ways to the Right, including strong elements in Blair's own approach, which share less with the centre-left, however defined. In this way, left and right divisions, as Bobbio (1996) argues, as well as those between liberals and communitarians, progressives and conservatives, have not been left behind. Such divisions also mark out social democratic paths taken beyond the United Kingdom, and underpin the reception of the Third Way elsewhere.

The Third Way Across the Pond, Over the Channel – and Before Blair

Tony Blair has had his moments of evangelism in trying to promote the Third Way abroad and these have not always fallen on the most open or unirritated of ears (Blair, 1997). But there is no doubt that across Europe and in many countries abroad the sort of Third Way ideas being pursued by Blair have caught on. Commentators such as Sassoon (1999a) and Vandenbroucke (2001) are keen to stress commonality rather than difference and there are notable similarities in agendas across Europe and other parts of the world. Blair has been keen to promote the Third Way abroad – not just through fitting in with Europe or playing a part in it, but through actively exercising leadership in creating a Third Way model that other European social democrats will go along with (Blair, 1997, 1998). But it is not only Blair who has helped these ideas to catch on. Many other centre-left parties were pursuing what have become known as Third Way policies before Blair. For some, commonalities around Third Way ideas are due to the fact that shared processes of globalization are leading to the same sort of logical adaptations (Giddens, 1998; Sassoon, 1999b). But there may be many other common problems that different national governments have been facing – pressures following from

European integration, or demographic change and other problems for European welfare states, for instance. We shall look now at common patterns in Third Ways across Britain, the USA and Europe, before moving on to examine the way national institutions and cultures lead Third Ways to take different forms in different places.

Some credit US President Bill Clinton as the first real popularizer of the idea and policies of the Third Way and with whose New Democrats Blair's New Labour came to have much in common. Both Clinton and Blair came to power against the backdrop of years of radical neoliberal governments, as moderates within their own parties convinced that modernization and a move to more central ground was necessary for electoral success, placing importance on globalization and the information economy and the priority for welfare reform, economic stability and fiscal prudence. Both tended away from isolationism on the international stage. Robert Reich, former Secretary of Labor under Clinton, declared in 1999 that 'we are all Third Wayers now' (Reich, 1999). Reich argues that Western Europe and the USA shared a commitment to reducing budget deficits and to deregulation (in the USA) or privatization (in Europe), an acceptance of globalization in trade and the mobility of capital, and commitments to flexible labour markets and reductions in welfare. The US Democrats and New Labour, he argued, were also committed to reducing burdens and regulations on business and accepted the growth of inequality. On these issues there may be some difference between the Anglo-American partners and their European counterparts, differences being an issue we shall return to shortly. Yet alongside this neoliberalism there is also a commitment to government activism, making the British and USA ways *Third Way*(s), departing from the old left but also more than just neoliberalism (Jaenicke, 2000). US and UK policies on social inclusion have both involved education and training, special support for families with children, and making sure that work is worthwhile for the poor, through tax credits for instance. In the US and the UK one factor that limited such attempts was an emphasis on fiscal prudence and restrictions on tax rises for those who benefited under two decades of Reagan and Thatcher (Reich, 1997, 1999), not to mention other institutional and political obstacles faced, especially in the USA (Weir, 2001; Jaenicke, 2000). Both Clinton and Blair's welfare reforms have also been marked by conservative emphases, imposing obligations in return for welfare rights, or in some cases limiting rights to, or amounts of, benefits.

But the spread of Third Way ideas and policies can be seen beyond Britain and the USA. Other leaders such as D'Alema in Italy, Gerhard Schröder in Germany and Cardoso in Brazil, not to mention leaders not of the left or centre, such as José María Aznar in Spain, have explicitly praised Blair's Third Way or allied themselves with it, attended Third Way conferences or developed written joint platforms with Blair reflecting Third Way policies (e.g. Blair and Schröder, 1999). This is not to mention policies which, named as Third Way or not, seem to match neatly with those of the Third Way. In the 1980s, 1990s and afterwards other parties have reinvented themselves in ways that could be seen as going in a comparable direction to Blair's (albeit with specifically national or some ideological differences) – the PSOE in Spain under Felipe Gonzalez, the Dutch PdvA under Wim Kok, and the Swedish SAP, for instance. Overall the political centre of gravity among social democratic parties has shifted to a more centrist position.

Beyond Britain, other social democratic parties have long been struggling to win middle-class and popular support outside their shrinking working-class constituencies. In Sweden, for instance, middle class support has always been central to the success of the SAP. By the mid-1990s Europe's social democrats were also in principle accepting the market economy they had long learned to live with in practice. For some, this path traces back to the 1950s, through Crosland and Gaitskell in Britain, *Bad Godesberg* in 1959 for the German SPD and through related reforms in this period in countries such as Italy, Norway and Sweden.

In some places, social democratic modernization preceded that recently carried out by the British Labour Party, seen by most as, for good or ill, presently the furthest down the road of liberalization. At the 1959 *Bad Godesberg* congress the German SPD broke with Marxism by accepting the market and a role for private ownership. The Dutch SDAP's conversion to the mixed economy and an electoral strategy that incorporated the middle classes happened as early as the 1930s. The Dutch PvDA (founded in the 1940s) shares a remarkable number of features with New Labour in the UK: the rejection of traditional welfarism and Keynesianism, and of planning and egalitarianism; an emphasis on combining economic efficiency with social justice; low taxation policies; competitiveness based on technological innovation; government intervention on social exclusion; a focus on labour and work as the basis for participation; partnership with the private sector; flexibility in worklife; and the importance of education and training (van den Anker, 2001). While Sweden has been noted for its high taxation and large universal welfare system, several of the characteristics of present day modernization were also exhibited by Swedish social democracy long before Blair had his day. And many of the criticisms of modernizing social democracy in the Netherlands are also comparable to those made of New Labour in Britain: too much emphasis on work as a solution to social exclusion and too much on opportunities at the expense of equality and redistribution, for example (van den Anker, 2001).

Third Way Economics and Welfare Beyond Britain

While Thatcherism left New Labour with a neoliberal inheritance, Maastricht and budget deficits were key factors that forced fiscal conservatism on other European social democrats. Social democratic parties across Europe were talking in the 1980s about the combination of social justice with economic efficiency and individual entrepreneurialism. In the 1980s and 1990s low inflation and stability replaced Keynesianism and full employment as the main goals, leading to the rethinking of economic, employment and welfare policies. Many European social democrats were well ahead of the British in their moves in these directions. Before Tony Blair became Labour leader, the Dutch social democrats were adopting their pragmatic approach to the market and regulation, and promoting deregulation, privatization and internal markets. They were practising sound public finances, implementing tax reductions and promoting the work ethic, flexibility and training initiatives in the labour market and reallocations of funding from social security to other areas, such as education. The Dutch social democrats have argued for and seemingly achieved what Blair aspires to: the combination of many of these liberal economic reforms on one hand with social cohesion and social justice on the other (de Beus, 1999). Others such as the Spanish PSOE put inflation above unemployment as an economic policy priority (Clift, 2001).

Across European social democracy, nationalization has generally been discarded. Many social democratic governments talk of a constructive partnership between business and government and are pursuing more ambitious privatization programmes than Blair or their own conservative predecessors (Sassoon, 1999b). An openness to private enterprise and a non-dogmatic attitude to state ownership has long been part of Swedish social democracy. As a small country dependent on exports, Sweden has accommodated itself to free trade and international competition for some time (Lindgren, 1999). Well beyond Britain, social democrats propose active government, rather than the direct state intervention or *laissez-faire* of the first and second ways; business-friendly practices, such as lower business taxes, and increasing labour market flexibility are pursued; and restraints on public expenditure are being widely implemented in response to pressures such as EU convergence and the perceived globalization of capital. Keeping inflation down is generally accepted as a prime target across Europe. Fiscal stability and curbing tax-and-spend policies are general commitments, as are the use of supply-side measures, subsidies and incentives to tackle unemployment. It is not only in the UK that small businesses and industrial innovation in hi-tech sectors are being promoted as the cutting edge of future growth. All this sounds very much like Blair's Third Way recipe for Britain.

The French socialists make the strongest noises about national uniqueness and a more traditional social democratic road. But beyond their policy for a 35-hour work week some see differences from Blair in hard policies often as not fundamental (e.g. Sassoon, 1999b). From this point of view, Britain has moved, albeit more weakly, in the direction of restricting working hours. Negotiations on Jospin's reductions to the working week have actually led to agreements on greater labour market flexibility. While the British are reluctant to increase income taxes, there is widespread feeling in Germany that tax rates are too high and there are concerns to restructure the tax system. The principle of central bank independence has been broadly accepted, implemented in Sweden at the same time as in the UK and part of the German scene for decades (Sassoon, 1999b). Across Europe, from Jospin to Blair, social democrats wish to pursue reforms to international financial organizations.

Although welfare problems vary from nation to nation, comparable agendas of welfare reform are being discussed by many European social democrats across national boundaries (Vandenbroucke, 2001). The Swedes have for decades been at the forefront of developing 'workfare' and active labour market policies based on education and training. While they remain attached to universalism, they are shifting away from the idea that the state should shoulder all the costs. The fiscal deficit and an increasing proportion of pensioners and students in the population have led Swedish social democrats to limit rises in social security (Lindgren, 1999). Across Europe employment is seen as a key to welfare reform. It is perceived that welfare needs to be more responsive to changes in the family and gender roles and more attuned to balancing work and family life. Welfare is seen as being as much about investment in education as spending on benefits (Vandenbroucke, 2001). It is not just in Britain that welfare reform imposes obligations on the unemployed: the German SPD, for instance, has also been thinking along such lines. The advocacy of tough crime measures, the tying of rights to responsibilities and the prioritization of education and training as routes to employment and fairer chances are defining features of New Labour that have also been rehearsed in the talk of other European social democratic parties.

Third Ways and National Paths

But the story is more complex than this. Despite globalization and European integration, national differences are important. A commentator like Clift writes that 'European social democratic parties are more similar now than at any time this century' (2001, p. 71). But he still makes the central aim of his essay on this topic explaining how the most notable feature of the European social democratic landscape remains difference along national lines. Vandenbroucke stresses 'theoretical convergence' among European social democratic parties in terms of the policy commonalities we have discussed, but also sees divergence in actual national models and policies: 'convergence of view on this level of thinking will not necessarily lead to convergence on practical measures between countries due to their very different starting points' (Vandenbroucke, 2001, p. 163; see also Kelly, 1999; White, 2001 part III; Lovecy, 2001; Martell et al., 2001).

For a large part of the 1980s the story was of Labour lagging behind its sister European social democratic parties in the march towards modernization. It was attached to nationalization, Keynesianism, unilateral nuclear disarmament, close links with the unions and a less than full-hearted embrace of European integration. Yet in the 1990s Labour is seen as having leapfrogged European social democracy in the race to 'modernize'. For some he has taken the politics of catch-up a little too far. At meetings of European social democrats Blair and Gordon Brown have tried to promote the virtues of liberalization and free trade, labour market flexibility, welfare reform and cuts in regulation of business in pursuit of productivity and employment. Blair is said to have irritated fellow European social democrats who see him as lecturing them to adopt what is effectively just warmed-up Thatcherism.

The British Third Way has often been seen to contrast with the politics of those, like the former French Prime Minister Jospin, who are not so opposed to the virtues of labour market regulation and public spending on job creation. Some social democrats among the Italians, French and Germans (but not many of their leaders) have argued for demand management (at a coordinated European level) to boost employment where British modernizers have focused more on advocating supply-side measures, arguing that the world has been changed so much by globalization that Keynesianism is dead (Clift, 2001; Giddens, 1994, 1998; Vandenbroucke, 2001). At the same time the European Central bank, supported by most social democratic governments, has pursued a very tight and conservative monetary policy in recent years. It has been the Anglo-American central banks in the UK and US that have pursued a more active and growth-oriented monetary policy by aggressively cutting interest rates. In Britain, inclusion in the job market is seen as occurring essentially through private sector jobs whereas other European social democrats, like the French, have put greater emphasis on public sector job creation. The French socialist policy has been to decrease the average working week to 35 hours while the British have trouble legislating for anything lower than 48 hours. Jospin argued 'yes to the market economy, no to the market society', an approach within which he pursued widespread privatization and deregulation but also the shorter working week and continued state intervention in the economy (Bouvet and Michel, 2001; Jospin 1999).

Meanwhile, the 'social' in Germany's social market seems to require goals that go beyond inclusion and equality of opportunity to more egalitarian values and beyond *laissez-faire* to a more collaborative approach (Meyer, 1999). In France, Germany, Sweden and elsewhere partnerships with the unions remain important, while New Labour has attempted to divorce itself from any special relationship with the unions, who emerged much weakened from the Thatcher years. For the Dutch and Swedes, politics is embedded in a social democratic political culture, emphasizing consensus and continuity – the 'polder model' as it is known in the Netherlands – quite different to the competitive individualism and Conservative domination of the British context (van den Anker, 2001).

Welfare problems vary across Europe: pensions dominate the debate in Italy, Sweden, Germany and France; health expenditure – too low in Britain, too high in Germany; disability benefits in the Netherlands; unemployment in Germany and France; and poverty and exclusion in the UK (Kelly, 1999). In Sweden there remains a stronger attachment to universal welfare than in some other places (Lindgren, 1999). In Germany issues of citizenship and immigration take a particular form. The emphasis in foreign policy and in attitudes to the EU varies by nation. Britain's response to economic globalization emphasizes national incentives to attract mobile capital and less so harmonization and proactive supra-national political coordination advocated elsewhere in Europe. In Europe Britain has tended to resist moves towards a European social model. Britain places special rhetorical emphasis on national interest in domestic arguments for EU integration.

Like the Swedes, the British remain open to economic globalization but cautious about European political integration. Yet, at the level of rhetoric at least, Britain is more pro-American, which contrasts especially with the attitude of the French who like to cultivate their own 'exceptionalism'. And Blair has been explicitly interventionist and active in military coordination, as evidenced by his leading role in the Kosovo war, European defence and the war against Afghanistan. Other social democrats in Europe have remained neutral and true to national traditions, or shown greater qualifications about pursuing international military intervention or alliances with the USA.

Why National Third Ways? Models of Capitalism

Why do differences happen? Different countries have their own historically developed economies, social structures, political systems and cultures which will affect rhetoric and policy (Vandenbroucke, 1999, 2001; Martell et al., 2001). For some, Blair and the US Democrats find a lot in common because they share the same Anglo-American tradition of capitalism: individualistic, *laissez-faire* and with limited government; flexible, less regulated with weak unions; and a market-based and short-termist financial system. The Anglo-American model has relatively low unemployment but high inequality and poverty. This is seen to contrast with the 'Rheinland' model of capitalism predominant elsewhere in Europe where economic and political culture is more collaborative and corporatist, unions and partnership more important, finance is less market-based and longer term, and employment is more skilled, secure and better paid – in short where there is more of a 'social market' approach (Albert, 1993; Hutton, 1995). In Germany and other European countries there are more statist or collaborative political cultures reflected, for example, in the Blair/Schröder document (1999) by references to partnership with the trade unions. Such sentiments rarely feature in New Labour statements. France has a tradition of centralized government and state involvement in public services, much of this still intact despite the Jospin government's privatization programme. In Sweden and the Netherlands political culture is predominantly social democratic, consensual, solidaristic and mutual in contrast to the relatively more conservative, competitive and individualist culture of Anglo-Americanism. Furthermore, language, image and concepts differ according to national traditions. The French are much happier talking the language of solidarity, regulation and the state and the Germans of partnership and neo-corporatism, for example, than the British.

So while reform of the Labour Party in the late 1980s looked to European social democracy for ideas, with Blair's accession to the leadership in 1994 Clinton and the New Democrats in the USA became a bigger influence and closer partners – and such differences between Anglo-Americanism and European models were probably reinforced (Clift, 2001). More recently a key factor in national political differences has been the reconstruction of the economic and political landscape by Thatcherism. The USA, like Britain, went through a radical right-wing experience under the Republican government of Ronald Reagan. Throughout the 1980s Labour was forced to confront the reforms of Conservative governments: fiscal conservatism, anti-inflationary policies, trade union legislation, privatization, deregulation of the labour market and reforms to health, education and housing. Blair's Third Way is a post-Thatcherite project, defined by inheritance of the Thatcherite legacy alongside a reaction against it in policies geared towards devolution and communitarian inclusion (Driver and Martell, 1998). The context that has led to this configuration has not existed to the same extent in other European countries. There governments of the right in the 1980s did not carry out experiments as radical as those in Britain and the USA. Blair's rhetoric is more pro-market and friendly to private business than, say, Jospin's in part because of the economic and political landscape he has inherited and had to work upon. This landscape also makes Blair more left-wing in the UK context than he would be in other European countries – reforms which may seem less notable in other European countries amount to a shift in a leftwards and pluralist direction in the UK compared to the Thatcherite past.

Why National Third Ways? Political Influences

Elsewhere in Europe there are other pressures on social democrats that do not exist to the same extent in Britain and these may also affect the different emphases of political rhetoric between countries and the varying forms that common policy agendas may take in practice (Lovecy, 2001). Because of the first-past-the-post British political system, Blair has an absolute majority of seats. Blair does not have to compromise with left-wing or green coalition partners as in France, Germany, Italy, Denmark and Sweden (in some places these are formal coalitions, in others minority governments with *ad hoc* cooperation). Moreover, coalitions or not, there are no significant parties to the left of Labour in the UK. As such Blair can dictate his own agenda to a greater extent and is less constrained by left-wing or green inputs or competition for votes from the left. Demand management and environmental concerns get a higher profile in the Blair/Schröder document, for example, than they would in most New Labour statements on the Third Way, in part a reflection of the greater strength of the left and greens in the German government. Jospin's rhetoric was, to some extent, an attempt to keep his five-party centre-left coalition on board. He needed to 'talk left' to appeal to his socialist, communist and green 'gauche plurielle' (Bouvet and Michel, 2001).

Blair is also not held back from his 'modernization' programme by a significant left-wing faction in the Labour Party and the political opposition – the Conservative Party – remains weak and ineffective. It should also be added that in systems where proportional representation requires coalitions, the decline of a party to a small vote does not necessarily lead it into the sort of oblivion that often entails radical modernization, as happened with the UK Labour party in the early 1980s. Small parties can still wield significant government influence in such coalitions. The Labour Party sank to 27.6 per cent of the vote in 1983 leading to fears of permanent electoral annihilation and the road to modernization. The French socialists came into government and held the Prime Ministership after having gained only 26.5 per cent of the vote in 1997 (Lovecy, 2001). The pressure for modernization, because of electoral decline at least, was not as great.

Germany faces further complications beyond its coalitional system. The SPD is a decentralized and fragmented party making it more complex for a leader to negotiate policy reforms of the sort carried out in Britain between 1987 and 1997. In Germany there are more points of potential hindrance. Once in power governments in Germany face a federal decentralized system with the devolved Länder system of government and strong interest groups representing employers and unions so that power is diffused and there are many potential obstacles to reform (Busch and Manow, 2001). Similarly the consensual culture we have mentioned in the Netherlands is embodied there in a system of politics that requires coalitions and negotiation with formally empowered non-state organized interests. The politics of a 'grand design' is not possible. The PvdA is less autonomous when it comes to policy reform and is restrained by the need to pursue change in a negotiated way (Hemerijck and Visser, 2001).

Blair's and Others' Third Ways

So, it appears today (and maybe the appearance is deceptive) that the British Labour Party is in the vanguard, if that is the right word, of modernizing social democracy. In other countries, such as Germany, the journey to modernized social democracy is a more difficult process, the government being subjected to a number of forces which affect what it can do. The need to combine moderate electoral appeal with more radical appeal to coalition partners, the social market culture, and the devolved nature of the German political system and institutions lead to different outcomes there compared to other countries where institutional and cultural pressures diverge. In Britain there is a more centralized state, a political system, which gives the modernizers greater control, and a *laissez-faire* market culture, for example (Lees, 2001). Similarly the Netherlands has embedded in its culture consensual norms that counteract or balance some of the more economically liberal developments in social democracy there and elsewhere. And the Dutch PvdA places more emphasis on individualization and liberalization and less on moral communitarianism than Blair, drawing on a greater social liberalism and less on conservative communitarianism than found in the UK (van den Anker, 2001). In France, of course, the rhetoric is sometimes hostile to modernizing social democracy for reasons of national tradition (French exceptionalism and the statist and public sector tradition, for instance, which transcend partisan boundaries) and politics (such as the need to hold together a coalition of the left). The French have been more inclined to spending on job creation and regulation of the market.

For some, there are lessons that different countries can import from one another. There are those in Britain – Will Hutton (1995) is one – who would like to see Tony Blair adopting an approach that imports more from, say, the German situation – more of a *social* market approach. In fact, Blair himself once made short-lived noises about the desirability of a stakeholder model that could have been interpreted as going towards the German model (Driver and Martell, 1998; Blair, 1996). Conversely, there are industrialists and SPD modernizers in Germany who would not be averse to a greater dose of competitive individualism to shake up economic life. But Hutton's words fell on deaf ears and Schröder's collaboration with Blair had to be swiftly downplayed in Germany when it was published. Blair, meanwhile, became keener on exporting Anglo-Americanism to Europe than importing the German model.

Across Europe social democratic parties are discussing or implementing more flexible labour markets, privatization, welfare reform, cuts in business regulations and taxes, low inflation and macro-economic stability and supply-side policies alongside continuing social democratic concerns for social inclusion and minimum social standards. But the contexts in which such issues are being addressed vary and so the outcomes of comparable theoretical agendas differ from nation to nation: dependent on factors such as the degree of centralized control or devolution in political systems; the extent to which modernizers monopolize power or have to share it with the left or other parties; and historical traditions of statism, consensus or economic liberalism. So even if different social democratic parties are all experimenting with Third Ways between neoliberalism and old-style social democracy, these are Third Ways in the plural, there being different Third Ways rather than just one, varying by national background among other factors. As these instances show, the Third Way is diverse and contested. Between them, nationally specific factors lead to rhetorical and policy divergence – to Third Ways rather than a Third Way.

References

Albert, M. (1993), *Capitalism against Capitalism*, Whurr, London.
Blair, T. (1995), 'The Rights We Enjoy Reflect the Duties We Owe', *The Spectator Lecture*, London.
Blair, T. (1996), 'Speech to Commonwealth Press Union', Cape Town, South Africa (14 October).
Blair, T. (1997), 'Speech to the European Socialists' Congress', Mälmo, Sweden.
Blair, T. (1998), *The Third Way: New Politics for the New Century*, Fabian Society, London.
Blair, T. (1999), 'Facing the Modern Challenge: the Third Way in Britain and South Africa', Speech in Capetown, South Africa.
Blair, T. and Schröder, G. (1999), '*Europe: The Third Way/Die Neue Mitte*', Labour Party, London.

Bobbio, N. (1996), *Left and Right: the Significance of a Political Distinction*, Polity Press, Cambridge.

Bouvet, L. and Michel, F. (2001), 'Pluralism and the Future of the French Left', in S. White (ed.), *New Labour: the Progressive Future?*, Palgrave, Basingstoke.

Brown, G. (1997), *The Anthony Crosland Memorial Lecture*, 13 February.

Busch A. and Manow P. (2001), 'The SPD and the Neue Mitte in Germany', in S. White (ed.), *New Labour: the Progressive Future?*, Palgrave, Basingstoke.

Callinicos, A. (2001), *Against the Third Way: An Anti-Capitalist Critique*, Polity Press, Cambridge.

Clift, B. (2001), 'New Labour's Third Way and European Social Democracy', in S. Ludlam and M. Smith (eds.), *New Labour in Government*, St. Martin's Press, New York.

Coote, A. (1999), 'The Helmsman and the Cattle Prod', in A. Gamble and T. Wright (eds.), *The New Social Democracy*, The Political Quarterly/Blackwell, Oxford.

Dahrendorf, R. (1999), 'Whatever Happened to Liberty?', *New Statesman*, 6 September.

de Beus, J. (1999), 'The Politics of Consensual Well-being: the Dutch Left Greets the Twenty-first Century', in G. Kelly (1999), *The New European Left*, Fabian Society, London.

Dearlove, J. (2000), 'Globalisation and the Study of British Politics', *Politics*, Vol. 20(2), pp. 111–18.

Dionne, E.J. (1999), 'Construction Boom: It's No Accident that the GOP is Being Rebuilt By Its Governors', *Washington Post*, 14 March.

Driver, S. and Martell, L. (1997), 'New Labour's Communitarianisms', *Critical Social Policy*, Vol.17(3), pp. 27–46.

Driver, S. and Martell, L. (1998), *New Labour: Politics After Thatcherism*, Polity Press, Cambridge.

Dworkin, R. (2001), 'Does Equality Matter?', in A. Giddens (ed.), *The Global Third Way Debate*, Polity Press, Cambridge.

The Economist (1999), 'Tony Blair and liberty', 2 October, pp.19–20.

Freeden, M. (1999), 'New Labour and Social Democratic Thought', in A. Gamble and T. Wright, *The New Social Democracy*, The Political Quarterly/Blackwell, Oxford.

Gamble, A. and Wright, T. (eds.) (1999), *The New Social Democracy*, The Political Quarterly/Blackwell, Oxford.

Giddens, A. (1994), *Beyond Left and Right*, Polity Press, Cambridge.

Giddens, A. (1998), *The Third Way: the Renewal of Social Democracy*, Polity Press, Cambridge.

Giddens, A. (ed.) (2001), *The Global Third Way Debate*, Polity Press, Cambridge.

Giddens, A. (2002), *What Next for New Labour?*, Polity Press, Cambridge.

Gilmour, I. (1992), *Dancing with Dogma*, Simon & Schuster, London.

Gray, J. (1993), *Beyond the New Right: Markets, Government and the Common Environment*, Routledge, London.

Gray, J. (1996), *After Social Democracy*, Demos, London.

Gray, J. (1997), 'Speech to the NEXUS/*Guardian* Conference', London.

Hall, S. (1994), 'Son of Margaret', *New Statesman*, 6 October.

Hall, S. (1998), 'The Great Moving Nowhere Show', *Marxism Today*, November/December.

Hall, S. and Jacques, M. (1997), 'Blair: Is He the Greatest Tory Since Thatcher?', *The Observer*, Vol. 13, April.

Halpern, D. and Mikosz, D. (1998), *The Third Way: Summary of the NEXUS 'on-line' discussion*, Nexus, London.

Hargreaves, I. and Christie, I. (eds.) (1998), *Tomorrow's Politics: the Third Way and Beyond*, Demos, London.

Hattersley, R. (1997a), 'Just One Per Cent On Top Tax Wouldn't Hurt', *The Guardian*, 24 June.

Hattersley, R. (1997b), 'Why I'm No Longer Loyal to Labour', *The Guardian*, 26 July.

Hay, C. (1999), *The Political Economy of New Labour: Labouring Under False Pretences?*, Manchester University Press, Manchester.

Held, D., McGrew, A., Goldblatt, D. and Perraton, J. (1999), *Global Transformations: Politics, Economics and Culture*, Polity Press, Cambridge.

Hemerijck, A and Visser, J. (2001), 'Dutch Lessons in Social Pragmatism', in S. White (ed.), *New Labour: the Progressive Future?*, Palgrave, Basingstoke.

Hirschmann, A. (1996), 'Politics', in D. Marquand and A. Seldon (eds.), *The Ideas that Shaped Post-War Britain*, Fontana, London.

Hirst, P. (1999), 'Has Globalisation Killed Social Democracy?', in A. Gamble and T. Wright, *The New Social Democracy*, The Political Quarterly/Blackwell, Oxford.

Hirst, P. and Thompson, G. (1996), *Globalization in Question: the International Economy and the Possibilities of Governance*, Polity Press, Cambridge.

Hutton, W. (1995), *The State We're In*, Cape, London.

Jaenicke, D (2000), 'New Labour and the Clinton Presidency', in D. Coates and L. Jospin, *Modern Socialism*, Fabian Society, London.

Jospin, L. (1999), *Modern Socialism*, Fabian Society, London.

Kelly, G. (ed.) (1999), *The New European Left*, Fabian Society, London.

Latham, M, (2001), 'The Third Way: An Outline', in A. Giddens (ed.), *The Global Third Way Debate*, Polity Press, Cambridge.

Lawler, P. (eds.) (2000), *New Labour Into Power*, Manchester University Press.

Leadbeater, C. (1998), 'Welcome to the Knowledge Economy', in I. Hargreaves and I. Christie, *Tomorrow's Politics: the Third Way and Beyond*, Demos, London.

Leadbeater, C. (1999), *Living on Thin Air*, Viking, London.

Lees, C (2001), 'Social Democracy and the Structures of Governance in Britain and Germany: How Institutions and Norms Shape Political Innovation', in L. Martell et al. (eds.), *Social Democracy: Global and National Perspectives*, Palgrave, Basingstoke.

LeGrand, J. (1998), 'The Third Way begins with Cora', *New Statesman*, 6 March.

Levitas, R. (1999), *The Inclusive Society? Social Exclusion and New Labour*, Macmillan, Basingstoke.

Lindgren, A.-M. (1999), 'Swedish Social Democracy in Transition', in G. Kelly, *The New European Left*, Fabian Society, London.

Lovecy, J. (2001), 'New Labour and the "Left that is Left" in Western Europe', in D. Coates and P. Lawler, *New Labour into Power*, Manchester University Press, Manchester.

Marquand, D. (1998), in Halpern, D. and Mikosz, D. (eds.), *The Third Way: Summary of the NEXUS 'on-line' discussion*, Nexus, London.

Martell, L. et al. (eds.) (2001), *Social Democracy: Current Ideological Directions*, Macmillan, Basingstoke.

Marxism Today (1998), 'Wrong', November/December.

Merkel, W. (2001), 'The Third Ways of Social Democracy', in A. Giddens (2001) (ed.), *The Global Third Way Debate*, Polity Press, Cambridge.

Meyer, T. (1999), 'From Godesberg to the *Neue Mitte*: the New Social Democracy in Germany', in G. Kelly, *The New European Left*, Fabian Society, London.

Plant, R. (2001),'Blair and Ideology', in A. Seldon (ed.), *Blair Effect: The Blair Government 1997–2001*, Little Brown, London.

Reich, R. (1997), *Locked in the Cabinet*, Knopf, New York.

Reich R (1999), 'We are all Third Wayers Now', *The American Prospect*, Vol. 43, pp. 46-51.

Sassoon, D. (1996), *One Hundred Years of Socialism: the Western European Left in the 20th Century*, I.B. Taurus, London.

Sassoon, D. (1999a), 'European Social Democracy and New Labour: Unity in Diversity?', in A. Gamble and T. Wright (eds.), *The New Social Democracy*, The Political Quarterly/Blackwell, Oxford.

Sassoon, D. (1999b), 'Introduction: Convergence, Continuity and Change On the European Left', in G. Kelly, *The New European Left*, Fabian Society, London.

Scruton, R. (1996), *The Conservative Idea of Community*, Conservative 2000 Foundation, London.

Shaw, E. (1996), *The Labour Party Since 1945*, Blackwell, Oxford.

Shaw, E. (1999), 'New Labour's Third Way', *Inroads*, Vol. 8.

Shaw, E. (2000), 'What Matters is What Works', Paper to conference on 'The Third Way and Beyond' at Sussex University, Autumn 2000.

van den Anker, C. (2001), 'Dutch Social Democracy and the Poldermodel', in L. Martell et al. (eds.), *Social Democracy: Global and National Perspectives*, Palgrave, Basingstoke.

Vandenbroucke, F. (1998), *Globalisation, Inequality and Social Democracy*, IPPR, London.

Vandenbroucke, F. (1999), 'European Social Democracy: Convergence, Divisions, and Shared Questions', in A. Gamble and T. Wright (eds.), *The New Social Democracy*, The Political Quarterly/Blackwell, Oxford.

Vandenbroucke, F. (2001), 'European Social Democracy and the Third Way: convergence, divisions and shared questions', in S. White (ed.), *New Labour: the Progressive Future?*, Palgrave, Basingstoke.

Weir, M (2001), 'The Collapse of Bill Clinton's Third Way' in S. White (ed.) (2001), *New Labour: the Progressive Future?*, Palgrave, Basingstoke.

White, S. (1998), 'Interpreting the Third Way: Not One Road, But Many', *Renewal*, Vol. 6(2) Spring.

White, S. (ed) (2001), *New Labour: the Progressive Future?*, Palgrave, Basingstoke.

White, S. and Giaimo, S. (2001), 'Conclusion: New Labour and the Uncertain Future of Progressive Politics' in S. White (ed.), *New Labour: the Progressive Future?*, Palgrave, Basingstoke.

Chapter 4

D'Alema's Dilemmas:
Third Way, Italian Style

Vincent Della Sala

In June 1999, the central Italian city of Bologna elected its first centre-right mayor in over 50 years. The irony was not lost of having 'red' Bologna, for long the symbol of the Communist Party's strength in central Italy, electing a candidate from the right at the same time as the country was governed by its first prime minister from the Partito Communista d'Italia (PCI) or the parties spawned after its demise. Not surprisingly, the 'fall' of Bologna has intensified the debate about the state and fate of the left in Italy. There may have been purely local reasons for the defeat; mainly, the split between the established *Democratici di Sinistra* (DS) (which was the party that had replaced the *Partito Democratico della Sinistra* (PDS), which was the main party to emerge from the transformation of the old PCI in 1991) and the other parties of the centre-left. However, it was also seen as a sign of a problem within the left as it tried to reconcile legacies of the past with a search for a role to play in a increasingly globalized economy and society, at the same time as trying to govern in a broad centre-left coalition.

The election results, repeated by poor performances in the European Parliament elections in June 1999 and regional elections in April 2000, may be an indication that the search to create a new force of the left that breaks many of its social and historical ties and seeks out a 'Third Way' may not have widespread support on the left. They may reflect the dissatisfaction many on the Italian left had felt with three years of centre-left governments; and some of the dilemmas for the left in adapting to the constraints assumed with support for 'Euro-Europe'. It is an indication that the relatively uncontested path for monetary integration in Italy may have masked a much deeper resistance to some of its attendant macroeconomic policies and institutions. Much has been said and written about the dramatic shift in Italian budgetary and monetary policies in the 1990s, and about the role played by the 1993 agreement on incomes policy in that shift (Salvati, 1997). However, very little attention has been given to the ways in which the rush to monetary integration may have affected Italy's ability to deal with social conflict. This is all the more surprising given the extensive political changes in the decade that have led most to assume that the postwar constitutional and political order had come to an end.

The contradictions in the story of the Italian left's taste of electoral victory and governing since 1996 are no less rich than they are in other European countries. The bulk of support, about 30 per cent of the electorate, for the centre-left *Ulivo* (Olive Tree) coalition came from the area of the former Communist Party (PCI): with about 10 per cent of the total vote going to Communist Refoundation (PRC) and a little over one-fifth to the PDS (The Democratic Party of the Left).[1] Yet, the coalition in 1996 was headed by an economist and former Christian Democrat, Romano Prodi, and two of the key ministers, Lamberto Dini at Foreign Affairs and Carlo Azeglio Ciampi at the Treasury, had been, respectively, Secretary General and Governor at the Bank of Italy. The first government of the Republic that had its roots in the left was also the one that has been the most active in terms of restructuring the public sector, and in making the liberalization of the economy and society – including labour markets – the central point of its governing programme. Moreover, the coalition based its electoral campaign in 1996 on the premise that it was the instrument that would guarantee meeting the Maastricht convergence criteria and that Italy would be one of the founding members of the Euro.

The story of parties of the left in the 1990s governing on an agenda that seems to be dictated from the exigencies of global economic pressures and market liberalization is not new. Nor has the Italian left been spared the debate as to whether it needs its own 'Third Way' to reconcile the tensions between the traditional principles and objectives of the left, and providing a credible electoral alternative. As in other European countries, structural economic and social change has affected many of the pillars of support for the traditional parties of the left. The Italian left has not been immune to the question of whether there are alternatives to a programmatic shift from objectives aimed at redistributing resources to those that favour competitiveness and liberalization of markets.

There are a number of factors that distinguish the Italian case and raise the question of whether the left is another example of Italian exceptionalism, rather than a laboratory that may provide some insight into the possible routes for the left in the face of economic interdependence and liberalization.[2] First, and most apparent, is that the largest party of the left has been the Communist Party (PCI) and its heir, the PDS. As we will see shortly, the PCI has struggled to gain legitimacy as a party of government in a liberal democracy, and to become a part

---

[1] The Communist Party (PCI) became the PDS in 1991. A faction of the PCI opposed to the creation of the party formed the PRC. In 1998, the PDS sought to create a broader movement of the left that incorporated a wide range of parties, including the PRC. It was limited in its success as only a limited number of new forces joined the *Democratici di Sinistra* in February 1998. As the new party is essentially the PDS, the paper will use PDS/DS and PDS interchangeably for the period after February 1998. For a discussion of the transformation of the PCI, see Ignazi (1992).

[2] For an interesting discussion of Italian exceptionalism, see Diamanti and Lazar (1997).

of the family of European social democratic parties. It has meant that the question of what is the alternative on the left has never been quite entirely resolved in Italy.

Second, the share of the vote for the left has remained fairly stable in the postwar period, and the 1996 electoral victory was the result of an opening to the centre parties and political forces rather than a significant electoral realignment. In 1948, the combined forces of the left received over 38 per cent of the vote. This figure crept up slowly to a high of 48.9 per cent in 1976, with the PCI by far the largest party (34.4) in that year, as throughout the period.[3] The Communist vote declined slowly since its apex in 1976 but total vote for the left hovered between 40 and 45 per cent. In 1994, the first election with a new electoral system, with three-quarters of the seats assigned through a single-member plurality system and the rest by proportional representation, saw the parties divided into three blocks. The left gathered 34 per cent of the votes and the right 46.4, and the rest going to parties of the centre. In 1996, the vote assigned to the left increased to 43.4 (and 44.0 for the right), but this was due to the fact that there was no coalition of the centre. Some of the parties that were part of the centre in 1994 were now part of the centre-left coalition. Moreover, the votes for the centre-right do not include the 10 per cent of the vote received by the Northern League (NL), which had been part of the right coalition in 1994. The 1996 victory, then, was not the result of a major shift to the left but of a change in alliance partners, largely within the centre-right coalition of parties (Hellmann, 1997, p. 84). The long road to government for the left was the one travelled by almost every government in postwar Italy; that is, its fortunes were decided by the vagaries of coalition politics and not the result of a clear shift in the electorate demanding a new policy direction.

Despite features that might suggest exceptionalism, the Italian case is an interesting one for the discussion of the transformation of social democratic parties, from an emphasis on redistributive objectives and collective responses to social demands, to one on the instruments and technologies that centre on individual responsibility and market mechanisms. It may shed some light on whether the change has been due to some external factor, such as economic interdependence, that generates social and economic change, or whether it reflects political strategies rooted in the dynamics of party competition and structures of political and economic power (Garrett and Lange, 1991, pp. 539–64; Kitschelt, 1994). In the case of the former, the response is that there is no alternative to market-based strategies as the competitive demands of an open economy undermine the structural bases of support for social democratic parties. The latter, while not denying structural change, suggests that we focus on the historical and institutional context in which the left has made the decision to change its political strategy. More importantly, the Italian experience of the left in government is a

---

[3] The figures are for elections to the Chamber of Deputies; for the 1994 and 1996 elections, for votes cast on the basis of proportional representation.

useful case to examine the politics of the 'Third Way' of social democracy in the 1990s. This is especially the case since leading figures, such as Massimo D'Alema and Walter Veltroni, have tried very hard to associate the Italian experience in the 1990s with transformations underway throughout Europe.

Talk of a 'Third Way' for the left is not new in Europe. Social democracy was often presented as an alternative to capitalism and socialism. In Italy, 'Third Way' has particular resonance, as Eurocommunism in the 1970s was presented as an alternative not simply to capitalism and socialism, but to social democracy and Soviet-style communism. The latest version of Third Way arguments are rooted in the experiences of 'New Labour' under Tony Blair, as well as drawing inspiration from the New Democrats in the United States. Anthony Giddens has provided the call to arms for a revision of social democratic thought and practice along the lines of 'Third Way' politics. He points to what he calls the five 'dilemmas' that are forcing the left to revisit some of its basic tenets and policies: globalization, individualism, the meaning of left and right, political agency and ecological problems (Giddens, 1998, pp. 27–8). His basic premise is that to be on the left is to believe in a 'politics of emancipation' whose overall aim should be 'to help citizens pilot their way through the major revolutions of our time' (Giddens, 1998, p. 41 and p. 64). Giddens argues that these transformations stem not only from globalization but also to changes in the ways in which individuals construct their personal lives and in their relationship with nature.

According to Giddens, social democratic renewal requires a displacement of the authority and capacity of the national state towards other levels of government and to parts of civil society. Giddens assumes that this 'hollowing out' of the state will not lead to its decline, rather, it will enhance its legitimacy because there will be a better fit between expectations and capacity (Giddens, 1998, chapter 3). Third Way politics also emphasize 'positive' welfare, which may signal a move away from the principles of universality and social rights as they developed in the postwar era. Giddens, arguing along lines similar to those of Paul Hirst, claims that civil society may take on greater responsibility in providing and delivering social services (Hirst, 1997). This would be part of a broader programme aimed at the democratization not only of liberal democratic institutions but all arenas of public and private life. The emphasis on an active civil society, participation and democratization leads to parallels between Third Way politics and some radical democracy arguments.

While the centrality of democratization of all aspects of life is an attractive element for a programme of the left, Third Way politics faces similar problems as those of radical democracy and pluralism. First, there is no reason to assume that hollowing out will enhance the legitimacy of the national state. For instance, why would citizens turn over their tax dollars to a state that provides fewer social services but maintains, and even enhances, its repressive capacity, as measures such as fighting crime, tax evasion and enforcing means testing of social programmes are part of the Third Way agenda? This raises the broader question of how to hold accountable decisions that have a profound effect on individual and collective action. It highlights a number of unanswered questions about political authority and the role of the state in the 'Third Way' programme. It is not entirely clear what kind of political authority will replace the hollowed out state, and what kind of institutions and processes will be put in place to ensure accessibility, transparency and accountability. Parallels to the private sector are drawn, using terms such as 'stakeholders', but little is said of how to define who and what might have stake, nor in what they may have a stake.

Second, the programme for renewing social democracy has very little to say about how to deal with capital and to temper both its movements and its consequences. Vague references are made to a new form of regulation and a new international financial architecture, including some form of Tobin tax; but there is little questioning of the basic principles of economic liberalization. Moreover, there is a fundamental acceptance of market principles for most forms of exchange, from labour to capital, and even for the introduction of market principles to the provision of many forms of collective goods. It is hard to see how a 'politics of emancipation' can be reconciled with promoting a form of economic regulation whose competitive basis divides society between 'winners and losers'. Third Way politics have accepted many of the principles and instruments of supply-side macro-economic policy: tight money, budgetary austerity, flexible labour markets and few controls on capital. The politics of 'emancipation' seem to have an emphasis on disembedding macroeconomic policy instruments from social and political constraints, with few concrete proposals on how to deal with the consequences beyond enhancing the surveillance and repressive capacities of the state.

This chapter will argue that the Italian left is caught between the dynamics of the First Republic, shaped by the domestic Cold War, and the demands created by the pressures of globalization, as represented by the creation of the Euro. The collapse of the First Republic has not been complete, and the left has had to deal not only with new challenges but also many old ones as well. The left in Italy, particularly the PDS, sees economic liberalization as essentially a political instrument to dismantle the entrenched networks of power established with the occupation of the State and large parts of civil society by the governing parties during the First Republic. This provides a context that has been conducive for the major parties of the left to pursue strategies and programmes that are consistent with the 'Third Way' renewal put forward by Giddens and are the basis of the New Labour government in Britain.

The first part of the chapter will provide a very short description of some of the structures of the First Republic and highlight some of the factors that led to its decline. The second part will focus more closely on developments on the left in the 1990s that led to its electoral victory in 1996 and reveal some of the features of its programmatic shift. The final section will argue that this shift is part of a political strategy that aims to have broader political participation in all areas of social and economic life. One of the ways to achieve this objective is to liberalize the economy so as to make it more transparent and accessible, and to undermine the close-knit network of private and state capitalism that serve a narrow band of interests. However, many of the tensions within the Third Way programme are apparent within the Italian left, and especially for the PDS.

The Announced but Unconfirmed Death of the First Republic

It is impossible to speak of the left in government without some discussion of the period that saw the end of Christian Democratic rule and the crisis of the postwar order. The First Republic was a political and constitutional architecture that entrenched the power of the Christian Democrats and its governing allies, and gave space to the PCI in a consensual democracy that was highly permeable to social and political forces (Fabbrini, 1994). It highlighted the anomaly of Italian liberal democracy, that is, that the second largest party in the country, the PCI, was condemned to eternal opposition.

Italy's postwar constitutional settlement was born in a period of great tension and not without contradiction for the left. On the one hand, the parties of the left enjoyed an unprecedented legitimacy, especially in northern Italy, as a result of their opposition to the Fascist regime and their role in the Resistance. This led many to believe that it was possible for the 'historic bloc' of social and political forces to be mobilized, and that the revolutionary moment was at hand. On the other hand, some argued that a more gradual strategy was needed, and that the Republic, born from a narrow referendum result on 2 June 1946, required a broad consensus so that a liberal democratic order could be established and consolidated. Togliatti's speech at Salerno upon his return to Italy in 1944, in which he announced that the PCI would accept parliamentary forms of democracy, was an indication that the left was ready to adopt strategies and tactics that gave a priority to institutional and constitutional stability, rather than revolutionary impulses (Togliatti, 1973, p. 11).[4]

The Constituent Assembly, which met in 1946–47, reflected a wide range of political forces and tensions not only within the left but also between the left and Catholic and secular parties that had already begun with the domestic Cold War. The result was a written constitution that was based on a widespread consensus whose basis lay in the fear of a return to an authoritarian regime. But it did not provide clear indications on where effective power to govern was to rest and on what basis. This reflects a constant thread throughout the debates of the

---

[4] See also Togliatti's comments made in a speech to a group of Neapolitan Communists on 11 April 1944 in what has come to be known as the 'Salerno Turning Point' (Lange and Vannicelli, 1981, p. 32).

Constituent Assembly: the willingness on the part of the Communist and Socialist parties to avoid a direct confrontation with the more conservative forces.[5] At the same time, mutual distrust meant that neither side was willing to put in place institutions that could provide an opportunity for the other to capture political power. The result was a constitutional architecture characterized by a diffusion of decision-making power, and providing a number of access points for political and social groups. Moreover, a 'constitutional' spirit was fostered that suggested that major political decisions would involve most, if not all, political parties. The institutional fragmentation and the commitment to accommodation would serve as the basis for a consensual democracy that would establish and consolidate itself in the postwar period.

There were a number of features that characterized the Italian version of consensual democracy. First, a relatively 'frozen' electorate gave parties little reason to look very far beyond their traditional constituencies or subcultures to make an electoral breakthrough. For the PCI, the Gramscian notion of the 'war of position' was the basis of a strategy for a party with a mass base but still highly centralized and centred on party activists and officials. Moreover, what set Italy apart was that the left was not dominated by a clearly social democratic party but by the PCI. While the total percentage of the vote for the left has remained fairly consistent since 1948, it has been fragmented across an increasing number of parties.[6] This fragmentation was not limited to just the electorate but also to trade unions and social movements. It meant that the question of 'what is the left?' was never resolved in the First Republic.

Italian civil society in the postwar period has been described as weak and lacking autonomous structures.[7] Political parties, which were not only the interlocutors but also the principal political and social structures for distinct subcultures, filled the vacuum. Weak state structures and a party system that offered no alternatives to governments led by the DC and the other centrist parties, facilitated the gradual 'appropriation' (if not expropriation) of large parts of the state (Pasquino, 1985). State agencies, nationalized industries and even government departments were allotted to specific parties, and factions within each

---

[5] This was evident not only in discussions about the structure of political institutions but in a wide range of issues such as family policy and the protection of individual, including property, rights.

[6] For instance, the Social Democratic Party was formed in 1947 when it split from the PSI in opposition to its alliance with the Communists. This was the first of many scissions in both the PCI and PSI. By the mid-1990s, after the dissolution of the Socialist Party, there were at least three political groups that claimed some heritage in what had been the oldest party in Italy.

[7] Robert Putnam has shown that there was a rich associational heritage in some regions of Italy but, for the most part, there existed little at the national level, with the possible exception of Catholic organizations (Putnam, 1993).

party.[8] The left was not excluded from this distribution of resources, although its share was limited. For instance, the state television network was divided between three channels, each close to, respectively, the DC, the Socialists and the PCI. The 'available state' was a problem largely ignored by the left not simply because it was not entirely excluded from a share of the spoils. A permeable state was also an expansive one, making it easier to use state instruments, such as an industrial policy or an ever-expansive welfare state (Di Palma, 1980). The result was a level of state intervention and ownership that remains one of the highest amongst OECD countries.

Italian capitalism was another area of civil society that has been described as 'weak' in the postwar era. Italy's high rate of savings did not mean the development of extensive capital markets to finance the postwar boom. Rather, a large number of small banks were limited in their commercial exposure, and Italians preferred to place their deposits in some form of government treasury bills. Equity markets, essentially the Milan stock exchange, remained very small affairs with the bulk of financing for economic activity coming from a few merchant banks or the state. Moreover, the largest private industrial groups were usually controlled, if not owned, by a small group of families. The lack of diffused capital markets made it possible for a few institutions, and individuals, to be part of most major financing for both private and public industrial ventures (Sapelli, 1993). The best example of this is *Mediobanca*, the commercial bank that has been able to influence the direction of many industrial holdings by being the principal financial instrument for over forty years.[9] Another feature of Italian capitalism was the 'third Italy' model that gained so much currency in the 1980s. It too was based on family ownership and control, albeit of industrial activity of a much smaller scale.

Both these features of Italian capitalism raised challenges for the Italian left that went largely ignored. The lack of diffused capital markets, and the control held by a small group, was balanced by forms of state capitalism and ownership. However, this did little to create greater transparency and accountability for either the public or private sector holdings. Public sector managers acted, in the best of circumstances, in the interests of the firms or banks they ran, but most often with an eye to the political interests of the party that was responsible for their appointment. The diffused nature of the 'third Italy' model served the left well in many parts of central Italy, such as *Emilia-Romagna*. However, the PCI and the

---

[8] The Italian term for the distribution of parts of the state is 'lottizzazione', literally 'parceling out'. There was even a formula, known as the 'Cencelli manual', to determine the size of rewards for different factions within the governing parties.

[9] Enrico Cuccia, head of Mediobanca for most of the postwar period and still influential as its honorary chairperson, is famous for being able to place his people on the board of directors of companies his bank had financed. He is reported to have said that, 'We do not count shares, we weigh them' (Friedman, 1988).

PDS remained highly centralist in their approach to, amongst other things, models of economic development; the strong localist tendencies within the 'third Italy' would be exploited in the 1990s by the Northern League.[10]

Political parties, then, were able to penetrate both civil society and the state so that the First Republic was commonly called a *'partitocrazia'*. The left was an integral part of this regime, whether as one of the pivotal coalition partners as the PSI had become, or as the perennial opposition party such as the PCI. While the divisions remained at the ideological level, and the PCI's legitimacy as a democratic alternative was a central theme in every DC election campaign, most social and political forces were accommodated in one form or another (La Palombara, 1987). One consequence was that the major political questions were not those about grand themes such the capacity to change capitalism but more immediate ones such as choice of coalition partner or, in the case of the PSI, whether to remain in a governing coalition with the DC.

On the left, the First Republic was characterized by the uneasy relationship between the Communist and Socialist parties (De Grand, 1989). The antifascist experience made them partners in the immediate postwar period, but the events in Hungary in 1956 ensured the final break between the two. The PSI's search for space between the DC and the PCI led it to try to present itself as the party of reform in a centre-left coalition in 1963. The experience produced few concrete changes and, along with the social and political unrest of the late 1960s and 1970s, pushed the PSI to its lowest level of support of the postwar period in 1976. Under Bettino Craxi, the party began what it called the 'long wave' whose aim was to reverse positions of strength with the PCI. In the mid-1980s, this seemed inevitable (Di Scala, 1988). Craxi became the first non-DC Prime Minister, as well as one of the longest serving of the postwar period (1983–87). He sought to neutralize the PCI's base of support in the largest trade unions, and to isolate it politically. The election results for the two parties were going in opposite directions and it seemed that the PSI would overtake the PCI/PDS at some point in the 1990s.

By the mid-1990s, the PSI was dissolved, electoral support for the parties it spawned in the wake of its collapse was negligible, and Craxi was a convicted felon (Gundle 1996). He died in exile in January 2000 at his seaside resort in Tunisia, having been unable to return to Italy unless he wanted to begin to serve over twenty years of his various sentences for corruption and fraud. Craxi's 'long wave' was a failure because it had no programmatic or social basis, and was based largely on the leader's charisma and the party exploiting the spoils of power. It provided very little in terms of articulating a way to create a project for the left in

---

[10] Massimo Cacciari, who would become mayor of Venice in 1993 at the head of a left-wing coalition, urged the left in 1987 to begin to think of building an alternative on the local level. His call went largely ignored. Cacciari had not changed his position 11 years later and was warning of the alienation in northeast Italy (Cacciari, 1987, 1998, p. 9).

Italy, other then discrediting the PCI as a legitimate democratic party and presenting the Socialist Party as part of the European social democratic family (Gangemi and Riccanbini, 1997). In government, the Socialists were part of coalitions in the 1980s in which public spending spiralled out of control, as it was used as a way to mobilize electoral support, especially in the South.

The PCI/PDS did not have any greater success in seeking out political coalitions that might construct a project for the left. Moreover, it had to operate on more than one front as it had to pursue strategies that also aimed to make it a 'party like the rest'; therefore, it had to prove that it was a democratic alternative before it could address questions of the extent to which it would seek to work within the confines of liberal democracy and market capitalism. The PCI had two major initiatives to address these issues since the 1970s. In the early 1970s, in the wake of events in Chile, the leader of the party, Enrico Berlinguer, called for a 'historic compromise' in which all the progressive forces in the country would coalesce around a truly reformist project (Berlinguer, 1975). It was vague on details but essentially it was calling for a grand coalition that included the DC, effectively at the expense of the Socialist Party. Berlinguer's argument was that events in Chile had pointed out that the left could not count on simply an electoral victory to bring about political and social change, as this required the consent of forces beyond the traditional confines of the left.

The 'historic compromise' never fully materialized, although the PCI supported but was not part of the government from 1976–79. The DC was ambiguous in its reaction to Berlinguer's proposal, and openly rejected it after 1979. The PSI saw it as a threat, as whatever leverage it might have as a pivotal party would disappear in a grand coalition. The 1980s, then, saw the PCI pursue a strategy of trying to find some kind of common ground with the PSI as an alternative to the DC.[1] As the decade progressed and the prospects for success of the 'long wave' increased, relations between the two largest parties of the left continued to deteriorate. The PSI, no less than the DC, continued to raise questions about the PCI/PDS as a democratic alternative.

What is perhaps surprising given the perception of the First Republic as a highly ideologically polarized regime, is how little ideological and programmatic questions formed part of the debate within the left. For instance, the PCI's acceptance of NATO and the Atlantic alliance, as well as participation in the EMS in the 1970s did not lead to any major scissions within the PCI.[12] Nor was it the basis of the division between the Communists and the Socialists. One is hard pressed to find a policy issue on which the Socialists and PCI/PDS were so

---

[11] For an excellent review of the PCI in this period, see Hellman (1986).

[12] The question of European integration did not cause any major divisions within the PCI, especially since one of the architects of the European project was a member of the PCI, Altiero Spinelli.

divided that it prevented any consideration of a broader discussion on how to create a project for a united left. The policy questions that did emerge in the 1980s, such as the end of wage indexation, had their roots in Craxi's political strategy to undermine the PCI base of support, rather than ideological differences. The fundamental issues remained political, and reflected an institutional and political architecture that gave the major parties very little incentive to change strategy. So long as there remained the bases for a multipolar, multiparty system, the PSI could continue to pursue its strategy of the 'long wave', using the spoils of power that accrued to it as being a necessary pivotal party for the DC.

The brief discussion of some of the key features of the First Republic has tried to describe the development of a fissure that shaped postwar Italy. It was a tension that shaped relations not only between the governing parties and the major parties of the left, but also those between and within the Communist and Socialist Parties. A clear answer was never given to central questions such as the extent to which the PCI had accepted the basic principles and structures of liberal democracy and market capitalism. The PCI tried to maintain its revolutionary impulse but it also wanted to be seen as a source of stability for the fledgling democratic regime; it struggled to be recognized as a legitimate party 'like the rest'. The paradoxical result was that the PCI, whose exclusion from executive office was the linchpin of the First Republic, was central for the regime to survive.

It would be too simple to say that the collapse of the Soviet Union and the communist regimes in Eastern and Central Europe caused greater problems for the DC and the governing parties than it did for the PCI.[13] However, the legitimacy of their occupation of government for over forty years was based on the premise that the DC represented the bulwark against communism and the only democratic alternative. With no international threat to refer to, and the transformation of the PCI into the *Partito Democratico della Sinistra* (PDS) in 1991, it became difficult for the governing parties to claim that the future of the Republic depended on excluding the largest party of the left from government. This, along with a constellation of factors – such as changes to the electoral laws that introduced an element of majoritarianism to the electoral system, the completion of the single market in Europe, the rise of the Northern League and the growing corruption scandal – conspired to ensure that the elections throughout the decade (1992, 1994 and 1996) produced major changes largely unseen in the first 45 years of the Republic. The extent of the transformation is, at first glance, impressive. Not one of the seven major parties that fought in the 1987 election did so in 1994.[14] No less

---

[13] There has emerged an abundant literature that has tried to understand the political upheaval of the first half of the 1990s (Gilbert, 1995; Bufacchi and Burgess, 1998; McCarthy, 1997).

[14] The PCI became the PDS in 1991; the DC dissolved in 1993, and its left wing became the Popular Party (PPI) and the right the CCD, while the rest went to the CDU which became

impressive was the complete elimination of a governing class as historic figures such as Giulio Andreotti (Prime Minister seven times) and Arnaldo Forlani, leader of the DC, were forced to political exile in the face of criminal charges.

It was not only the changes in the parties and party leaders that led to the view that the First Republic was dead. It was also the fact that what brought its demise was not just the fall of communism or the activities of meticulous investigating magistrates but a burst of public outrage against the parties and popular support for change. This began with support for the Northern League, whose basis was less its belligerent positions on southern Italy and immigration, than its attacks on a highly centralized state and calls for the creation of a federal Italy (Marletti, 1997). Moreover, in 1991 and 1993, there were two referenda that did what the parties had been unable or unwilling to do: that is, change the electoral system (Bull and Newell, 1995). The votes were widely perceived as blows against the existing party system, and occupation of power by parties who governed for the private interests of their supporters.

The crisis of the First Republic was aggravated by the growing sense that it had lost not just its ability to represent the political demands of its citizens but also its capacity to be responsive and effective. The exponential growth in public spending in the 1980s had done little to stem the deterioration of public services and infrastructure such as transportation. The challenge of the single market, and Italy's reliance on trade in general, highlighted the gap between the private sector's capacity to compete and the obstacles, including a fiscal burden, presented by an ineffective state. In some instances, the lack of state capacity to impose its will, such as in the collection of taxes, helped competitiveness in the short run. But for the most part, it caused a crisis of legitimacy amongst large parts of the population; for instance, the Italian state is said to be absent in parts of the territory that are instead under control by elements of organized crime. Combined with the crisis of the political class, the perception of an ineffective state raised questions about the legitimacy of the constitutional order of the First Republic.

It is in this political and constitutional vacuum that the left has formed its first government in fifty years. The path that led to government was a stormy one, with electoral disappointments in 1992 and 1994. This was followed by the collapse of the centre-right Berlusconi government in 1994, after only six months, and its replacement with a government of technocrats supported essentially by what would be the winning coalition in 1996.

---

the UDR; the Liberal, Republican and Social Democratic parties disappeared for all intents and purposes; the PSI still contested the 1994 election but dissolved shortly after; and the neo-fascist MSI became the Alleanza Nazionale (AN).

The Road to Government and EMU

In a speech in July 1998 addressing a motion of confidence in his government, Romano Prodi raised the ire of some members of his coalition, who shared his background in the DC, when he said that Italy would never have been able to join the Euro under the First Republic.[15] He was referring to its tendency in its dying years to mobilize electoral support through public spending rather than on the basis of coherent programmes aimed at achieving clearly delineated objectives. Prodi may have added that the collapse of the First Republic was not due to the diligent prosecuting judges, the fall of communism, nor the rise of new parties but to the signing of the Maastricht treaty. The commitment to be part of the first members of the single currency undermined the 'cement of consent on which the old regime rested' and paved the way for new alternatives.[16]

The Maastricht treaty raised very little political debate in Italy. All the major parties at the time it was signed were strongly in favour of European integration, and little changed with the arrival of new political actors. The old parties of the First Republic had either not understood what the convergence criteria would mean for their basis of support, or perhaps they assumed that the criteria would not be important and that either they would be ignored or that they were so far out of reach for Italy, that they would not matter.[17] On the other hand, there were others, in the Treasury and the Bank of Italy, that pushed for the convergence criteria precisely because they saw it was the external pressure that would bring about political and economic change. On the left, *Rifondazione Comunista* did raise the question of who was to pay the cost for bringing Italy's public finances within the parameters of the convergence criteria. However, the PDS did not embrace this critique, and saw support for Italy's entry into the single currency as a vehicle to further its quest as a legitimate governing alternative. It repeatedly pointed to how close Italy risked financial collapse in 1992 as reason for seeking out government stability and discipline in budgetary matters.[18] It did not question who and what

---

[15] Camera dei Deputati. XIII Legislatura (1998), *Atti Parlamentar: Discussioni*, Vol. 394, 17 July, p. 18.

[16] The cement referred to was often literal as many of the corruption scandals involved construction contracts (Reviglio 1998, p. 13).

[17] It should be remembered that Giulio Andreotti was Prime Minster and Gianni De Michelis was Foreign Minister at the time of the treaty. It is hard to imagine two figures more emblematic of the last years of the First Republic. De Michelis was more famous for his book on the best places to go dancing in Italy than for his pronouncements on European or foreign policy. He too was forced to leave politics in the face of corruption convictions. For a broader discussion of the Italian positions at Maastricht (Dyson and Featherstone, 1996, pp. 279–99).

[18] For instance, see Fabio Mussi's speech to the Chamber explaining why his party supported the Ciampi government budget for 1994. He speaks of the 'incalculable consequences' of another crisis had the Ciampi government not survived and if its budget

defined the terms of the 'crisis', and the displacement of political power to centres that dictated the terms of 'crisis' and responses to it.

Arguably, the turning point came with the Amato government in 1992 and, more specifically, with the currency crisis in September that forced the retreat of the lira from the ERM. It is at this point in that year that we begin to see a concerted effort to arrest the growth of the deficit and begin to think seriously about meeting the targets set by the convergence criteria (Reviglio, 1998). Moreover, the emergency budget measures introduced for 1992, and the 1993 budget presented to Parliament shortly after the currency crisis, were the start of a series of measures that sought to bring about major structural changes to governing the Italian economy, and to the role of the state. For instance, approval was given to a bill that delegated to the government reform of four areas that were essential to the mobilization of consent for the First Republic: health, pensions, public sector employment and local and regional government administration.[19] Delegating decision-making power to the government, at the expense of Parliament, was seen as a way to insulate spending decisions from political pressures of parties and factions to serve the needs of their narrow interests.

The Amato government, then, might be seen as the beginning of the neoliberal turn in Italian economic policy. There was relatively little ideological debate about the change in direction; the resistance that was most apparent (with the possible exception of the PRC) came from the vested interests of the First Republic who saw that the pillar of support for the regime was crumbling. It seemed that the convergence criteria had given the political forces that sought to bring about change a sense of purpose that was missing in other areas, such as constitutional change. With the possible exception of the Berlusconi government between March and December 1994, every government since 1992 has made it a priority to bring the deficit under the 3 per cent barrier, and has done so primarily through cuts to public spending. Moreover, they (with the exception of the Amato government) have done so with the support of the PDS, either directly voting for measures when a majority could not be found otherwise or by abstaining.

The Amato government was important in that it marked the first serious attempt to put the control of public finances at the centre of government policy. However, it was the Ciampi government that followed Amato in 1993 that could be seen as a missed opportunity for the left to capitalize on the political, economic and ethical crisis of the First Republic. Ciampi was called to form a government of 'technocrats' from his position as Governor of the Bank of Italy, as so many of the leading figures in the parties supporting the Amato government faced indictments for crimes ranging from fraud to conspiracy to commit murder. The Ciampi

---

would not be accepted. (Camera dei Deputati. XI Legislatura (1993), *Atti Parlamentari: Discussioni*, Vol. 28, 6 December, p. 21080.)

[19] Disegno di Legge, n. 382, 1992.

government was a turning point for a number of reasons. First, the PDS had initially agreed not only to support it, but it was also going to be part of it. However, it decided to pull out its ministers when the Chamber of Deputies had refused to lift Craxi's parliamentary immunity to face corruption charges in April 1993. The public outcry was immediate and the legitimacy of the legislature was put in question. This occurred in the wake of the 18 April referenda, which were a vote against the old party system and in favour of a transformation of the bases of politics. There was a clear and strong demand for change coming from Italian civil society, and the PDS was ambiguous on how and where it was going to respond to it. In the end, it abstained in the vote of confidence on the Ciampi government, but supported it as a government of transition from the 'old to the new' and became its most reliable base of support in Parliament. The PDS primarily saw it as a government to implement a new electoral law, although Ciampi made clear in his speech to the Chamber that he also had other objectives.

Second, Ciampi, as head of the Bank of Italy, had been instrumental in pushing for the convergence criteria, not simply to arrest the growth in public sector borrowing, but also to bring about major changes in the structures of Italian capitalism. He made it clear that this was the objective of his government as well. He told the Chamber of Deputies that the link between major political and economic change in Italy was privatization, whose primary aim was not to bring badly needed funds to the public purse. Rather, privatization was essential to redefine the role of the state in the economy, and to bring about a fundamental transformation of the entrepreneurial culture of Italian capitalism. The PDS, which had opposed Amato's budgetary policies, tried to minimize the importance of Ciampi's economic programme, emphasizing that its primary aim was to introduce institutional changes. But, as Sergio Garavini, leader of the PRC at the time, pointed out, the left could not ignore who was the head of the government, and what it represented in terms of economic policy. He asked, rhetorically, whether the PDS was not embarking on a 'colossal retreat in a conservative direction'.[20] Moreover, it meant that the PDS had accepted that the terms of the political agenda would be dominated by the convergence criteria and the discourse of 'discipline', 'austerity' and 'flexibility'.

The Ciampi government was indeed one of transition, and therefore, provides some insight to the position of the left in the 1990s. The PDS chose, in effect, to support it, while the PRC remained firm in its opposition because it felt threatened not just by changes to the electoral law. The PRC leaders felt that support for a government that made little mention of employment or economic growth in the south in the midst of a recession was not one sympathetic to the left or its natural constituencies. The PDS argued that the left needed to act responsibly. The

---

[20] Ochetto, Camera dei Deputati. XI Legislatura (1993), *Atti Parlamentari: Discussioni*, Vol. 28, 6 December p. 13207.

country, after risking financial collapse at the time of the currency crisis in September 1992, could not risk what little credibility it had in financial markets by rejecting a government led by a central banker, and going to new elections. Moreover, an election risked leading to a right-wing government that exploited popular dissatisfaction with the previous regime, and politics in general.

This last fear became ever more apparent during the life of the Ciampi government in 1993–94. It had completed one of its primary objectives of changing the electoral law in August 1993. It also had been successful in bringing an element of stability to governing; especially important in this regard was an agreement with the major trade unions and employers in July 1993 that would limit salary increases. The left was in an enviable position in the autumn months of that year. There seemed to be no political force able to create a centre or centre-right coalition to fill the vacuum left by the collapse of the traditional parties. Municipal elections in November brought to power, under a new electoral law that allowed for direct elections, mayors supported by very broad coalitions of the left and progressive forces in Naples, Rome and Venice. However, it was the municipal elections that brought Silvio Berlusconi on to the political stage to create a right-wing coalition to contest the imminent national elections.

Berlusconi's ability to use the media and to introduce new means of communicating with voters was apparent from the start (McCarthy, 1996). Perhaps more importantly for the left was that he had recognized that the end of the Cold War meant not so much the end of questions about the legitimacy of the parties that had roots in the PCI – Berlusconi never ceased his anti-Communist rhetoric – rather, his strategy implied that the anti-fascist legacy that inspired the Republic had been surpassed. In concrete terms, it meant that it was possible to think in terms of an alliance with the reconstituted *Alleanza Nazionale* (Marletti, 1997, p. 69). In anticipation of the elections, he crafted two different alliances whose contradictions soon became apparent. In northern Italy, his party, *Forza Italia*, formed the '*Polo delle liberta*' (the Liberty Pole) with the Northern League. Its basis was its attack on the centralized state, with its welfarism and heavy taxation. In the south, FI formed the *Polo del Buongoverno* (the Good Governing Pole) *with Alleanza Nazionale* (AN). The attacks on state intervention were tempered here, as the AN base of support was much more dependent on state assistance of one form or another. Both alliances included the centre-right remnants of the DC, and drew votes from former Socialist voters.

Arguably, Berlusconi entered the political arena because he wanted to thwart the investigations into his own role in the corruption scandals of the First Republic.[21] His political strategy was to capture the void left by the centre of the

---

[21] Berlusconi was very close to Craxi, and was implicated in a number of schemes to funnel money to the PSI. He has since been convicted on three different charges, and is facing

political spectrum while trying to combine the traditional right of the AN with a right that was more neoliberal in its orientation. Berlusconi was trying to construct a political coalition of the right similar to the one that had formed in France in the postwar period. The fact that he had to do so through two separate alliances with very different parties indicates that it was not just the left that was not 'normal' in Italy.

The left was unprepared for the centre-right coalition it faced in the 1994 election. Perhaps it had not realized that a significant part of the electorate was ready to accept a governing coalition that included former neofascists. Or perhaps it had not understood that the new electoral rules required broader alliances and a more personalized campaign style, including making clear the nature of a future government and its leader (Bull, 1996). An electoral alliance of the parties and groups of the left was formed under the banner of the *'Progressisti'* (the Progressives). It was dominated by the PDS, with Communist Refoundation as a very junior partner. However, it did not include a large centre-left component as these coalesced largely around the *Patto per l'Italia*, dominated by the Popular Party (PPI).

The 1994 election campaign, which saw Berlusconi make heavy use of his three television networks, focused primarily on individual candidates, especially the leader of *Forza Italia*. The left did not seem to have a response to his attacks on the 'communists' and the obstacles they presented to individual liberties and a market economy (Bull, 1996). While the Cold War may have been over and the *Progressisti* thought they could engage in a debate on the best way to manage a market economy and retain some element of social solidarity, the centre-right returned to the old anti-Communist crusades. The electoral victory for the left, which seemed certain in autumn 1993 when the centre-right was fragmented and leaderless, turned into a bitter defeat in March 1994. Moreover, the new electoral laws seemed to guarantee a Berlusconi government for a five-year mandate.

The discussion on the electoral defeat within the left, and the PDS, did not centre on policy or programmes but rather on alliances and strategy. Massimo D'Alema, who had a long history in the PCI and the PDS, replaced Achille Occhetto as leader. The choice of D'Alema had important strategic consequences more than any significant impact on PDS policy positions. The party remained committed to Italy's entry into the single currency, and perhaps, more importantly, continued to speak strongly in favour of bringing public finances under control as well as liberalizing the economy. However, it had to first address the question of what sort of alliances or coalitions were necessary to defeat the centre-right. The question gained some urgency when the Northern League withdrew its support for the Berlusconi government in December 1994. The PDS became an important

---

charges that his company recycled money from organized crime syndicates as well as fraud charges in Spain.

anchor in Parliament for another government of 'technocrats', this time led by a former director-general of the Bank of Italy, Lamberto Dini (Bull, 1996). D'Alema and many others on the left had realized that without an opening to the forces of the centre, the risk of repeating the results of 1994 would be great. Moreover, there also was the recognition that the centre-left would need to coalesce around a candidate to head the government.

The centre-left coalition began to take form in 1995 with two related developments. First, the PDS and the centrist parties, such as the PPI and later one formed around Dini called Italian Renewal (RI), agreed to form a broad coalition that eventually was named, l'Ulivo (the Olive Tree). The PRC did not join and drafted its own programme but did agree to an electoral pact that would essentially have a single candidate of the left in most of the single member constituencies. Impetus for the coalition came, in part, from a second development. Romano Prodi, an economist with links to the DC left as well as a history as manager of state holdings, began an unofficial campaign to bring together the centre-left around his candidacy for the head of a coalition whose essence was defined by entry into the single currency. There seemed to be initial popular support for Prodi as he drove across Italy in his coach, and promoted local *'Comitati per l'Italia che vogliamo'* (Committees for the Italy that we want). The movement seemed to send a signal that there was popular support for a candidate who was clearly from the centre but whose base of support came from the left.

The coalition, including the electoral pact with Communist Refoundation, covered a wide spectrum, from Dini's RI to the Greens and former Communists. The intense negotiations that preceded the election were less about policy than about whose candidates would get the safest seats. The Ulivo platform, called 'le 88 tesi per la piattaforma programmatica', reflected the coalition's broad composition, but it did send out a clear message that the Ulivo would govern from the centre (Adinolfi, 1996). For instance, under the heading of 'Healthy finances for a healthy state', the coalition committed itself to: keeping inflation under control; the independence of the central bank to achieve that end; continuing to reverse public deficits and debts; and to the incomes policy agreements of 1992–93 that saw trade unions limit their wage demands. The programme made the usual statements, without any specific commitments, about the need to address unemployment, development in the South and preserving the bases of the welfare state. This contrasted with the very real commitment to bring Italy into the single currency. The inclusion of the greens in the coalition might help to explain why environmental concerns gained as much attention as the more traditional redistributive issues such as the south and employment.

The Ulivo's programme stood in even starker contrast to that of its electoral partner. The PRC platform, titled 'An Alternative that begins on the Left', shared little in style and substance with that of the Ulivo.[22] It challenged making the objective of achieving the convergence criteria a priority, and did not hesitate to speak of the single currency as part of a 'reactionary and hyper-liberal' project. Its primary objectives were full employment, the protection of the welfare state, and more state intervention to address the perennial problem of development in the South. The instruments to achieve these objectives included the 35-hour workweek, guaranteed employment for youth in the provision of collective goods and services, and a commitment to crack down on tax evasion.

It should come as no surprise, then, that the PRC was a skeptical ally of the government, and the centre-left government had a difficult time in maintaining its majority. The PRC decided not to join the government but committed its parliamentary votes that were decisive to gain a majority in the Chamber (but not the Senate). However, this did not prevent it from threatening a government crisis on a number of important issues. The first occurred in October 1997 when a crisis resulted from the PRC's objection to the Ulivo's budget for 1998 that would bring Italy in line with the convergence criteria.[23]Fausto Bertinotti, the party leader, was forced to retreat from his threat to bring down the government and possibly force an election in the face of criticism from within his own party, from both activists and rank-and-file members, and a severe reaction from the trade unions, including the left-leaning trade union, the CGIL (*Confederazione Generale Italiana del Lavoro*), which is where Bertinotti began his political career. Bertinotti was able to get a promise for the implementation of the 35-hour workweek at some point early in the next century.

Bertinotti's first attempt to push the political centre of the government to the left failed primarily for two reasons. First, the government could still call upon the 'European' card to justify its budgetary choices, including further cuts to spending, even to its basis of support on the left. There were few political leaders who would risk challenging the objective of entrance into the single currency. Bertinotti may have miscalculated how committed not just the government, but also trade unions and other social actors were to meeting the Maastricht criteria (at least the deficit target of 3 per cent). The effort to meet the criteria was significant in the 1990s, and there was the sense that it would be lost at such a crucial stage. It is important to note that while economic growth by the mid-1990s helped restore revenues, along with tax increases, the bulk of the change has come through cuts in public spending. Moreover, governments supported by the PDS carried these out (Della Sala, 1997). Second, Bertinotti underestimated the extent to which the PDS was committed to the coalition with the centrist parties. There was the danger for the

---

[22] PRC, 'Ricominciare da sinistra per l'alternativa', found at URL, http://www.rifondazione.it/eprog.html.
[23] This occurred at about the same time that the PRC and the Ulivo were engaged in a bitter by-election campaign for a vacant Senate seat in Florence in one of the country's safest constituencies for the left.

PRC that the Ulivo would find other centrist allies to support the government in Parliament, thereby reducing its bargaining power. This is precisely what happened twice in the first months of 1998 as the PRC opposed the government on its position on Kosovo and the enlargement of NATO.

In June 1998, the instability caused by the lukewarm attachment of the PRC to the coalition led to a round of negotiations before Parliament considered a motion of confidence in the government. It followed an important vote on NATO enlargement that the government was able to carry thanks to the votes of a new centrist party led by former President, Francesco Cossiga. The PDS had repeatedly called for Cossiga to be impeached when he was President, and the irony of the coalition (of which it was the largest component) relying on his support was not lost on many commentators. It did highlight the question of how to deal with the PRC. The centrist forces in the coalition complained that Prodi was hostage to the PRC, while the latter refused to endorse the government completely, calling its vote in favour as 'decisive but not complete support' (Bertinotti, 1998, p. 5). Bertinotti claimed that the real test would come with the 1999 budget the government would present to Parliament in September 1998. He pointed to demonstrations by unemployed workers in Napoli and Milano shortly after the vote of confidence as a sign that the autumn would be one of social unrest; and he urged the government to address the problems of unemployment and the South. The PRC conditions for continued support for the government were for the State to use its agencies to hire youth and long-term unemployed in the South, and for the government to restore spending in social programmes such as health. The classic Keynesian solution contrasted with the PDS approach, which proposed to reduce labour costs by cutting employer contributions to social programmes and for increased flexibility.[24]

Bertinotti eventually led the PRC into the opposition benches in October 1998, leading to a new government led by D'Alema and a split amongst the Communists. The D'Alema government included members of Cossiga's party (which then split into two parties), and a faction of the PRC that opposed Bertinotti's move. At first glance, the decision to leave the government over the 1999 budget, which introduced only minor measures, after supporting the two previous budgets that resulted in cuts of US$ 60 billion seems like a futile resistance to the changes introduced in the 1990s. However, it reflects the tensions within the left over how to respond to the challenges that result from the commitments assumed at Maastricht, and from globalization in general, and about what kind of left will emerge from the transformations taking place. D'Alema's problems did not end with the new coalition and government. His new allies now included former Christian Democrats, who claimed to be centrists. They opposed their coalition

---

[24] 'Agensud, scuola, lavoro: I documenti a confronto', *La Repubblica*, 8 July 1998, p. 7.

partners on issues such as the rights of common-law couples, *in vitro* fertilization and parental leave. Moreover, they pushed for equal treatment of Catholic schools. They did support the government's economic policies, including plans to create more labour market flexibility. The D'Alema government, then, had sacrificed the support of the left of the coalition because of its economic policy while opening up to centrist forces who essentially opposed new openings to definitions of the family and individual choices.

The coalition remained fragile, and D'Alema was forced to form a new government that distanced Cossiga but brought in the Democratici in December 1999. The latter grouped the centrist political forces that identified closely with Romano Prodi, who had taken up his new position as head of the European Commission. But even this attempt to balance the power of the ex-DC in the centre of the coalition could not sustain the D'Alema government. The regional elections in April 2000 brought a major defeat, especially in northern Italy. The centre-right alliance, with the Northern League once again in the fold, took hold not only of the major northern regions, but also Lazio (the region where Rome is located). D'Alema had staked his leadership on positive electoral results, so he resigned immediately and was replaced by Giuliano Amato. The coalition is no more cohesive than it was under D'Alema, and the questions remain about what principles, values and structures, not to mention electoral candidates, will hold it together.

There are divisions within the PDS/DS itself, between those who would like to see a re-constituted Ulivio strengthened and eventually become a broad party of the centre-left akin to the Democratic Party in the United States and those who oppose this idea. D'Alema's main rival, and successor as leader of the PDS, Walter Veltroni heads the group that favours a united centre-left. The balance in this instance would be tipped towards the centre as it is unlikely that the PRC would find room within a big tent that would include Dini and large parts of the left of the DC. D'Alema, on the other hand, has resisted attempts to create a new party based on the governing coalition, and has looked to the DS as becoming the party to coalesce the left (Ranieri, 1998, p. 608). He has tried to assemble all the forces that are clearly on the left, especially the former Socialists such as Giuliano Amato, into a new political force. However, the new *Democratici di Sinistra* has not generated a movement to bring together all social democratic, Christian social and communist forces. It is unlikely, for both ideological and political reasons, that the PRC would join such a movement or party. For instance, it would be hard to imagine the PRC agreeing with D'Alema's claim that making the health of public finances a priority was not something clearly of the left or the right. He recognized that it would be difficult to include the PRC in his project as it continued to see the presence of two lefts in Italy, the reformist one that was part of D'Alema's project, and a radical one that had its roots in the PCI and now rested within the PRC.[25] The trials of the D'Alema governments have highlighted the questions about how to aggregate the broad and disparate forces of the left.

D'Alema looked to aligning his governments closely to the 'Third Way' as a force of modernization that would constitute the centre point of a new left. This political force would embrace economic liberalization, flexible labour markets and 'positive' welfare.[26] Discussion about a project to aggregate the forces of the left, whether its centre is the Ulivo or the ex-PCI, leads to the question about the bases of division within the Italian left. The collapse of communism and European integration have raised in Italy, as elsewhere, the questions of what it means to be on the left, let alone why there should be divisions within it. There are clearly ideological divisions between the PRC and the PDS/DS. The latter have adopted the discourse, policies and style of governing that is not so different from parties of the right that have pursued market-based solutions to collective problems. There is a great deal of rhetoric about social solidarity and tempering inequalities that result from economic liberalization, but the reference point to solving collective problems, whether it is unemployment or the welfare state, is to create the right competitive conditions. Some of the strongest advocates within the government for introducing more competitive pressures both in the economy and society, such as Vincenzo Visco and former Public Administration Minister Franco Bassanini (both senior figures in the D'Alema government), are from the left, and more specifically, the PDS. For instance, resistance to privatization within the government has come more from some of the old Christian Democratic sections of the coalition than from the PDS/DS. This did not prevent the Prodi government from pushing ahead with privatization, increasing the value of sales of state holdings from close to US$7 billion in 1996 to over $21 billion in 1997 (Bemporad and Giannino, 1998).

While the fault line on the broad contours of political economy may fall between the PRC and the rest of the left, there are numerous ways in which the left is split on political and constitutional questions. The PDS/DS stands largely on its own in support of changes to the electoral system that will lead to greater aggregation and a bipolar, if not two-party, party system. In addition, the other parties of the centre-left coalition and the PRC are opposed to proposals that would strengthen the executive, an objective that forms part of the PDS/DS's

---

[25] See D'Alema's speech to the 'estates general' that launched the DS in Florence on 12 February 1998. Bertinotti also made the 'two lefts' the centre of his speech to the third congress of the PRC in 1997, see Partito della Rifondazione Comunista, *III Congresso Nazionale: innovare la politica per cambiare la societa*, Roma, 12–15 December 1996, (Roma, 1997), p. 15.
[26] For instance, see 'Blair and D'Alema urge labour reform', *Financial Times*, 18 March 2000, p. 2.

constitutional position. It is easy to understand why the smaller parties on the left would oppose any changes that might lead to a greater aggregation of decision-making power within constitutional structures. The disproportionate strength of the PDS compared to the rest of the parties generates the fear of a loss of autonomy and identity both to the right and to the left of the PDS/DS. However, with only one-fifth of the total vote, the PDS/DS is not in a position under the current rules of the game to exert its strength and create a sense of cohesion for the left (Hellman, 1996, p. 87). The parties of the left are also divided on the question of how to deal with the judicial questions resulting from the bribery and corruption scandals that brought down the previous political class.

It would seem that it is the lingering questions of the First Republic – constitutional and judicial – that have served to fragment the parties of the left beyond the divisions on political economy. The question of Europe and entry into the single currency has not been one to cause new or permanent divisions. The forces to the left of the PDS/DS have been, at times, the strongest proponents of closer integration. For instance, *Il manifesto*, the independent daily that still calls itself communist, has reorganized its layout so that domestic news is reported in the section on the 'provinces' of Europe so that readers find out about the latest developments of the D'Alema government under, 'Provincia-Italia'.

Concluding Remarks: The Third or Lost Way of the Italian Left?

Is the case of the left further evidence of Italian exceptionalism or an indication of trends that may be found, or may emerge, elsewhere in Europe? The major party of the Italian left, like its European counterparts, has accepted to govern on the basis of market principles but continues to use the rhetoric of social solidarity and collective responsibility. Was this a case of 'TINA'; that is, there is no alternative in a globalized economy and an integrated European market? Given the state of Italian public finances at the start of the 1990s and the demands of the convergence criteria, it was easy to make a case for adopting market-based technologies to liberalize the economy. For the PDS, intent on creating or enhancing its image as a responsible party of government in the tradition of European social democracy, the crusade to join the single currency provided goals upon which to focus and mobilize support. Opposition to fiscal austerity and even changes to the welfare state was muted in the name of the 'sacrifices' that needed to be made for Italy to get its finances in order, and assume its rightful place at the heart of Europe. The PDS, beginning with the Ciampi government, essentially adopted the line that there was no alternative to the neoliberal turn.

However, there are indications that the programmatic shift for the PDS and the left was shaped not simply by economic changes but also by political considerations. For the PDS, and the Ulivo, meeting the convergence criteria was a sign of not just the modernization of the Italian economy but of politics and society as well. Prodi's claim that the First Republic would not have entered the single currency is part of a broader strategy that tries to present the emergence of a new left that breaks with the past. It is a political force that seeks to bring transparency, efficiency and accountability to all areas of public life, and to make this the basis of a more participatory democracy. Public finances were presented as the vehicle through which First Republic party elites used the state to generate support from specific parts of the electorate. Tackling the debt and deficit was not just an exercise to meet the Maastricht criteria but also to dislodge an economic and political oligarchy.

It also may be argued that the discussion of the use of the state to promote private interests is a thread that has been present in the PCI/PDS for some time. In 1981, Berlinguer talked of addressing the *'questione morale'* (the moral question) in Italian politics, that is, of the loss of a sense of political power as an instrument of collective purpose. Moreover, it is no coincidence that the word 'democratic' appeared in the new name given to the party that replaced the PCI. Occhetto told the congress that dissolved the party that socialism was a process of the 'complete democratization' of all parts of society (Bull, 1994, p. 42).

The theme of democratization is present in almost every statement that is made by members of the PDS/DS when speaking about Italian political economy. For instance, Franco Bassanini spoke of constitutional and political decay of the First Republic stemming from a 'political-business' oligarchy that had operated beyond the rules of law, markets and democracy. In this way, he linked not just the political class of the First Republic to the scandals that had undermined the regime, but also to the financial crisis of 1992 and the disastrous state of public finances.[27] Compared to the secret deals of the First Republic, done not even in boardrooms but in more obscure settings, equity markets were presented as democratic arenas that were accessible and transparent, operating according to rules that were fair and equal for all. Privatization and pension funds, then, became a means of democratizing the economy and taking power away from the private interests and party factions that continued to occupy state holdings.[28] The same argument is made in terms of restructuring the welfare state. A more 'efficient' welfare state is seen to be more transparent, and outside the control of vested interests and accountable to representative institutions and not party elites. The debate about pension reform is particularly illustrative on this point. The target has been the

---

[27] Camera dei Deputati. XI Legislatura (1993), *Atti Parlamentari: Discussioni*, Vol. 17(6), May, p. 13201.

[28] It is not surprising, then, that the PDS/DS has been one of the strongest advocates of the creation of pension funds to ensure that privatized firms do not continue to fall under the control of the narrow group of large capital. See Camera dei Deputati. XII Legislatura (1994), *Atti Parlamentari: Discussioni*, Vol. 1(2), June, p. 468; see also an editorial by Sergio Cofferati, the leader of the CGIL, the largest trade union (Cofferatti, S. (1999), 'Il capitalismo e I fondi pensioni', *La Repubblica*, 28 February, p. 13).

'seniority pensions' that have allowed workers to collect pensions after 35 years of contributions and as young as 55 years old. A series of reforms has been introduced in the 1990s to scale back these pensions, but some argue that change is too slow and not drastic enough. The D'Alema government has sent out signs that it agrees or, at least, some of its members agree. The argument against the pensions is that a small group of privileged workers is taking money away from 'positive' measure such as worker retraining and education. The unemployed and usually well-educated youth, who wants an opportunity but is held back, is contrasted to the middle-aged worker who is ready to collect a pension and feed off public finances for a long time. Third Way politics, then, is presented as providing the tools to help individuals become more competitive on labour markets, and dismantling the privileged position of a narrow group that had a vested interest in a regime in need of modernization and democratization.

A good illustration of the governing left's emphasis on markets as mechanisms for democratization is the case of Telecom Italia. The telecommunications giant provided an opportunity for both the Prodi and D'Alema governments to highlight some of their major initiatives: privatization and restructuring Italian capitalism. The privatization of Telecom Italia in 1997 was significant not simply for its dimensions, roughly US$15 billion, but also for the nature of the new ownership. Unlike the privatization of the state-held banks a few years earlier, small investors, many of whom had previously put their money in treasury bills that had lost their shine because of improving public finances, were at the heart of the privatization of Telecom Italia. It signalled a shift away from the small circle that had controlled most financial and economic transactions in the postwar period. More importantly, it was hoped that Telecom Italia would become a 'public company' in the Anglo-American model, managed in the interests of its shareholders in an open, transparent process. Olivetti's public takeover bid, with an offer to all shareholders in February 1999, was taken as proof that something was happening to the world of Italian capitalism. D'Alema joined the chorus of praises for a new form of 'corporate governance' that was emerging; one that would be based on an assessment of the management of firms rather than the machinations of an economic and financial oligarchy (Gianola, 1999, p. 10). Olivetti's successful bid had large financial backing from an emerging entrepreneurial class in northeast Italy, who had few links with the traditional economic-financial and political centres in Rome and Milan.

Democratization and politics through markets, presented as the Italian 'Third Way', are not without their problems. They are useful strategies for the PDS/DS on two fronts. It provides a discourse that allows for the adoption of markets without accepting that they are necessarily part of a neoliberal strategy, and can even allow the left to reconcile it with arguments about redistributive justice. Second, it can allow the left to appeal to moderate elements of the centre while continuing to make arguments about the transformation of economic power. However, the PDS/DS has not addressed some of the tensions that may appear as a result of such a strategy. First, it has been glad to transfer to central banks power over monetary policy; and has even been the base of support for governments of technocrats led by central bankers. So while it may see markets as democratizing structures of economic power, it has accepted the 'hollowing out' of the authority of political institutions. Second, the faith in markets seems almost naïve. While there may be no doubt that there has been little transparency in economic and political decisionmaking, the PDS/DS ignores the concentration of power that follows economic liberalization. This stems, perhaps, from the fact that it has not articulated a vision for the state and its role in economic and social life.

The Italian left in government has embarked on the 'Third Way', at times making clear references to the term and to other European experiences. The path was made easier by the objective of gaining entry into the single currency, and the political vacuum of the 1990s. These developments allowed the PDS and the left to embrace economic liberalization as part of a democratization without any large degree of resistance from within its own ranks. The emphasis on democratization of institutions and giving greater space to civil society, along with 'positive' welfare, have all been important elements of the Prodi and D'Alema governments. However, they have not addressed the questions of the legitimacy of the state while it is being 'hollowed out', nor have they provided any responses to questions about what to do about highly mobile capital and how to temper it. It would seem that without answers to these fundamental issues, it is not clear exactly where the 'Third Way' will lead the left, leading to questions about whether it might not be the lost way of the left.

References

Adinolfi, M. (ed.) (1996), 'Le 88 tesi per la piattaforma programmatica dell'Ulivo', in M. Adinolfi (ed.), *Guida Ragionata ai Programmi Elettorali e dell'Ulivo*, Banzi, Roma.

Andreotti, O. (1993), Camera dei Deputati. XI Legislatura. *Atti Parlamentari: Discussioni*, Vol. 17, 7 May.

Bemporad, S. and Giannino, O. (1998), 'Storia di un'illusione italiana: Come e perche banche e aziende rimangono di Stato', *Liberal*, 16 July 1998, pp. 11–15.

Berlinguer, E. (1975), 'Riflessioni sull'Italia dopo I fatti del Cile', in E. Berlinguer, *La questione comunista* 1966-1975, Editori Riuniti, Roma, pp. 609–39.

Bertinotti, A. (1998), 'Ma quali elezioni siamo gia nel semestro bianco', *La Repubblica*, 9 July 1998, p. 5.

Bufacchi, V. and Burgess, S. (1998), *Italy Since 1989: Events and Interpretations*, St Martin's Press, New York.

Bull, M.J. (1994), 'Social Democracy's Newest Recruit? Conflict and Cohesion in the Italian Democratic Party of the Left', in D. Bell and E. Shaw (eds.), *Conflict and Cohesion in Western European Social Democratic Parties*, Pinter, London.

Bull, M.J. (1996), 'The Failure of the Progressive Alliance', in R. Katz and P. Ignazi (eds.), *Italian Politics: The Year of the Tycoon*, Westview Press, Boulder, Co.

Bull, M.J. and Newell, J. (1995), 'The Italian Referenda of April 1993: Real Change at Last?', *West European Politics*, Vol. 16(4), pp. 607–15.

Cacciari, M. (1987), 'Il morte del riformismo', *Micromega*, Vol. 2, pp. 15–21.

Cacciari, M. (1998), 'Il Nord-Est deluso rischia di esplodere', *La Repubblica*, 13 July 1998, p. 9.

D'Alema, M. (1998), 'Relazione Introduttiva', *Stati Generali della Sinistra*, Florence, 12–14 February, pp. 4–8.

De Grand, A. (1989), *The Italian Left in the Twentieth Century: A History of the Socialist and Communist Parties*, University of Indiana Press, Bloomington.

Della Sala, V. (1997), 'Hollowing Out and Hardening the State: European Integration and the Italian Economy', in M. Bull and M. Rhodes (eds.), *Crisis and Transition in Italian Politics*, Frank Cass, London.

Diamanti, I. and Lazar, M. (eds.) (1997), *Stanchi di Miracoli: Il sistema politico italiano in cerca di normalita*, Guerini e Associati, Milano.

Di Palma, G. (1980), 'The Available State: Problems of Reform', in P. Lange and S. Tarrow (eds.), *Italy in Transition*, Frank Cass, London.

Di Scala, S. (1988), *Renewing Italian Socialism: Nenni to Craxi*, Oxford University Press, New York.

Dyson, K. and Featherstone, K. (1996), 'Italy and EMU as a 'Vincolo Esterno': Empowering the Technocrats, Transforming the State', *South European Politics and Society*, Vol. 1(2), pp. 279–99.

Fabbrini, S. (1994), *Quale democrazia: L'Italia e gli altri*, Laterza, Roma.

Friedman, A. (1988), *Agnielli and the Network of Italian Power*, Harrap, London.

Gangemi, G. and Riccanbini, R. (1997), 'Introduzione', in G. Gangemi and R. Riccamboni (eds.), *Le elezioni della transizione*, UTET, Torino.

Garrett, G. and Lange, P. (1991), 'Political Responses to Interdependence: What's Left for the Left?', *International Organization*, Vol. 45(4), pp. 539–64.

Gianola, R. (1999), 'Telecom, Opa da 100 mila miliardi', *La Repubblica*, 20 February, p. 10.

Giddens, A. (1998), *The Third Way: The Renewal of Social Democracy*, Polity Press, Cambridge.

Gilbert, M. (1995), *The Italian Revolution: The End of Politics Italian Style?*, Westview Press, Boulder, CO.

Gundle, S. (1996), 'The Rise and Fall of Craxi's Socialist Party', in S. Gundle and S. Parker (eds.), *The New Republic: From the Fall of the Berlin Wall to Berlusconi*, Routledge, London.

Hellman, S. (1986), 'The Italian Communist Party Between Berlinguer and the Seventeenth Congress', in R. Leonardi and R. Nanetti (eds), *Italian Politics – A Review*, Vol. 1, London.

Hellman, S. (1997), 'The Italian Left After the 1996 Elections', in R. D'Alimonte and D. Nelken (eds.), *Italian Politics: The Center-Left in Power*, Westview Press, Boulder, CO.

Hirst, P. (1997), *From Statism to Pluralism*, UCL Press, London.

Ignazi, P. (1992), *Dal PCI al PDS*, Il Mulino, Bologna.

Kitschelt, H. (1994), *The Transformation of European Social Democracy*, Cambridge University Press, Cambridge.

Lange, P. and Vannicelli, M. (eds.) (1981), *The Communist Parties of Italy, France and Spain: Postwar Change and Continuity*, Allen and Unwin, London.

La Palombara, J. (1987), *Democracy, Italian Style*, Yale University Press, New Haven, Conn.

Marletti, C. (1997), 'Perche non siamo ancora un paese normale', in I. Diamanti and M. Lazar (eds.), *Stanchi di miracoli. Il sistema politico italiano in cerca di normalità*, Guerini e Associati, Milano, pp. 69–82.

McCarthy, P. (1996), 'Forza Italia: the New Politics of Old Values in a Changing Italy', in S. Gundle and S. Parker (eds.), *The New Italian Republic*, Routledge, London.

McCarthy, P. (1997), *The Crisis of the Italian State*, St. Martin's Press, New York.

Pasquino, G. (1985), 'Partiti, Societa Civile e Istituzioni', in G. Pasquino (ed.), *Il Sistema Politico Italiana*, Laterza, Bari.

Putnam, R. (1993), *Making Democracy Work; Civic Traditions in Modern Italy*, Princeton University Press, Princeton, N.J.

Ranieri, U. (1998), 'Il deficit culturale della sinistra di governo', *Le ragioni del socialismo*, Vol. 111(1), pp. 608–20.

Reviglio, F. (1998), *Come Siamo Entrati in Europa (e perche' potremmo uscirne)*, UTET, Milano.

Salvati, M. (1997), Moneta unica, rivoluzione copernicana, *Il Mulino*, Vol. XLVI(1), pp. 5–23.

Sapelli, G. (1993), *Sul capitalismo italiano*, Feltrinelli, Milano.

Togliatti, P. (1973), *La Nostra Lotta – Organo del Partito Comunista Italiano* [1944], in, A. Colombi, (ed.), *La Nostra Lotta: Organo del Partito Comunista Italiano: 1943–1945*, Edizioni del Calendario, Milano.

Chapter 5

The Third Way in France:
Tertium Non Datur?

Serenella Sferza

Introduction

At the turn of the twenty-first century, thirteen of the fifteen countries that make up the European Union had a left government. At no prior time has the left enjoyed such power. Yet, perhaps never before have its identity and purpose been so much in question. The issue is not a lack of good reasons for the left's success: high unemployment rates and rising insecurity and inequalities are plausible enough grounds for the trashing of governing parties and for left voting. The problem, rather, is that there are increasing reasons for believing that doing so does not make any difference.

In most European countries, the social, organizational and policy criteria by which we used to identify the left are in tatters. The working class is both shrinking and deserting the left. In the most recent French presidential election, the candidate who attracted the largest working class vote on the first ballot was neither a Communist nor a Socialist, but the extremist right-wing politician Jean Marie le Pen. Everywhere, albeit at a different rate, trade unions are losing members and, even more important, the moral authority to speak for the general interest. The solid institutional ties with organized labour that were once a necessary condition of left strength, have now come to be seen as a severe handicap left parties are seeking to minimize. In Britain, 'New' Labour has largely rebuilt its image and its electoral strength by breaking free from its close ideological and organizational ties with the Unions. Left parties that prided their mass-class character have turned into flimsier, leadership-centred, electoral organizations that strive for a 'catch-all' appeal. In Italy, for example, state 'moralization', and economic normalization were two of the major reasons for the left's victory in 1998. New alliances, best illustrated by red-green governments that have ruled in various European countries, including Germany and France, have further blurred the left's image and agenda. Last, but not least, the instruments on which the left has historically relied to promote growth and equality, from welfare and social policies to macroeconomic stimulation, have become unaffordable or unviable for a variety of reasons that range from population aging to global competition and regional integration. The last government of the left that seriously tried these instruments in full – the

Mauroy government in 1981 France – had to beat a hasty retreat that taught its successors and other European lefts a major lesson in moderation, which has not yet been forgotten.

These changes, it is often suggested, have not only transformed the left, but have emptied it of its substance. Ironically, this hollowing is also seen as a major factor in the left's comeback in the 1990s. The left parties that are doing best are the ones that have more effectively walked away from their sectoral working class appeal toward 'New Politics' issues and groups; put their fate in the hands of young and often charismatic leaders with a strong personal and mass media appeal; and consented to the 'marketization' of their economies and societies.[1] Thus, New Labour, which claims to have entered a new course – a 'Third Way' that would increase efficiency and equity while avoiding state- and market-domination – is practically sailing through its mandate. By contrast, the German Social Democrats, who, in spite of their search for a 'New Centre', still resemble a classic northern Social Democracy, have had a much rockier time in power (Dalton, 1999). As the left discovers that, independently of what it intends to do, there is little it can do; long entrenched differences across lefts may eventually fade. The resignation of Oskar Lafontaine – one of the most vocal spokesmen of old-style Keynesian measures and redistributive policies – from his post as Germany's finance minister illustrates this point.[2] As one major historical study of the European left has concluded, the fin de siècle left has become unprecedentedly homogenous and modest (Sassoon, 1996).

To the question: how much is left of the left? The answer seems to be: not much.[3] From such a perspective, the left's late 1990s comeback has little practical meaning or significance, other than as a sign of widespread disappointment with tightening international constraints and slow economic growth. At best, left governments will bring a fuller understanding and legitimation of market values and rules, a younger and less stuffy leadership, and a greater openness to post-materialist concerns; at worst, they will slow Europe's adaptation to global competition and unification.

---

[1] On the recent evolution and transformation of European Socialist Parties, see Kitschelt (1994).

[2] Other left politicians – and notably France's Finance Minister Dominique Strauss-Kahn – share similar views, but Lafontaine was seen as the one with the greatest chance to have them adopted at the European level. Yet, his bullying failed to convert either the German or the European Banks. Following his resignation, German stocks surged by 5.4 per cent and the Euro experienced its biggest gain against the dollar since its creation (*New York Times*, 3/13/1999, and 3/15/1999).

[3] Even political theorists who maintain the left has a distinct identity – rooted in its committment to equality – which remains highly relevant in contemporary societies, admit to major problems when shifting from principles to policies. See the exchange between Norberto Bobbio, 'At the Beginning of History', and 'A Sense of the Left, A Reply to Norberto Bobbio', *New Left Review*, n. 231, September/October, 1998.

In this article I take a different position. There is more left of the left than is usually suggested, I contend, for two reasons. First, the record of the contemporary left on the redistributive agenda, with which it has been historically identified, is not as bad as it is made to be. A new wave of scholarly research shows that traditional left constituencies, issues and objectives are still important in contemporary societies, and in the programmes of most lefts, and that left governments have found new ways of pursuing their old egalitarian goals. Whereas the left may lack a grand project, an argument can be made that the glass is still half full (cf. Boix, 1998, Garrett, 1998; Clayton and Pontusson, 1998).

Second, and, most important, I want to make a 'this is an altogether different beast' type of argument. What we think is left of the left, depends on how we look at it. Dominant views of the left, past and present, are distorted because they include only one of its faces, the economic one, while leaving out its other equally important face, the political one. When we take both the economic and political faces into consideration, developments that appear to signal the unmooring of the left from its historical legacy, suggest instead a shift in emphasis between the two components of this legacy.

From its beginning, I contend, the left has been as much about issues of political equality as about socioeconomic ones. At the time in which Socialist parties were formed, most European countries were dealing with a set of highly contentious issues centring on the location of power, access to political rights and the constitutional form of the state. These battles and issues pitted supporters of universal suffrage and parliamentary regimes against supporters of limited voting and executive-centred regimes, and laid the foundations of what I term the 'authoritarianism/democracy' cleavage. Over time, the expression, focus and constituency of this cleavage have changed, as this primordial conflict has spilled over to other issues concerning the location of, and access to, political power.

The 'authoritarianism/democracy' cleavage enduringly shaped the ideology and organization of left parties. In countries where the battles between supporters of authoritarianism and democracy were more salient, competitive and prolonged, like in France and other Southern European countries, Socialist parties from their inception tended to be 'citizens'' parties with relatively universalist ideologies and open organizations. By contrast, in countries where the authoritarianism/ democracy cleavage was salient, but where Socialists did not face much competition in representing the democratic pole, as in Germany, or where the authoritarianism/democracy conflict had been by and large resolved by bourgeois parties prior to the formation of a Socialist party, as in Britain, left parties displayed the materialist ideology, tightly-knit subculture, and mass organization associated with 'workers'' parties. As a result, the 'political' face of the left was differentially incorporated in the repertoire of various left parties: most prominent in the citizens' parties, and much less so in the workers' ones.

If we take into account both faces of the left, a new interpretation of recent left trends becomes possible. The programmatic shifts that many left parties are undergoing today, which often are major departures from their historical legacy, may indeed be signs that the left's genetic stock is running thin. However, an alternative and, I would suggest, equally plausible interpretation, is that they represent the sometimes divergent, sometimes convergent efforts by different strands of the left to revitalize and incorporate, each in its own way, aspects of the left's heritage that, for reasons having to do with the country-specific historical circumstances of party formation, were weaker in their genetic pool. This 'borrowing' may well lead to the revitalization of the left rather than to its demise. The question, then, becomes whether and how the democratic and the egalitarian face of the left can be combined, and how parties that had never fully incorporated both traditions can now do so.

Answering these questions is beyond the scope of this article. My goal here is to provide some support for the perspective I have outlined, and some clues on the questions it raises, by discussing the case of the French Socialist Party since the left's legislative victory of 1997 and the formation of a Socialist-led government in its aftermath. A major left 'winner' of recent years, the PS epitomizes the broader left's trajectory from radicalism and grand projects to moderation and conformism. At the same time, the French Socialist Party is a 'citizens'' party, which has never been historically successful in pursuing traditional left economic and social goals. On both counts, it provides an ideal observation point for analyzing what is left of the left and taking a closer look at a left strand which is arguably being grafted onto other, and genetically quite different, European lefts.

A 'Citizens'' Party: The French Socialist Party

The French Socialist Party has long intrigued analysts and commentators, first as a historical underachiever that never lived up to its promise, and since the 1970s for its remarkable success and unexpected resilience.[4] At a time in which its European counterparts were on the defensive, the PS staged a phoenix-like comeback that brought it to power in 1981 amidst widespread expectations that its victory would 'change life'. Since then, the PS has been more or less continuously in power until 1993, and then again from 1997 until 2002. In these years, the PS has weathered many changes and a variety of moral and policy failures, notably its inability to prevent unemployment from rising. Initially viewed as a test of whether radicalism could work, the Socialists' first years in power turned into a conclusive proof that it could not, and the French Socialists took the lead of a broader process of left modernization and marketization.

In the aftermath of its brutal defeat of 1993, however, the PS partially retreated from its newly found economic orthodoxy. The cause of left modernization found new pioneers in the British and Italians, and the whereabouts of the French left attracted notice more for what they said about the peculiarities of

---

[4] For a standard account of the PS's trajectory, see Bell and Criddle (1984). On the left's governmental experience, see Ross, Hoffmann and Malzacher (1987) and Daley (1996).

French politics than for what they could say about the left.

The left's unexpected 1997 victory attracted little attention, primarily as providing further proof that left victories had little policy implications and that French Socialists had fallen out of the step with left modernization. On the first count, the left's victory was dismissed as a victory by default, both in the sense that it was the byproduct of President Jacques Chirac's ill-fated decision to call for anticipated elections in order to force his right-wing majority to fall into line behind his Prime Minister and his austerity measures, and in the sense that the electorate had voted against an extremely unpopular Prime Minister, rather than for the left. Whatever the 'voters'' reasons, the left government was said to be up against such tight international constraints that it would practically have no policy choices. Unexpectedly, it would be up to the left to finish the dirty job the right had been so reluctant to do by bringing 'France's' public deficit within the limits of the Maastricht Treaty, but the outcome would be the same. On most issues, anyway, the so-called 'Plural Left' that composed the government was viewed as too diverse to agree on anything. With some help from Chirac, the composite mixture of Socialists, Communists, Greens, Citoyens and Radicals in the Jospin government was expected to implode at the first misstep, and many were expected.

On the second count, the programme – more jobs – the means – statism – and even their leadership on which the left won, were all seen as evidence of the French left's hopeless archaism. Lionel Jospin – the architect of the left's comeback, and France's current Prime Minister – is a lifetime left activist who lacks the charismatic brilliance, congeniality and media appeal of some of his counterparts, like Tony Blair and Gerhard Schröder, or the 'novelty' appeal of a boundary crosser like Romano Prodi. As a result, he has been often portrayed as a second rate leader, and a somewhat parochial French bureaucrat.[5] Even worse, Jospin – an early opponent of Mitterrand's austerity measures – remains committed to the old notions of left and right. After Tony Blair announced to the French National Assembly that 'there is not an economic policy of the left and an economic policy of the Right, but only a good and a bad policy', for example, Jospin hastened to correct him by noting that 'things are more complicated...there are good left policies and bad left policies, and good Right policies and bad Right policies'.[6] The comparison between an 'archaic' left – Jospin's – and a 'modern' one – Blair's – has been the common staple of articles on the European left, until the German Social Democrats began to steal the French's role.

What I would like to suggest in this article, is that the best way to understand the record, past and present, of the French Socialists is not by looking at them as 'ahead' or 'behind' other lefts, but as illustrating the strength and weakness of a

---

[5] Jospin's lack of interest in the 'Third Way', and his absence from the international meetings on the subject organized by Bill Clinton, Tony Blair, Romano Prodi and Henrique Cardoso, was taken as further proof that the French left had stepped back into its past.

[6] *Le Monde*, 3/26/98.

distinctive left strand, the 'citizens'' party. More universalist than class oriented, more focused on political issues having to do with the democratization of power than on social or economic ones, and more loosely and democratically organized – but as egalitarian and as radical – as workers' parties, the French Socialist Party has had a better record as a spokesman of democracy than of labour. Still, the PS is neither a centrist, nor a catch-all party.

The Constituency

One of the reasons why so little is said to remain of the left has to do with the disappearance of old cleavages, and the shrinking of the left's working class constituency. Together these developments are said to have produced a volatile and competitive market in which major parties can win only by presenting bland programs that appeal to centrist voters, and in which electoral victories have no programmatic content.

Whether this analysis applies to the French case is questionable. In 1997, the socialist electorate was more educated, richer and more sheltered than in the Mitterrand years: Support for the Socialists had declined among blue collar workers and increased substantially among public sector employees and cadres. Still, this electorate had a distinct sociological, and most important, ideological profile. Left voters attributed their vote to values and issues – 'society, morality, equality' – entirely different from those of right voters – 'liberal, market, national tradition, immigration'. The foundations of left/right divide have shifted, especially among younger voters, with new stands, notably a universalistic acceptance of immigrants and Europe, displacing old ones, notably support for nationalization, as signposts of left positions (Boy and Mayer, 1997; Dupoirier and Parodi, 1996). When viewed against rising support for the National Front and the xenophobia that goes with it, these values are hardly bland, uncontested, or extraneous to the left's historical legacy.

Similarly, France's electoral landscape hardly resembles the volatile, centrist-leaning market that is seen as a major cause of the left's obliteration. Many shifts have undermined structural and ideological bases of partisanship: economic and cultural transformations; the creation of new parties, like the Front Nationale and the Verts (Green Party); the appearance of new issues, like unemployment, immigration and European unification, all cut across partisan blocs. Other issues such as nationalization, which used to define the left, have been neutralized. French voters have begun to question the notions of left and right, and, as illustrated by repeated alternation between left and right, some of them are now willing to travel unprecedented distances along the political space, trampling across what had once been a clearly drawn left/right divide.[7] Still, a majority of the French think of the political landscape as divided between these blocs, readily place themselves and the candidates in one of the two camps, and vote in keeping with this self placement.[8] Accordingly, mobility within blocs is actually quite low: over the last three elections only ten per cent of the electorate has crossed the left/right divide, primarily to the advantage of the National Front. The centre, by contrast, remains very small: The number of French voters who place themselves in the middle of the political spectrum has decreased in the past thirty years.[9]

In short, whereas the French political landscape has certainly changed, it still hardly resembles a real 'market'. Further, the motivations and concerns of the Socialist electorate are more consistent with the egalitarian, inclusionary legacy and society-centred preoccupations of a citizens' party, rather than with the consensual, individual-centred appeal of a 'catch-all' one.

The Programme

A 'demand' for left policies does not necessarily imply a left 'offer'; in 1997, however, the two appeared to match. Jospin's campaign emphasized three themes: job creation, the restoration of the Republican pact between citizens and the state, and the preservation of national sovereignty as an instrument of social citizenship, which wove democratic and social issues into a distinctively left package.

Jospin's major promise was to reduce unemployment – a goal which had eluded left and right governments since the late 1970s – through two state sponsored measures: the promotion of 700,000 five-year non-renewable youth jobs in the so-called 'social' sector, and the shortening of the workweek to 35 hours, so that by working less, more people would work. Both measures were criticized as more or less malignant, but equally ineffective, examples of left 'assistentialism' and disdain for economic constraints. Other European lefts openly questioned the impact of the shorter week on job creation; objected to the method through which it was to be introduced – legislation rather than concertation; or viewed it as an

---

[7] At the 1995 presidential election, for example, 28 per cent of the voters who had supported Jean Marie Le Pen – the leader of the extreme right wing party, Front Nationale – intended to vote for the Socialist candidate Lionel Jospin at the second ballot.

[8] Between 79 per cent and 97 per cent of French voters consistently place themselves and their politicians along a left/right continuum (Jaffré and Muxel, 1997).

[9] In 1994, fewer voters (26 per cent) located themselves at the centre of the political spectrum than 30 years before (36 per cent). Further, the electorates of the two major presidential candidates has actually grown more distant from each other in 1995 then they had been in 1988 (Chiche and Dupoirier, 1996). Electoral mobility strengthened the extremes, on the right, with the Front Nationale now consistently polling about 15 per cent of the vote, but also, to a lesser extent, on the left, with extreme left increasing from 2 per cent in 1978 to 6 per cent in 1995 (Boy and Mayer, 1997).

obstacle to industrial competitiveness.[10] Gerhard Schröder dismissed the 35 hours as the French left's 'great present to German industry'; French industrialists announced their strenuous opposition to any legislative reform on this matter; and President Chirac spoke of it as 'hazardous'.[11]

These controversial measures sent a very clear message about Jospin's priorities, and his willingness to engage his credibility and imagination on a cause that most other politicians viewed at lost. Throughout the campaign, these measures became Jospin's best, and constantly hammered, selling points, and particularly the 35 hours, his most distinctively left ones.

The restoration of the Republican pact between the state and the people was Jospin's second major campaign theme. While this promise has become very common among French politicians, Jospin nevertheless gave it a distinctive left twist by emphasizing the democratic character and inclusive scope of the Republican pact, and the centrality of the state as the guardian of universalism and equality. In keeping with this view, Jospin promised to privatize only when strategically beneficial to the specific industry and under close state supervision, maintain public ownership of all basic services – from transportation to education and electricity – and introduce positive discrimination in the financing and pricing of these services to make them more truly universally accessible.[12] Power was to be made more transparent, accountable and widely distributed through a change in leadership style and a variety of political reforms, which ranged from non interference in judicial matters and severe limitations on the number of offices politicians could combine, to institutionally enforced 'gender parity' in political office. Most controversially, Jospin pledged to restore the state to its universalist obligations by returning to *jus soli* as the sole condition of citizenship and to forms of immigration control which would respect the immigrants' individual rights.[13]

Some of these promises were designed to make the best of Jospin's reputation as an unbending man who spoke his mind, kept his word, and remained untouched

---

[10] In Italy, where the 35-hour work week was part of the Ulivo's electoral promises, Jospin's determination raised serious fears of contagion. When the legislation passed, the Union movement took its distance from this measure, on the grounds that it had been adopted through legislation rather than negotiation.

[11] *Le Monde*, 10/20/97.

[12] Whereas this was clearly a retreat from Mitterrand's 'neither...nor' stand, which rejected both further nationalization and privatization, it set some principled boundaries to the latter, and prepared the stage for the highly *dirigiste* approach to privatization the Jospin government has thus far successfully practised. The allocation of more resources to schools located in underprivileged neighbourhoods and the reform of family allowances, are examples of 'positive discrimination'.

[13] The Pasqua-Debré Laws had made access to French citizenship for individuals born in France conditional to a variety of requirements; subjected the immigrants' right to bring into France their close relatives to strict conditions and bureaucratic impediments; and considerably increased the power of the police to control the identity of suspicious looking individuals.

by scandals in spite of his past proximity to power, while differentiating him from both Mitterrand's Florentine style, and Juppé's technocratic absolutism. Still, Jospin's emphasis on universalism, egalitarianism and reliance on the state as the protector of both, clearly placed him within the political tradition of the French left. Interestingly, these roots also inspired Jospin's riskiest electoral bet: the return to *jus soli* as the only source of citizenship compatible with this tradition. Considering Le Pen's success in imposing his view of immigration as a threat to economic security and national identity, the strong anti-immigrant feelings of the popular electorate, and the considerable number of Le Pen's voters who had supported Jospin at the second ballot of the 1995 presidential election, Jospin's decision to enter the fray and reframe the debate on citizenship and immigration in terms of universal obligations and social issues was a rather courageous one.[14]

Jospin's third theme, the pledge to defend national sovereignty and the social rights that went with it against the threats posed by globalization and European unification played a relatively minor role in the campaign. Jospin's suggestion that a left government might reconsider France's commitments, were the EMU's stabilization pact to conflict with its priorities, resonated with a substantial component of the popular electorate for whom European unification had become synonymous with austerity, and, together with immigration, a major cause of xenophobia.[15] However, because of France's engagements, the President's traditional primacy on international matters, and significant differences within the plural left on this issue, Europe remained on the backburner.

The Policies

The most powerful argument for the demise of the left is that the policies with which it has been traditionally associated no longer work. In this respect, the Jospin government was viewed as doubly doomed: its commitments were unrealistic, and its internal diversity was going to block their implementation.

Prior to the 2002 elections the Jospin government had gained considerable weight and credibility. Contrary to what happened in Germany, where intense conflicts within, and between, the SPD and the Greens riveted the left government, the more internally diversified French left discussed and disagreed on a variety of issues, but in a relatively collegial way and without paralysing the government.[16]

---

[14] In the recent past, the left had alternated between very generous and very repressive stands, from Mitterrand's support for the immigrants' right to vote to Edith Cresson's extradition charters (Ireland, 1996).

[15] Many Socialist voters, especially its more popular electorate, opposed the Maastricht Treaty, as shown by the defeat of the Maastricht referendum in some socialist strongholds like the North region.

[16] The Greens were remarkably quick in grasping the constraints and opportunities of their governmental role, and the PCF has only haltingly and not very successfully tried to present

Surprisingly, even the PS – a legendarily fractious party – stood behind Jospin.[17] Further, the government was relatively unaffected by two other causes of instability – street protest and presidential whims. Cohabitation made it impossible for the President to dismiss a popular Prime Minister; and social and protest movements were deflated by the left victory and by the government's skilful use of legislation to take the wind out of street mobilization.

Second, the government was quite popular. In January 1999, nearly two thirds of the French approved of Jospin's action; key ministers had a more positive image than the principal right-wing leaders; and confidence in the left stood at a rate unseen since the early 1980's – 21 points higher than that enjoyed by the right.[18] What is more, the local elections of March 1998, showed that approval for the government translated into partisan support for its components, and especially for the PS.[19] The European election of June 1999 confirmed this trend.

Third, the government stuck to its agenda. Much of the promised legislation, and notably some of its most controversial measures were approved. The government passed new laws on citizenship and immigration as part of a broader effort to recast immigration-related issues as social, rather than as security or identity, issues, and to reframe the question of national identity in universalistic Republican terms. The outcome was a compromise between the left's principled universalism and its determination not to alienate its working class constituents. On immigration, the government realistically acknowledged that immigration cannot be stopped, but also that it is a source of insecurity, especially among low income groups, and hence needs to be tightly regulated according to the national interest, although in ways that respected individual rights.[20] On citizenship, sons and daughters of foreign parents born and living in France were, once again, given automatic access to French nationality, but only at the age of eighteen.

---

itself as the spokesman of 'le social' and as 'the left of the left'. Efforts at differentiation increased with the approaching of the European elections, and relationships between Jospin and the Greens became more tense with the appearance of Daniel Cohn-Bendit and the launching of his European campaign.

[17] Aptly labelled the 'peace congress', the Socialists' 1997 Congress of Brest witnessed the consensual election of François Hollande as the party's secretary and the official disappearance of factions, with the exception of the very small *Gauche Socialiste*.

[18] At the beginning of the year, different polls put Jospin's positive rating at between 49 per cent and 68 per cent 44 per cent of the French had confidence in the left (*Le Monde*, 1/3-4/1999).

[19] At the 1998 local elections, the 'Plural left' outscored the Republican right by 5.77 per cent (*Le Monde*, 3/18/1998).

[20] Thus, for example, asylum rights were expanded; immigrants who returned to their countries of origins were given access to their pension funds; family regroupments, as well as professional and scientific exchanges, were eased; but the administration was authorized to detain illegal immigrants for 12 days, and remained in charge of their dossiers. The laws and the debate on immigration and nationality were profoundly shaped by the rapport presented by Patrick Weil, an academic close to the PS (Weil, 1995).

Both reforms were quite divisive. No compromise could be reached with the Right and, in the end, most communist and green deputies abstained on the new nationality code because it failed to grant citizenship at birth.[21] Further, as undocumented immigrants, backed by a wide array of religious, humanitarian, green, and union associations and prominent left-wing intellectuals, staged a number of highly dramatic protests in the hope of obtaining legal immigrant status, the left split between principled hardliners – who did not want to set the wrong precedent – and humanitarians – who sympathize with the immigrants' individual plights – with Jospin walking a tightrope in between.[22]

Still, by seizing the initiative the government effectively challenged the National Front's monopoly over nationality and immigration issues, and even reduced its influence. A majority of the French approved of the new laws, and in a highly symbolic victory, a Socialist conquered the National Front's only legislative seat.[23] The fact that political analysts, commenting upon the new laws a year after their approval, wondered why such moderate measures had seemed so divisive, is a further indication of the government's progress in changing the terms and tone of the debate.

On the job front, the government passed the two measures Jospin had promised. The Aubry law, named after Martine Aubry, the Employment and Solidarity Minister, proposed the creation of 700,000 minimum-wage and largely state-financed jobs, half in the private and half in the public sector. Reserved to youths who never worked long enough to qualify for unemployment, these jobs of a 'third type' consisted of five-year non-renewable contracts, which seek to 'marry social demand and labor supply' by addressing needs which are not covered by the public or the private sector.[24] By May 1998, 100,000 posts had been identified, and 60,000 filled, in the public and voluntary sectors, and the government was hoping to reach a total of 150,000 jobs by the end of the year.[25] In contrast, nothing seems

---

[21] See J.M. Colombani (1997), 'Jospin, Acte 2', *Le Monde*, 10/14/97. In the end, the two laws passed with very few changes. Whereas the Minister of Justice consented to give access to French nationality to individuals aged 13, upon specific request and with family consent, the Minister of Interior agreed to lift the obligation for immigrants who sought to reunite with their relatives to obtain a 'housing certificate' from their mayors.

[22] *Le Monde*, 11/27/98.

[23] In the aftermath of the new legislation, 52 per cent of the French approved the Chevènement-Guigou laws, including the automatic acquisition of French nationality at eighteen. Even more encouraging, support for Le Pen's suggestion to send back all immigrants had declined to 15 per cent, and 42 per cent approved the regularization of the undocumented immigrants (*Le Monde*, 12/24/97). The Socialist victory against the Front National took place in Toulon, in a 1998 remake of the 1997 legislative election.

[24] Local and national experts have identified 22 professions that respond to these criteria, primarily in education, culture, housing, health care, mediation of urban conflicts and the environment, and in order to keep the programme close to the ground, local governments are responsible for its implementation (Cole, 1999).

[25] *Le Monde*, 5/30/98.

to have happened in the private sector.

Whereas state-financed jobs, of whatever type, are relatively uncontroversial in France, the 35-hour workweek was surrounded by controversy. The French public was moderately supportive; experts could not agree about its overall effect on jobs and productivity; unions worried about its impact on wages and work regulations; industrialists denounced its costs while maintaining it would not create jobs.[26] By the fall of 1997, the 35-hour workweek had become a major *casus belli* between the government and the various employers' associations. Upon learning that the government intended to go ahead as planned the president of the CNPF – France's largest business association – for example, resigned in protest; his successor portrayed his mission as 'the killing of Jospin', and contacts between the patronat and the government were suspended for six months.

In this context, many expected the 35-hour work week would join the long list of highly symbolic, yet unfulfilled, promises of the French left. When, in February 1998, however, the government legislated the 35-hour week, beginning in January 2000 in firms with more than 20 workers, and in 2002 in all firms, with the exception of the public sector, the law struck even the left as a somewhat divine surprise. All the more so, since its timely passage effectively took the unemployed off the street, putting an end to a mobilization which was beginning to harm the government's popularity.[27]

In addition to these state-centred efforts at job creation, the government also passed redistributive welfare and fiscal policies – two areas on which left and Right are supposed to diverge, but which past left governments left relatively untouched. In both areas, the government took advantage of the inequities and inefficiency that permeate the French tax and welfare systems, to reroute resources to low income groups at no extra budgetary costs (Levy, 1998). Thus, the budget deficit – a major cause of the 1997 election – was brought within EMU limits by raising business and corporate taxes. The fiscalization of health insurance contributions, and the subordination of family allowances to income-testing that exclude the rich, are further examples of revenue- and expenditure-neutral reforms, which have shifted burdens and benefits in markedly redistributive ways (Levy, arts. cits.; Ross, 1997). Like other left governments at times of fiscal restraint, the Jospin government managed to turn 'vice into virtue' by 'targeting inequities within the welfare state that are simultaneously a source of inefficiency'.

Even on its supposedly weakest front – the international one – the left government had something to show, from an agreement on the statute of New Caledonia, which had long eluded its predecessors, and some achievements on Europe. Italy and Spain have been admitted into the EMU, as demanded by the

---

[26] *Le Monde*, Dossiers, Les 35 heures, 12/02/1998.

[27] In 1997, the unemployed staged numerous and highly symbolic occupations of public and private spaces, from the École Normale to the restaurant La Coupole, culminating in a 20,000 demonstration on 17 January 1998.

French government, if not necessarily because of it; Europe now officially has a social dimension, and its members have agreed to a major campaign against unemployment. Whereas some of these changes are symbolic, the Jospin government nevertheless managed to convey the impression that European integration is an interactive process with some room for negotiation (Ross, 1997).

Assessment and Prospects

Few analysts would deny that the Jospin government had done much better than expected. The debate on the reasons of this success, however, is wide open. A popular argument emphasizes luck and leadership. Unlike his left predecessors, Jospin won office on the eve of an unexpected economic upswing – not to mention France's World Cup victory – which gave his government much needed breathing space. Whereas Chirac had felt compelled to call for early elections to secure support for the budget cuts required by Maastricht, the left managed to meet the criteria for admission to EMU in a seemingly effortless, and, as we saw, redistributive way. With the economy growing at rates unknown in the past decade – from 2.3 per cent in 1997 to three per cent in 1998 – Jospin was able to lower the deficit and please the voters. Spending on left priorities, like employment, education and justice increased. The disposable income of wage earners went up by 2.5 per cent in 1998. Best of all, unemployment began to come slowly down, from 12.6 per cent in June 1997 to 11.5 per cent in January 1999 – a small but significant change that brought the total number of unemployed under the highly symbolic milestone of 3,000,000.[28]

A very skilled leadership got the best mileage out of this lucky start. Whether we look at the quality and size of the government, the upkeeping of the Plural left coalition, or the government's relationship with civil society, Jospin revealed remarkable skills, as well as unsuspected capacity to market them as what has become known as the Jospin 'method'. Based on 'diagnosis, dialogue, decision', this method stems from the assumption that listening and discussing do not undermine authority. Thus, the government discussed and disagreed, and Jospin arbitrated, on a variety of controversial issues, like nuclear energy, privatization, citizenship and family allowances without coming to a halt.[29] The government's unusually small size; the absence in ranks of socialist notables; the presence in key posts of men and women with a reputation for being honest, capable and imaginative; moderation in claiming the political spoils which come with office; and the obligation for members of the government to forego executive local office,

---

[28] *Le Monde*, 5/2/98.

[29] Thus, for example, Jospin catered to the Greens' environmental concerns by cancelling a controversial canal between the Rhone and the Rhine, and stopping the Super Phenix nuclear generator, and partly soothed the Communists, who are in support of nuclear energy, by keeping the Phenix nuclear generator working.

all added substance to this decisional style.[30]

Even when applied to the relationship between the government and interest groups, associations and spokesmen of civil society – a terrain on which French governments have treaded gingerly, alternating between a principled disdain for sectoral interests and surrender to street protest – the Jospin 'method' worked well. While open to consultation, the government yielded relatively little under pressure, as illustrated by its interaction with groups as diverse as the undocumented immigrants seeking regularization; business associations opposing the 35-hour week; prominent business leaders attempting to impose their own view of privatization; the unemployed demanding higher compensation; or, more recently, teachers opposing school reform.[31] As an anonymous commentator put it, in Jospin France found, once again after Mitterrand, a leader who 'does politics'.[32] Even better, the unusual combination of accessibility and firmness with which the Jospin method has become identified has earned its creator praise for being both democratic and effective.

French voters eventually do tire of their Prime Ministers and luck does not last forever. In this case, the high rating of Jacques Chirac suggested that Jospin's appeal was weakening, and the Asian crisis and economic disturbances in Latin America forced the government to lower its growth forecast for 1999.[33] What is more, the government may have already cashed in most of the benefits its policies are ever going to produce: credit for keeping its electoral promises is in, while blame for their possible failure is not. For different reasons, the Aubry laws, the 35-hour week, Social Europe may all end up making little difference; the government's firmness in dealing with business and in reshuffling taxes may have

---

[30] Dominique Strauss-Kahn, the powerful minister of economy, in particular, is widely praised for being a realist without being conservative, as indicated by his support for Maastricht but also for the 700,000 youth jobs and his five-year jobs for unemployed youth. Strauss-Kahn has also spoken in favour of left-wing economic and financial policies aimed at helping productive, high risk investments and high technologies while penalizing rents (*Le Monde*, 8/20/97).

[31] *Le Monde*, 01/09/98.

[32] Quoted by Chemin, A., *Le Monde*, 10/24/97. The undocumented aliens have also staged dramatic protest actions, primarily within the Church building they have occupied, and have created a remarkably extensive and highly visible support network.

[33] The estimate went down from 3.2 per cent to 2.7 per cent, a rate which many analysts see as too optimistic. Jospin's interview in *Le Monde*, 1/7/1999. Were France's economic performance to deteriorate further, two of the government's job creation policies, whose high costs have not yet become fully operational, may be in jeopardy. The cost of the 700,000 youth jobs has been estimated at 35 million francs, to be financed partly through existing credits. The government will also provide substantial fiscal incentives to firms which shorten the workweek. A firm which cuts its worktime by 15 per cent and increases its labour force by 9 per cent, for example, is to receive 13,000 francs per additional worker in the first year, and, progressively, 1,000 francs less each year for five years. Similar incentives apply to firms which cut their worktime in order to prevent the loss of jobs.

hindered job creation; and the scandals surrounding key figures of the 'Mitterrand years' may have seriously undermined the credibility of the Jospin method.[34] Indeed, disillusionment was bound to be greater since the government's early achievements raised higher expectations about its future actions.

The 35-hour week illustrates well the uncertainty which surrounded some of the government's initiatives. The actual content of the reform depends on ongoing union-business negotiations as well as on future legislation. Economic experts suggested that the 35 hours could create a substantial amount of jobs, but only if accompanied by wage moderation and more flexible work hours.[35] At the time, this seemed unlikely. Business continued to oppose the reform, and has taken advantage of a divided and extremely weak union movement to negotiate branch agreements that violate its spirit.[36] The content of these agreements, in turn, prompted the government to contemplate punitive measures against firms that counter the 35 hours with extended overtime; strengthened the workers' opposition to wage moderation in exchange of (unlikely) jobs; lowered public confidence in business and union organizations, and increased trust in the government.[37] In keeping with France's tradition, the fate of a reform whose viability hinges on flexibility and negotiation will be decided by the state.[38]

My own assessment of the Jospin government, does not deny the importance of luck, leadership and time, but suggests that Jospin's achievements can best be understood as part of a broader picture. In particular, on several fronts, Jospin reaped the reward of the 'Socialists'' record as a 'citizens'' party, a record that was confirmed and revitalized in the 1970s by the PS's commitment to 'autogestion' and the promise to democratize and equalize power across genders and sites.[39]

---

[34] See J.M. Colombani, 'Tout va bien...,' *Le Monde*, 11/24/98.

[35] 710,000 over three years, according to a report by the Banque de France, or 450,000 by 2000 according to a more optimistic estimate by the OFCE (*Le Monde*, 22/1/98).

[36] A majority of workers (54 per cent), however, apparently wishes for significant wage increases even if they were to imperil the 35 hours, as against one third which opts for self-restraint in order to contribute to the success of the 35 hours (BVA Poll, cited by B. Mery and A. Monnot, *Le Monde*, 6/26/98). Of all the Unions, only the CFDT appears intentioned to trade wage increases for shorter hours. In the early summer, wage centred labour conflicts were increasing. By the fall, 51 per cent of the French did not believe shortening the work week would create jobs, 48 per cent of wage earners supported the 35 hours only without wage cuts against 34 per cent who supported them even with cuts, and 4 per cent supported them only if they came with wage cuts (CSA Poll, Oct. 1988, *Le Monde*, 12/02/98).

[37] Trust in business organizations and unions went down by 5 and 9 points respectively: 58 per cent of the French distrusted business organizations and 44 per cent distrusted the unions. By contrast trust in government went up from 49 to 52 per cent (*Le Monde*, dossiers, 'Les 35 heures', 12/02/98).

[38] Lebaube, A., 'Le piège des 35 heures refermé', *Le Monde*, 10/17/97, and 12/02/98.

[39] The promise to give power back to the citizens, was a key – although often obscured by nationalization – aspect of Mitterrand's 1981 victory, and more broadly, of the PS's renaissance

Thus, for example, the relatively smooth integration of the Greens in the government, while eased by Jospin's understanding of coalition politics, is largely a byproduct of the substantial overlapping – in terms of organizational styles, culture, policies and electorate – between these two formations. Similarly, the appeal of Jospin's 'method' is certainly rooted in Jospin's personal quality, but the search for a distinctive governmental practice is a longstanding theme of the French left. French Socialists have always defined themselves vis-à-vis the management of power, as much as that of the economy, and this may well turn out to be the major achievement of the Jospin government (Bergounioux and Grunberg, 1992).

At the same time, the current left government has displayed remarkable determination in pursuing traditional left issues, from job creation to redistribution, which have never been the number one concern and guiding principle of left governments in France. Still, the instruments through which Jospin is pursuing this 'new' agenda are typical of the French left: top down legislation, and state centred programmes combined with some doses of Keynesianism. As with other universal rights, so it seems, the French left is not yet willing to trust the market with providing jobs. Whether the state can command the solidarity its reforms presuppose and seek to expand, of course, remains to be seen.

Discussion and Conclusion

This article has shown that in terms of constituency, programme and governmental record, there is still something left to the French Socialists. The source of this unexpected resilience is partly the continued centrality of the traditional distributive concerns and issues of the left, and the 'state's' ability to deliver in these areas. However, in large measure it also stems from a relatively ignored reservoir of left identity and policies: the 'left's' historical commitment to political democracy and equality. In the French Socialist party, the political roots of left identity have been stronger than the economic ones. Jean Jaurès, and to a lesser extent, Léon Blum are revered more for their stand on democracy, as exemplified by the Dreyfus Affair and the Riom trial, than for their stand on social and economic issues. Even when in power, French socialism has never been particularly successful or rigorous in its pursuit of traditional left-wing policies: Mitterrand's two terms barely altered 'France's' fiscal and welfare policies and industrial relations. By contrast, the French Socialists have developed a discourse and an organization which have been extremely adept at absorbing and voicing demands for a more universal treatment and equal access to power, across sites, gender and generations, and at incorporating the groups which have raised these

---

in the 1970s. For an analysis of what the Socialists were up against, see Berger (1979); for an analysis of why they were so successful in responding to these challenges, see Sferza (1996).

themes.[40] The full turn to an institutional strategy of the French feminists, as illustrated by the Gender Parity Movement, and the overlapping of 'Socialists' and Greens illustrates these points well (Jenson and Sineau, 1995). This association with democracy is the most persistent source of the Socialists' long term resilience. The Jospin government is building on this political strand of the left, but owes some of its unexpected success to its pursuit of the left's most traditional, yet, in France, less prominent, economic strand.

The 'PS's' achievements raise the interesting question of whether left parties may be facing an opportunity to recombine their genetic material in similar ways. Historically, national lefts have been primarily associated with one or the other of the two traditions of economic or political equality, depending on the relative salience of political and economic conflicts during the critical juncture of party formation and early development. These early patterns have thus far proven to be stable and enduring, as evidenced by the relative imperviousness of the 'workers'' parties to democracy and power-related issues. By contrast, 'citizens'' parties have been less adept at dealing with traditional employment and distributive issues.

There is some evidence, across time and countries, that the graft between the two strands can 'take'. Some of the most successful left parties, notably the Swedish Social Democrats, owe their success to their ability to be both a citizens' and a workers' party. Their capacity to do so, however, is fraying. In the past, citizens' parties which have sought to become more like workers' parties have not been very successful. These days, the most sought after transformation is in the opposite direction, but this does not make it necessarily easier. For unadulterated workers' parties, credibility on democratic issues is likely to entail major changes in discourse and organization. Privileged and nearly exclusive alliances might have to go, a process that, as shown by British Labour, may take quite some time. What is more, new alliances will have to be constructed. This is not going to be an easy task anywhere, since political democratic issues have a more shifting constituency than class ones. An effective and charismatic leadership may act as a substitute for more institutional societal linkages, but not indefinitely. In some countries, furthermore, these issues may have been captured by a different party, either a Liberal, or more likely in these days, a New Politics one. Even under the best circumstances, there are inherent tensions between the universalist and inclusive inspiration of the left and its egalitarian commitment. The current debates on immigration and citizenship illustrate this point. In sum, new citizens' parties like the old ones, are likely to be at constant risk of being destabilized, either by sectoralism or 'catch-allism'.

The recent trajectories of the French and British lefts in recent years are cases in point of how this grafting is working, or not working, in the real world. Both

---

[40] On the relationship between the socialists and the women movement, see Jenson and Sineau (1995) and Mazur (1995); on the increased presence of women in the legislature, primarily in the Green and Socialist parties, and in the government, see Gaspard (1997).

formations, albeit to different degrees and in different directions, appear to be breaking with their respective pasts. While, as described above, the French Socialists – historically a citizens' party which has fared much better on democracy than on economic and social issues – have focused on traditional economic issues and policies, the British left – an unadulterated workers' party which has long been a paragon of such a focus – has shifted its emphasis towards democratic power reforms. In both cases, these shifts paid off electorally, as both Blair and Jospin remained quite popular for some time after their victories. Yet, whether the graft has taken remains to be seen.

As a citizens' party the PS has long had an ideological and organizational repertoire that can accommodate old and new quality of life concerns. Even the Green party poses a small threat to the Socialists' strong position on democracy related issues: in terms of agendas, discourse, voters, organizational styles and tolerance for street politics, the overlap between the socialist and the 'New Politics' is much more pronounced in France than in many other European countries. Still, past attempts by citizens' parties, including the PS, to pursue social and economic goals associated with workers' parties have consistently failed for lack of domestic institutional support, and the type of policy instruments chosen by Jospin largely reflects these failures. A similar fate may well await recent reforms aimed at job creation, and notably the 35-hour work week.

When we look at the seemingly unshakable popularity of the British Labour government since its return to power, it would seem that the shift from a workers' to a citizens' party is both feasible and highly rewarding. Although it has taken 'New' Labour a long time to rebuild its internal organization and its discourse along more universalist lines, much of this transformation, it would seem, can be carried out by leadership alone. Further, in a country where citizens are still subjects, and where voting was recently, if briefly, taxed, Labour's promise to create a 'radical democracy' entails quite substantial changes. From the reform of the House of Lords to a substantial power devolution to Scotland and Wales that may effectively end the United Kingdom, these are hardly 'catch-all' measures. Still, even a citizens' party needs to reach out to society other than through its leader, and the capacity of Labour to do so remains untested. Whereas the old is mostly gone, the new is not yet in place, and is meeting with some resistance; whatever the final mixture of old and new will be, their coexistence is bound to create tensions in the Labour Party. Finally, as a new citizens' party, New Labour is perhaps even more at risk than its older counterparts of losing sight of the egalitarian drive, which is the other side of the left's democratic mission.

In sum, these attempts to bring together separate left traditions may not succeed. But then, looking back, the left has never really had full solutions to its quests, nor has it been always successful in pursuing them. In trying to figure out whether it has a future, we should not be blinded by a somewhat nostalgic, and misleadingly optimistic, picture of its past.

References

Bell, D.S. and Criddle, B. (1984), *The French Socialist Party*, Oxford University Press, New York.

Berger, S. (1979), 'Politics and Anti-Politics in Western Europe in the Seventies', in *Daedalus*, Vol. 108(1), pp. 27–48.

Bergounioux, A. and Grunberg, G. (1992), *Le long remords du pouvoir*, Fayard, Paris.

Boix, C. (1998), *Political Parties, Growth and Equality*, Cambridge University Press, Cambridge.

Boy, D. and Mayer, N. (eds.) (1997), *L'électeur a ses raisons*, Presses de la Fondation Nationale de Sciences Politiques, Paris.

Chiche, J. and Dupoirier, E. (1996), 'Echelle gauche-droite et choix politiques', in E. Dupoirier and J.-L. Parodi (eds.), *Les indicateurs socio-politiques aujourd'hui*, L'Harmattan, Paris.

Clayton, R. and Pontusson, J. (1998), 'Welfare State Retrenchment Revisited: Entitlement Cuts, Public Sector Restructuring, and Inegalitarian Trends in Advanced Capitalist Societies', *World Politics*, Vol. 51(1), pp. 67–98.

Cole, A. (1999), 'French Socialists in Office: Lessons from Mitterrand and Jospin', *Modern & Contemporary France*, Vol. 7(1), pp. 71–88.

Daley, A. (ed.) (1996), *The Mitterrand Era*, Macmillan, London.

Dalton, R. (1999), 'Germany's Vote for a "New Middle"', *Current History*, Vol. 98(627), pp. 176–9.

Dupoirier, E. and Parodi, J.-L. (eds.) (1996), *Les indicateurs socio-politiques aujourd'hui*, L'Harmattan, Paris.

Garrett, G. (1998), *Partisan Politics in the Global Economy*, Cambridge University Press, New York.

Gaspard, F. (1997), 'Les Françaises en politique au lendemain des élections législatives de 1997', *French Politics and Society*, Vol. 15(4), pp. 71–85.

Ireland, P. (1996), 'Race, Immigration and the Politics of Hate', in A. Daley, *The Mitterrand Era*, Macmillan, London.

Jaffré, J. and Muxel, A. (1997), 'Les repères politiques', in Boy, D. and Mayer, N. (eds.), *L'electeur a ses raisons*, Presses de la Fondation Française des Sciences Politiques, Paris.

Jenson, J. and Sineau, M. (1995), *Mitterrand et les Francaises: un rendez-vous manque*, Fondation Nationale des Sciences Politiques, Presse de SC.PO, Paris.

Kitschelt, H. (1994), *The Recent Transformation of European Social Democracy*, Cambridge University Press, New York.

Levy, J. (1998), 'France in a Globalizing Economy: The Shifting Logic of the Welfare State', Paper presented at the Center for European Studies, Harvard University, 11/23/98.

Mazur, A. (1995), *Gender Bias and the State: Symbolic Reform at Work in Fifth Republic France*, Pittsburgh University Press, Pittsburgh.

Ross, G. (1997), 'Jospin So Far', in *French Politics and Society*, Vol. 15(3), pp. 9–20.

Ross, G., Hoffmann, S. and Malzacher, S. (eds.) (1987), *The Mitterrand Experiment*, Oxford University Press, New York.

Sassoon, D. (1996), *One Hundred Years of Socialism: The West European Left in the Twentieth Century*, I.B. Tauris, London.

Sferza, S. (1996), 'The Shifting Advantages of Organizational Formats: Factionalism and the French Socialist Party', in A. Daley, *The Mitterrand Era*, Macmillan, London.

Weil, P. (1995), *La France et ses etrangers: L'aventure d'une politique de l'immigration de 1938 a nos jours*, Gallimard, Paris.

PART III

CULTURE, IDEAS AND POLITICAL SPACE – WHERE DOES THE THIRD WAY COME FROM AND WHERE WILL IT GO?

Chapter 6

Still a Third Way, or, At Least Any Alternatives to World Capitalism?
Some Remarks on the Fundamental Split Between the Intellectual Critique of Capitalism and Real Political Powers

Michael Th. Greven

The Cold War seemed to split the political world into two competing systems of *actually existing socialism* in the Soviet way, and *actually existing democracy* in the western capitalist way, yet a Third Way was nevertheless always present. This Third Way was framed as an alternative to both dictatorial state socialism and free market capitalism – ergo, by its very definition it appeared to present some alternative. Historically and in the present, various groups and individuals have frequently employed the connotation of this concept.[1] The equal optimization of two political and social principles form its normative core: on the one hand, it connotes a belief in at least as much political and individual freedom as has already been guaranteed by western liberal democracies; on the other hand, it advocates the maximum possible distribution of equality and justice, usually aimed at a strategy involving a mixed economy and an interventionist welfare state. However, for as long as this Third Way tradition has existed, doubts about its viability have been expressed. The strongest critiques perceive equality and freedom as contradictory aims in a kind of zero-sum-game[2] – one triumphs at the expense of the other.[3]

In practical political life – following the split of the formerly more or less

---

[1] The concept 'Third Way' during the 20th century also has been used by liberal and pro-capitalist authors, most prominently by Franz Oppenheimer (1932), Wilhelm Röpke (1942) and Alexander Rüstow (1949); this tradition of inner-liberal revisionism will be excluded in this article, which further on refers only to left traditions of the concept.

[2] For Germans most authoritatively Johann Wolfgang Goethe: 'Wer Gleichheit und Freiheit zusammen verspricht, ist ein Phantast oder Charlatan', quoted by Franz Oppenheimer (1938), who in his 'scientific last will and testament' promised exactly to have 'finally' proven the opposite.

[3] See for a recent well-elaborated version of this argument Kersting (2000).

unified working class in the wake of World War I and the Bolshevik revolution in Russia – this Third Way was very influential on the programmes and policies of the Social Democrats. The history of welfare state policy making in western democracies shows the extent to which socio-economic systems and governmental policies have substantially driven these societies away from being pure capitalist market societies. Such alterations suggest that Social Democrats have been politically successful in implementing at least bits and pieces of their programme. The clear categorical dichotomy between capitalism 'here' and socialism 'there' was challenged by political societies such as the Swedish *folkethejm* that could not be categorized in this crude dichotomous manner. Thus, Social Democrats successfully claimed to be the actually existing Third Way in practice, convincing many including some of its neoliberal critics.

The success of this 'revision' of Social Democracy was quickly faced by a revisionist critique. For the most part, this critique has been an *intellectual* endeavour, lacking its own organizational backbone and at times manifest as some intra-party minority opposition.[4] The competition for who 'truly' represented or represents the Third Way continues to rage between the political leadership of various Social Democratic parties, and various 'socialist' intellectuals. To some extent, this dispute reflects the ubiquitous tension between a genuine working class labour movement – or at the very least, politicians with genuine working class backgrounds – on the one hand, and idealistic academics and intellectuals on the other.[5] Given that Soviet style anti-capitalism and its hegemonic strategy towards the so-called 'Third World' has finally disappeared, and Red China has developed a new mixture of authoritarian rule and capitalist economic strategy, Third Way claims seem lost. Neither some powerful democratic alternative to a Marxist-Leninist or Maoist strategy of anti-capitalist power politics, nor some socialist economic alternative to the excesses of global capitalism seem realistic alternatives given the contemporary socio-political landscape.

But, nevertheless, the political split between some intellectuals and the Social Democrats – who governed most West European societies in the late 1990s – persists. Increasingly, intellectuals and governing Social Democrats fundamentally disagree over what kind of government constitutes the so-called Third Way. While the big European Social Democratic Parties, especially when they are or were in power, still claim to represent the Third Way,[6] many intellectual critics throughout

---

[4] Radhika Desai, in her convincing study 'Intellectuals and Socialism' (1994), argues, that for a relevant period in British politics, a group of such intellectuals and their influence had been critical for the Labour Party.

[5] For the somewhat paradigmatic German case see Auernheimer (1985).

[6] Explicitly this has been done in the 'Blair-Schröder paper'; but also internationally recognized authors like Anthony Giddens understand their version of the Third Way (1998) more or less as an intellectual support and programme for the Labour Government.

Europe and Britain denounce this claim.[7] For the most part, Social Democratic governments in practice, such as Blair's in Great Britain, Jospin's in France, and/or Schröder's in Germany have already shifted towards the neoliberal programme to such an extent that many remaining differences between these programmes are irrelevant. In fact, this debate is nothing but a weak continuation of the political discourse and social protest against the victorious capitalist system that first arose in the early nineteenth century. With the remarkable exception of the United States, these anti-capitalist forces remained embedded for a century in powerful working class movements, whose power was manifest in their parties and trade unions. These forces went on to gain political power over almost half of the world's population for a period of seventy years, in the *Imperium Sovietcum* and later in Mao's Red China and a few satellite states and neighbours.

However, outside of Fidel's Cuba and a few other remote hangers on, the anti-capitalist forces of today have faded into history. Ergo, the historical burden of such a project falls back to where it all began in the early nineteenth century; on the weak shoulders of intellectuals and their notorious incapacity to organize political influence and governmental power. Because such anti-capitalist movements no longer have class-based labour movements to back them, this critical project often turns into an intellectual exercise that increasingly becomes an integral part of the cultural and liberal *discourse* of modern pluralist societies, rather than real political challenges manifest inside or outside political parties and other mass organizations. So-called 'left' critiques of recent capitalist developments, especially those chattering around popular tropes of 'globalization' in global conferences, are at times extremely successful authors of international bestsellers and their 'critique' is effectively disseminated by the mass media throughout the intellectual world. No talk show on the problematic aspects of 'globalization' would be without these left-wing media stars, making these prominent critics of 'globalization' into global players themselves.

The contemporary status of left critiques and what has come to be referred to as the Third Way demands a re-evaluation of the basic philosophy of anti-capitalism by scholars and intellectuals. Are the reasons for such an opposition still justified? Are the analytical and theoretical premises of their conception of the history and nature of capitalism still valid? Does a practical alternative in the foreseeable future exist? How is the practical relationship between such an intellectual opposition and the real political powers of the social democratic parties? The discussion presented here is not the place to argue in detail or give empirical evidence with respect to these aforementioned questions; however, some

---

[7] For a German version of this denouncement see for example Joachim Hirsch (1998) or most of the contributions to his *Festschrift* (Görg and Roth, 1998); the most popular French author to represent this critique of the actual social democratic policies is nota bene Pierre Bourdieu (1998); for Great Britain see for example the writings of Bob Jessop (1998).

brief comments are in order.

Reflecting on what the anti-capitalist New Left or Third Way has become over the years has been the domain of intellectuals, arguing the relevance, downfall or solvency of these forces in hundreds of pamphlets, articles and books. The political consequences of this intellectual adventure have been to produce new intellectual opponents to capitalism, which over years of education have become either frustrated scholars (and professionally established) or incurable dogmatics. The ongoing success of mobilizing students and younger academics for some kind of anti-capitalist project in the guise of more traditional critical elements (classical anarchist, Marxist-Leninist, Trotskyite, Maoist, et cetera) or more 1968-like style (neoanarchist, feminist, situationalist, et cetera) seems to have a common ground. These groups and ideological streams differ from each other as much as *individuation* would assume in post-modern societies. However, what they all have in common is their impertinent opposition against the capitalist reality of the states in which they live. But, this raises a further point: is such opposition completely justified?

On the one hand, the anti-capitalist critique posed by intellectuals seems both unrealistic and beyond social justification given the status of victorious capitalist systems. The second half of the last century witnessed not only progress and wealth among welfare state capitalist projects – especially when compared to *actually existing socialist societies* – but also the almost total acceptance of this system by their populations, including endorsements by the remains of the working class. Nonetheless, on the other hand capitalism still appears to be the key factor of recently growing inequalities in living standards within these wealthy societies. Obviously, to be poor in a western OECD society does not usually lead to starvation and the complete deprivation of welfare support. Yet even in these societies, social and/or ethnic background is still an important condition that influences the educational and career options for youths. Moreover, for many young people in these capitalist welfare state societies, becoming a wealthy successful member of such a society remains nothing but hollow ideology.

When one adopts a more global perspective, one comes to the realization that the kind of society developed in the capitalist north cannot act as a template for the rest of the world. The dependence on the exploitation of limited natural resources extracted globally from hinterlands, leading to major waste and pollution makes such a model undesirable and impossible for the rest of global civilization. Thus, world capitalism, seen as an ideological development programme with the shining examples of successful OECD nations is nothing but an illusion for the people of the poor south. They cannot and never will *in toto* achieve what the better off segments of western populations have achieved in this historical moment; not in terms of energy, or protein, or even sheer per capita water consumption.

While well known but often suppressed knowledge about the negative consequences of the capitalist economy can be easily explained, it is not as easy to explain why anti-capitalist critiques brought about by younger and more ethically responsible people often merge with theories and political programmes that – in my eyes – have long since proven to present no practical answer to the global mobilization of capitalism. Ergo, given the justification for fundamental critiques of capitalism in its apparent destructive or at least ambivalent mode of development, the answer to the second aforementioned question is by no means evident. Surely contributions to the field of *cultural studies* explore in some detail theories of present day capitalism.[8] Such discussions explain in many different ways capitalism's genealogy, all its negative internal and external, social, economic, political, and psychological effects, often drawing all kinds of scenarios about its further development. However, none of these theories and approaches matches their theoretical critiques with their practical implications. When Marx, Lenin, and Luxemburg, and even first generation revisionist critiques of capitalism from Bernstein and Hilferding formulated their 'theories', such critiques were written as guidelines for revolutionary practice of certain collective actors – be they parties, trade unions, or spontaneous upheavals of the masses.. On the other hand, political opposition in our days – that is, critical theory of any kind – in practice addresses no relevant political actor(s). Other than the mobilization of some students, recent critiques lack substantial hints as to whom such critiques would at least potentially mobilize as practical challenges to the present state of affairs. When Marx claimed that (his) 'Scientific Socialism' would be *the* valid theoretical critique of capitalism, he expected to be proved correct by the revolutionary mass movement carried by the working class. He and other revolutionary intellectuals mentioned above despised academic consent and never searched for it. The proof of their 'theoretical' critique had to be found in political practice. After the Second World War very few authors continued to criticize capitalism in the ways authors had previously. Typically, these post-1945 authors were part of anti-colonial movements, such as the most famous among them: Franz Fanon. As a representative of a more academic opposition, the late Herbert Marcuse in the sixties and seventies really seemed to believe in the existence of a practical revolutionary perspective for various new social movements, and thus, shared their political illusions instead of criticizing them.

Since the withering away of Soviet-like communism, or its western 'Eurocommunist' variants – aside from these almost exotic outsiders in the late twentieth century – no critical intellectual approach to capitalism that expresses a potentially revolutionary u-turn in capitalist development has existed. In this respect, critical theory is no longer a practical or political endeavour, making the decision by academic booksellers and publishing companies to classify most

---

[8] Just thirty years ago – in a more optimistic period of fundamental critique of capitalism – the topic has been 'late capitalism' or at least the 'crisis of capitalism', what has not changed is the fundamental disagreement with the given reality of world capitalism in this type of literature.

critical scholarship under the heading of *cultural studies* not at all puzzling.

Taking this situation into account in practical and political terms, the critique of capitalism in practice is relegated with those reformist and gradual approaches represented today by the big Social Democratic parties and their affiliated organizations such as trade unions. Since more radical academic critiques of their political programmes and policies by intellectuals quite often implicitly refer to a revolutionary perspective (which does not really exist), its practical implications are close to zero. And, it is not at all surprising that the governing Social Democratic leaders of Great Britain, France and Germany, given the electoral and public support they enjoy for their policies, often ignore their critical commentators from the academic world. On the other hand, and this is the remaining valid element in Marxians' claim of practical truth – critical intellectuals have to face the truth: whatever they hold as true in their radical critique of capitalism today is only accepted by politically irrelevant minorities of the democratic electorates. The so-called masses may always be critical towards many aspects of their existing societies and those politicians, who only gradually tend to correct and compensate certain negative effects of capitalism through political intervention, but almost nothing in the popular mass conscience reflects the radical approaches of the academic critique. This critique is written in an *iron cage* and becomes relevant only beyond it in the cultural and educational sphere.

Against this very general judgement it may be argued that new social movements and more recently so-called Non-Governmental Organizations (NGOs), on national as well as on transnational and international levels *de facto* represent the kind of collective actor who puts anti-capitalist theories into an equivalent political practice. Much emphasis in intellectual and scholarly writings in recent years has been intended to show that certain new social movements and/or NGOs practically represent the fundamental dissent against the capitalist world system that various theories pretend to have already theoretically grounded. But this claim easily proves false when confronted with a more empirically informed picture of most of these informal or non-governmental actors.[9] For the most part, these collective actors appear – especially when compared with the systematic and inclusive perspective of critical theories – to be oriented at only single issues.[10] These movements and NGOs have developed strategies of action

---

[9] See for a recent and well informed critique of this NGO-emphasis Ulrich Brand et al. (2000).

[10] The 'Charta 2000' by the French initiative 'Raison d'Agir', inspired by Pierre Bourdieu, recently formulated again such a theoretically framed perspective of bringing the whole pluralistic universe of new social movements, informal groups and dissenting individuals together for forming *one* common 'force mobilisante' against world capitalism and its neoliberalist company; the former empirically grounded sociologist Bourdieu ought to have known better why this will remain just another powerless playground for the intellectual

that in most cases combine public protest with more silent professional cooperation with governments and international organizations, but are largely restricted to single issues in their focus. The most famous examples of such actors are Amnesty International, Greenpeace, and Medico International. Some single issue strategies have been very successful, such as the campaign of the ICBL that finally led to the international ban on landmines in the so-called Ottawa Convention of 1997. This example suggests that combining effectual agenda setting, the mobilization of an international public and wide-ranging coalition building can lead to overthrowing the resistance of mighty governments. But if we talk about a fundamental alternative and opposition against world capitalism, even those groups who were successful with their protest against the WTO in Seattle and who target international finance capital and its representatives, are far away from any theoretically grounded or at least ideologically coherent anti-capitalist programme and practice. If regulating international financial transactions ever becomes a reality in the future, exactly those types of intergovernmental regimes and institutions at which various informal actors and groups have directed much protest and action will no doubt carry it out.[11]

It seems presently that nobody is imaginative enough to see in these punctual protests carried out by NGOs and other alliances, the equivalent to a revolutionary movement on a global level.[12] In short, it seems impossible to imagine a real power strategy that would seriously challenge further capitalist development. If something actually challenges the future of capitalism in our days, it will more than likely not be some collective political actor or coalition that is framed in the familiar historical pattern of the 'revolutionary subject' – i.e. the (international) proletariat. It seems that theories, which either since the nineteenth century predicted some looming crisis or breakdown of capitalism have been as wrong as theories of revolution against the capitalist order that owe their construction to the experience of the French Revolution in 1789. The revolutions of czarist Russia in February to October 1917 could to some extent follow that classical pattern, since both the social and institutional conditions in Russia during that period were similar to the conditions in revolutionary France. It certainly shares more with this experience than the experience of contemporary modern mass democracies and interdependent society. Today, such a dramatic change of social power and economic conditions by revolutionary action plus the necessary public support for such change is no longer conceivable, not to mention the extent to which such

---

opposition. For more information see <www.raisons.org>.
[11] See for an historical overview and some optimistic proposals Louis W. Pauly (1997).
[12] To escape this consequence even such post-modern deconstructivist pacemakers like Jacques Derrida sometimes – strangely enough – retire to not less but an explicit 'messianic eschatology' of the 'in future coming revolution', voluntaristically grounded in nothing else but the *confessio*: '...*it doesn't work differently*' (Derrida, 1995, p. 100).

revolutionary action depends on the sovereignty of separated nation-states that has also passed away. The integration of the global capitalist economy that has contributed greatly to this denationalization has also thrown the idea of national revolution – regardless of aims – into the garbage can of history. And against the international capitalist economy or international regimes, public protest is possible and may have in some cases measurable success; but nobody can overthrow international capitalism and international regimes by some kind of transnational revolutionary action. As every historical system has changed over time, so too the present form of capitalism may one day no longer exist. Today, contrary to what Francis Fukuyama (1992) suggested in his international bestseller, we are not experiencing some contemporary version of eschatology or the 'end of history'. Whether those who presently advocate some Third Way will at this end of capitalism be able to take some credit for its downfall is questionable. It seems as if future change on this level no longer results from intentional political action, be it revolutionary or revisionist. Furthermore, assuming that capitalism reconfigures itself internally as much as it has over the last centuries, it may also turn out that capitalism is far away from the limits of its own potential development. This would mean that ever since Marx and his fellow critics of capitalism and dissenting thought we have been subjected to an intellectual tradition and attitude of *revolutionary impatience*[13] that has seduced intellectuals time and again into a kind of wishful thinking that assumes the end of capitalism is already on the agenda.

In our context two consequences seem to follow from such a brief and sketchy evaluation of capitalism's present situation. First and foremost, because a direct theoretically designed anti-capitalist political strategy does not have any relevant counterpart in practice, the necessary and permanent struggle against the anti-human and anti-social effects of this kind of economic system has to be and remain internally reformist. In the absence of a practical anti-capitalist strategy a fundamental critique of reformism that is implicitly grounded on such a fictional alternative is unjustified and contradicts the ethical maxim: *nemo posse nemo posse obligatur*. This is especially relevant in the field of academic education, where younger students ought not to be seduced into believing altogether unrealistic judgements. However, continuing to argue for the immanence of political interventionism, aiming only at compensating for the negative consequences of the capitalist economy seems to entail just such a project. Still, the 'Third Way' comes very close to such an ethical *sacrificus intellectus* since it suggests more radical alternatives in practice than are actually possible in the present stage of history.

---

[13] The term 'late capitalism' ('Spätkapitalismus'), indicating the final stage of its development, has been coined not in the late sixties of the 19th century, but already by Werner Sombart at the end of the 18th century.

Secondly, the intellectual critique of capitalism and its consequences must not stop only because a practical alternative in a revolutionary sense seems impossible. On the contrary, intellectual critique becomes even practically more relevant when it is based on a valid and empirically grounded analysis of the present situation, in contrast to the kind of wishful thinking briefly mentioned above. If this analysis leads to the consequence that neither Second nor Third Ways of anti-capitalist strategies in the traditional and hitherto discussed manner are practically feasible or ethically recommendable, than this intellectual opposition must still not merely affirm the bad realities of capitalism or end up in some form of *quietism*. Critique and intellectual dissent can continue to be as radical as the negative and unjust effects of capitalism demand, fighting for recognized global normative standards like human rights and principles of democracy as much as they do today in many sectors of western societies and the world as a whole. Those who might argue that both human rights and democracy form only bare and abstract minimal standards of evaluation and critique of present day societies and politics should nevertheless accept, that demanding more and going further in programmes of global political development, can under no circumstances justify any violation of these minimal standards. Because at least majority support for political regimes and proposed programmes is a necessary minimal standard following from both principles, many intellectual critics during the last century as well as in this new century continually confront the actual danger of ignoring these principles for the sake of a theoretically grounded *blueprint* of an imagined future. To cope with this temptation in a democratic manner and simultaneously remain a non-affirmative critical intellectual in the present capitalist world order should render intellectuals more careful with easy visions of Third or whatsoever numbered new ways to an old and everlasting dream of human beings.

References

Auernheimer, G. (1985), *'Genosse Herr Doktor': Zur Rolle von Akademikern in der deutschen Sozialdemokratie 1890 bis 1933*, Focus, Giessen.
Bourdieu, P. (1998), *Gegenfeuer: Wortmeldungen im Dienste des Widerstandes gegen die neoliberale Invasion*, Universitätsverlag, Konstanz.
Brand, U. et al. (2000), *Global Governance*, Westfälisches Dampfboot, Münster.
Derrida, J. (1995), *Marx' Gespenster. Der verschuldete Staat, die Trauerarbeit und die neue Internationale*, Fischer, Frankfurt am Main.
Desai, R. (1994), *Intellectuals and Socialism. 'Social Democrats' and the Labour Party*, Lawrence & Wishart, London.
Fukuyama, F. (1992), *The End of History and the Last Man*, Free Press, Toronto.
Giddens, A. (1998), *The Third Way. The Renewal of Social Democracy*, Polity Press, Cambridge.
Görg, Ch. and Roth, R. (eds.) (1998), *Kein Staat zu machen*, Westfälisches Dampfboot, Münster.

Hirsch, J. (1998), *Vom Sicherheitsstaat zum nationalen Wettbewerbsstaat*, ID-Verlag, Berlin.

Jessop, B. (1998), 'Die Erfahrungen mit New Labour – Eine Politik des Postfordismus', in Ch. Görg and R. Roth (eds.), *Kein Staat zu machen*, Westfälisches Dampfboot, Münster, pp. 71–94.

Kersting, W. (2000), *Theorien der sozialen Gerechtigkeit*, J.B. Metzler, Stuttgart/Weimar.

Oppenheimer, F. (1932), *Weder Kapitalismus noch Kommunismus. Der Dritte Weg*, Fischer, Jena.

Oppenheimer, F. (1938), *Das Kapital*, A.W. Sijthoff's Uitgeversmaatschappij N.V., Leiden.

Pauly, L.W. (1997), *Who elected the Bankers? Surveillance and Control in the World Economy*, Cornell UP, Ithaca/London.

Röpke, W. (1942), *Die Gesellschaftskrisis der Gegenwart*, Eugen Rentsch Verlag, Erlenbach-Zürich.

Rüstow, A. (1949), 'Zwischen Kapitalismus und Kommunismus', *ORDO*, Bd. 2, Helmut Küpper Verlag, Godesberg.

Chapter 7

From the 'Anti-Revisionist Left' to the 'New Centre': Reflections on the Ancestry of 'Modernized' Social Democracy

Frank Unger

More than 30 years ago, a new generation of young Europeans who were born and raised in the forties and fifties shocked their elders by fervently demonstrating against the U.S. war in Indochina and pursuing an iconoclastic rebellion against the decorous boringness of their post-World War II welfare state cultures together with their authoritarian-elitist systems of higher education. Astonishingly similar events took place in many European countries, such as France, West Germany, the United Kingdom, Holland, Italy, and not to be forgotten, in Czechoslovakia, where the rebellion was directed against the communist variety of post-World War II authoritarianism. As 1968 happened to be the year of the most spectacular events – with the May events in France being the most noteworthy – the entire cohort became associated with it, earning themselves the ambiguous denomination '68ers'.

In the Federal Republic of Germany, the rebellion was perhaps the widest in scope and the deepest in effect. Although initiated at the time by a minority, it certainly affected over time the ways in which the entire generation of younger Germans began to look at the world. It definitely changed the hierarchy of values for the generations who came after them: from their attitudes towards authority, to their work ethics, to the style they brought up their children, and even the way they perceived other cultures.[1] Over the years, the ambiguity in the meaning of 68 faded; the 68ers came to be seen (and saw themselves, of course!) as the best and brightest of the postwar generations, instrumental in finally transforming West

---

[1] Daniel J. Goldhagen, for instance, believes that the 'generational replacement' in the Federal Republic has produced 'a decline and a fundamental change in the character of antisemitism' (Goldhagen, 1997, p. 483).

Germany into a truly modern and democratic post-fascist polity. Due to their pressure from below, many West German universities were substantially reformed, granting co-determination to lower status faculty, students, and in some cases even secretaries and maintenance workers.

In the late seventies, some of the most radical activists – many of them organized in self-declared 'Communist Leagues' and similarly named outfits – decided they wanted to give up the 'Leninist' revolutionary fight and partake in regular parliamentary politics with their own party. Realizing the increasingly bipartisan appeal of environmentalism, they decided to call it the Green Party, assuming that environmental issues were the most promising causes by which to win mass support for anti-capitalist policies. The more 'realist' or those with social democratic family backgrounds joined the Social Democratic Party of Germany (SPD), conventionally as Young Socialists (*Jungsozialisten*, the official SPD-organization for party members under 35). Many of them saw themselves as being on the left of 'really existing socialism'! In the theoretical battles with their peers, most of them (like the current German chancellor, Gerhard Schröder) wore the badge of 'anti-revisionism', by which they meant they were part of the 'revolutionary left', but strictly opposed to Eastern European socialism, whose leaders in their view were 'revisionists' because they had deviated from the true Marxist path towards revolutionary transition to socialism, which, among other things, would have to include the abolition of money, a political system of council democracy and the withering away of the state!

Once in federal and regional parliaments, the young anti-revisionists no longer pushed their 'Maoism Lite'. But their cohort soon made themselves heard as outspoken critics and challengers of Chancellor Helmut Schmidt. In accordance with certain shifts in public opinion at the time, they succeeded in undermining Schmidt's position as chancellor and party leader, painting him as, among other things, a 'cold warrior' and a 'technocrat'. But then it was not they who reaped the immediate benefits from this leftward shift within the SPD. The conservatives under the leadership of Christian Democrat Helmut Kohl and Free Democrat Dietrich Genscher rose to the occasion, and – by taking advantage of the internal strife within the left camp – engineered a parliamentary turn to the right in the country.

The eighties, shaped by consecutive chancellorships of Helmut Kohl together with his congenial foreign policy collaborator Genscher, soon came to be known as 'the conservative decade'. The new CDU/FDP regime was sold to the public as a deliberate counter project to the 'excessively' liberal-reformist seventies – an intellectual (spiritual) moral turnabout. In the freshly reformed universities, the old hierarchies were quickly restored; student representatives, junior professors and other low-ranking instructors were put in their place again. But the turnabout was intended to go even further and deeper: The entire postwar regime with its philosophies of government moderated class compromise and relative egalitarianism came under fire now. The welfare state was suddenly presented as 'too expensive', and West German work laws that provided a certain amount of job security for full-time personnel were attacked for putting West German employers at a competitive disadvantage in the global economy. A new crop of 'neoconservative' Zeitgeist-shapers presented money making and pursuing a career as the new objectives for an increasingly 'realistic' and 'materialistic' younger generation.

In real politics, profitable public companies and other public assets were prepared for sale to private investors; cultural institutions and universities were downsized and/or stripped of funds, which rendered them dependent on additional funds to be solicited from foundations or the private sector. The declared objective was to increase their 'efficiency', but to suggest that the intention to impose some control over system-critical research agendas was also at work here could hardly be denounced as a nasty insinuation. The 'deregulation' philosophy – meant to create an optimal climate for the innovative endeavours of imaginative entrepreneurs – began to replace the 'security and prosperity' philosophy – meant to preserve the approval of the masses for the 'social market economy' – as the government's central domestic policy objective, if not immediately in full practice, then at least in relentless public agitation (Hirsch and Roth, 1986).

Meanwhile, the Greens established themselves as a serious parliamentary party and soon challenged the Free Democrats for the status of the 'third force' in the country. Likewise, 68ers continued to define the agenda of the SPD as the main opposition party; they, slowly but surely, became the heart and soul of the party. Encouraged by the broad popular support which the peace movement had enjoyed during the early eighties in its fight against the stationing of new US nuclear missiles on West German territory and by the widespread popularity of anti-nuclear energy positions, younger social democrats introduced anti-nuclear environmentalism and opposition to American Cold War strategies to the mainstream of the party.[2] In the wake of it, self-declared Marxist or radical democratic groupings and individuals gained a certain nominal influence in some local and regional party organizations. But the radicalism had to be 'condensed' in order to be feasible in everyday politics and reflect the general attitudes and objectives of their younger voters. By the mid eighties, the actual common denominators among 'the left' in Germany were issues of gender equality, opposition to the nuclear arms race, the fear of nuclear power plants and some general concern about the poor nations in the so-called Third World. This left had curiously little interest in the domestic system changes that the CDU/FDP coalition and their – as we know now – clandestine financial supporters from the business

---

[2] The change in the foreign policy positions of the SPD as a result of the debates on the 'modernization' of US nuclear theatre weapons stationed in Germany was – this should be mentioned here – as much driven by the older statesmen Bahr and Brandt as by the younger generation. For an authorative account see Hofschen (1989, p. 523ff).

community[3] were working at.

The March Through the Institutions and the Illusions of the Gorbachev Years

The longer the CDU/FDP carried out their neoliberal reforms, the more realistic and popular became the (initially rather utopian) idea of an SPD-Green Party coalition as the only feasible alternative to CDU rule. Among trade unionists, it was hailed as a necessary precondition for revising the despised 'turnaround' and for re-establishing the old structural hegemony of the 'left', as enjoyed in the seventies by the SPD/FDP coalition under chancellor Willy Brandt, when the slogan of the day was 'let's wage more democracy'! By supplementing the old social-liberal project with fresh ideas and young personnel taken from the 'new social movements' and the environmental movement, this anticipated 'turnaround of the turnaround' served to vindicate the endeavours and merits of the 68ers in postwar West German history.

The 1989 Berlin Programme of the SPD – passed unanimously (!) by the delegates of the Berlin Party Congress after a total of seven years of discussions and re-writings – read like a call to arms for old activists. It represented a radical rhetorical departure from the famous 1959 *Godesberg* Programme, which had firmly presented the SPD as a pro-Western and pro-capitalist party. The new programme employed sometimes openly anti-capitalist rhetoric, as if the student revolutionaries of twenty years ago wanted to show proudly to the world that they had arrived. Whereas the *Godesberg* Programme intended to move the party towards bourgeois respectability, the *Berlin* Programme defiantly articulated positions of a self-assured radical left, curiously at odds with what was actually going on in Germany at the time.

The *Berlin* Programme contains, for example, a staunch commitment for the cause of economic democracy, defined here as a regime in which 'social objectives take precedence over the blind mechanisms of profit-seeking capital'. It also calls for 'internationally binding rules and regulations for socially acceptable ways of producing and trading', and it pledges for 'the completion of women's emancipation, which means not the integration of women in a man's world, but the transformation of society to a truly human society, i.e. overcoming the man's world'. In summary, the document's objective was to initiate the 'ecological-social transformation of our industrial society'. In the commentary section, the authors explicitly criticized the hitherto untouchable objective of economic growth as the

---

[3] This refers to the recently revealed and widely disseminated information about how Chancellor Helmut Kohl had a constant flow of illegal contributions from big private interests at his disposal, a system of money laundering that reaches back to the time when he was a regional boss in the Rhineland-Palatinate (Semler, 2000, p. 13).

main strategic precondition for a social democratic welfare policy. 'Emancipation' and 'quality of life' were regarded as higher objectives. 'Emancipation' meant the humanization of society, 'progress' insinuated a greater role for the caring state, and 'modernization' was generally understood to refer to processes that fostered greater equality and democratization (Wehr 1998, p. 128 ff).

Before it could stand any real test, however, this project for 'modernization' was delayed by the dramatic shift of events which led to the internal collapse of the East European socialist regimes. The final effects of Gorbachev's perestroika turned out to be much different from what some dreamers among the traditional Western left had hoped for. Instead of providing a boost for 'democratic socialism' everywhere, he dealt it a nearly fatal blow. Instead of democratizing the socialist Soviet regime, Gorbachev only paved the way for the forces who later pushed the entire Soviet system towards ruin. Instead of eliminating the tyrannical character from Soviet socialism, he eliminated the socialist character from Soviet tyranny. Instead of helping to remove the stigma of political authoritarianism associated in the West with actually existing socialism, he only added to the stigma of socialism by exposing it as a system of losers. In the end, his successors transformed the half corrupt, stagnant socialist system into a fully corrupt, contracting 'market democracy' in which the former state managers simply elevated themselves to property owners. These events destroyed the Soviet Union as a state as well as a global power.

One of the many spin-offs of these developments was the unification of Germany in 1989–90. Politically as well as ideologically, it was driven less by nationalist passion than by anti-socialist venom. The younger generation of East Germans wanted to get rid of the degrading controls and paternalistic regulations, especially restrictions on travel to the West, which were the most annoying attributes of their socialism run by an insecure and paranoid bunch of septuagenarians. Not only did they want to escape the drag of GDR life, but they also hated the embarrassment of being treated as 'lesser Germans' on the rare occasions when they were travelling in their socialist brother states (Maaz, 1995). Joining West Germany appeared simply to be the fastest and most comfortable way to achieve these goals, even if this would clearly mean giving up on their own state. Whereas the actual 'dissident' movements explicitly called for a democratically improved GDR, the majority of East Germans simply wanted to join a winning team. An immediate union with West Germany (*Anschluss*) promised the greatest rewards in the shortest possible time. West German chancellor Kohl – who was single-minded in his pursuit of unification – particularly encouraged those East Germans who were longing for quick material rewards.

For West Germany as a whole, this was acceptable, even though there was widespread skepticism among its population (Baier, 1990). However, this skepticism was soon pushed aside by campaigns in official patriotism that reminded Germans that this unification was exactly what every good German had been waiting for over a period of forty years. For the West German left, this proved to be disastrous. First of all, leading Social Democrats like Oskar Lafontaine warned against immediate unification on the basis of a currency union. He correctly foresaw the inevitable destruction of East German industry as a result of such a policy. At the time, however, he simply appeared as unpatriotic. His behaviour apparently underscored the old saying that the left has no fatherland! And furthermore, since standing up for unification was hailed as the ultimate 'politically correct' sentiment and 'socialism' implied the continued division, everything only vaguely connected with socialism, even when it just meant the very moderate variety of Western social democracy, could – at least implicitly – be defined as bordering on high treason.

Carrying out the SPD-Green Party-led 'turnabout of the turnabout' project, with all its rhetoric of economic democracy, domestic ecological regulation, and solidarity with the World's South, suddenly appeared like trying to block the path of history which was obviously heading for the ultimate vindication of Germany and/or the final triumph of unbridled capitalism. So the 'turnabout of the turnabout' had to be abandoned, while Chancellor Kohl, who clearly appeared to be on his last legs by the late eighties, enjoyed an unexpected new surge of popularity in the united Germany for nearly another decade.

At the turn of the millennium, 13 out of 15 European Union (EU) member states were run by 'left of centre' governments, the great majority of them being successors of former rightist-conservative regimes (Perger, 1998, p. 23). On paper, this appears to be a huge comeback for European social democracy. Undoubtedly, at the century's end the majority of EU voters wanted change, and they attempted such change by casting their ballots for an end to the conservative/neoliberal policies. Furthermore, former 68er 'revolutionaries' were in key positions in many of these governments. Was now the time to translate the old dream of the 'march through the institutions' into praxis; to create an economically just and environmentally protective society where, at last, 'social objectives take precedent over the blind mechanism of profit-seeking capital'? Many people who had fallen victim to economic polarization brought about by neoliberal policies hoped for this, even more so since the communist regimes had collapsed ten years ago and consequently would not be available as a bogeyman for conservatives anymore.

Nothing of the kind happened. In Germany, as in other parts of the EU, we can see no substantial political initiatives for revising the conservative/neoliberal policies of the eighties and nineties. On the contrary, the new 'left of centre' governments seem to see their objective in securing and sometimes even expanding the structural changes initiated by their conservative predecessors! They continue to undermine the regulating powers of the nation states without seriously attempting to create institutions on the EU level which could compensate for it. National monetary policies which could be used by national banks for fighting unemployment in their countries are now rendered impossible due to their subordination to an 'independent' European central bank. In the rhetoric of modernized social democracy, the latter is seen as 'internationalist', therefore 'progressive'! Social Democrats now hail the retreat of the 'regulating' state in the face of 'globalization' as progressive developments, quite similar to the way Marxists used to see the march towards socialism as a 'law of history'. And they implore the national pride of their traditional voters by urging them to understand the 'need to stay competitive as a location in the ever faster growing world of globalized production' ('*Standortkonkurrenz*'). That is, to refrain from demands for higher wages, greater job security or shorter working hours (Jessop, 1993).

Modernized Social Democrats now demand 'flexibility at the workplace', meaning weekend work, night work, irregular working hours, low payment and low job security, i.e. the employers' right to arbitrarily hire and fire whenever 'the market' calls for it. These liberties have always been part of employers' dreams since the earliest times of capitalism. However, the century-long struggle of trade unions and other organizations of the working class in industrial societies resulted in considerable concessions on many of these points. Now they are coming back with a vengeance, heralded as the ultimate trend in our ever 'modernizing' world. The most a Social Democratic government is willing to do now for its traditional voters from the working class is to provide some subsidies for professional training and point to the self-employed as a new role model.

On paper, the 1998 'Red-Green' government was considerably left of centre. As a matter of fact, some of the same people who wrote the *Berlin* Programme were now ruling Germany. One would therefore expect that the spirit of the Berlin document, passed unanimously only a decade ago, would have informed government policy. In reality, though, the new government not only completely disregarded the *Berlin* Programme, but it actually exceeded the policies of the Kohl government when it came to neoliberal reform. After the Schröder government introduced its new plans for tax reform and a reorganization of the pension system, the Christian Democrats criticized them and presented themselves as the more socially minded party! 'Innovation and social justice' was the slogan by which the government tried to sell its policies to the public, but they did not mean to invoke classical social democratic contents anymore. Instead, they now opted for selling public property, privatizing state-owned enterprise, charging fees for higher education, and cutting taxes for businesses and higher incomes in order to provide 'incentives' for investment (Schmidt, 1999).

The Destruction of the Traditional Party Structures

The campaign to regain hegemony and acceptance for unbridled capitalism started simultaneously in the leading western nations at the end of the 1970s and the beginning of the 1980s. In varying degrees, Reagan, Thatcher and Kohl all represented the same 'spiritual-moral turnabout' from the orthodoxies of the postwar regimes. In Europe, the British led the way. Helped by the jingoism created during the time of the Falklands/Malvinas War, Margaret Thatcher was able to terminate the British accommodation between the classes, namely the corporative welfare state and the trade unions' role in politics. Reworking the phrases of the political vernacular, the Thatcherites provided classical social-liberal terms like 'change', 'modernity' and 'reform' with new meanings. With the willing assistance of the national media (many of its leading figures became her privileged advisors), Thatcher was able to systematically tar those who would defend the interests of organized labour, and the position of its 'functionaries', as sticks in the mud blocking human progress.

Slick media pundits and eager academics supported this restoration by eulogies on the self-healing powers of 'the market' and its heroic Black Knight, the daring and innovating 'entrepreneur'. Those who know just a little about the history of economic thought cannot but feel embarrassed sometimes by the jadedness of these 'theories'. In their original forms, they go back to economists like John Ramsay McCulloch or Jean-Baptiste Say, who can lay no other claim to fame than having distorted Adam Smith in the service of the chambers of commerce. At the turn of the 19th century (another historical high mark for globalization)[4] they were picked up by 'neoclassical' economists like Leon Walras and Alfred Marshall, in more recent times by 'libertarian' conservatives like Ayn Rand and George Gilder, by 'neoliberal' economists like F.A. Hayek and Milton Friedman, and – perhaps the most zealous of them all – by New York Times columnist Thomas Friedman (Friedman, 1999). For several decades after the war – when Keynes was the theoretician of choice – libertarian thinkers were regarded as fringe ideologists. In the course of the last two decades of the 20th century, they became respected mainstreamers. Margaret Thatcher used the advice and inspiration of F.A. Hayek extensively in her successful attempt to smash the British trade unions and destroy their stake in British industrial society.

Once the neoliberals had successfully reworked the meaning of 'modern' and 'progress' as unbridled capitalism Anglo-American style, Europe's social democratic parties faced a crisis of legitimization. For a while they were effectively portrayed as last year's model overcome by the advance of history. Cornered in the opposition, they searched for new ways. At first, most of the Social Democratic governments were trying to adapt their politics to the pressure from the right while still keeping their old rhetoric. The German Social Democratic leadership, for example, indicated their approval with CDU projects like abolishing the right of political asylum, legalizing the tapping of citizens' phones by the police, and allowing the German *Bundeswehr* to take part in out-of-area-missions. However, in doing this they came across as inconsistent and two-faced. Some

---

[4] The stunning similarity of today's hype for 'globalization' and the magical powers of the 'market' with the one that was prevalent at the turn of the past century has been observed by more than one author. Two of them – from different political camps – shall suffice here: Soros (1995) and Amin (2000, p. 2).

power conscious politicians then went a step further. They finally adapted their rhetoric to the new ideological mood. They understood that in a political climate aggressively influenced by neoliberal rhetoric they would receive better press by obeying the powers that be. Their traditional clientele would still believe that it would be better to vote for them than for 'them'. So they 'modernized' their rhetoric. At first, it may have started as a Machiavellian thought, as a ruse to win back power. But this begs the question of who is fooling whom. Soon Social Democrats everywhere were trying to save the village by destroying it.

The earliest recorded case so far of rolling back a really existing welfare regime in the name of 'modernized' social democracy was the *coup d'etat* carried out by the New Zealand Labour Party and its Finance Minister Roger Douglas during the eighties. Within a short time, New Zealand – left out in the cold by Britain's turn towards Europe – was miraculously transformed from one of the world's most prominent welfare states to its most decidedly 'free market' laboratory, hailed by US commentators as an example for every country in the world. Today, the transformation has resulted in much improved profitability for New Zealand businesses, but also in a much higher crime rate and a dramatic drop in the quality of the country's public services.[5]

In Europe, Tony Blair led the Labour Party back to power after 18 years in a historical landslide victory. Nobody who was witnessing his triumph on 1 May 1997, will ever forget the general feeling of elation that accompanied the total defeat of a Conservative Party whose regime was so compromised by corruption and other vices that it truly felt like the *ancien regime* before the French Revolution. Blair demonstrated his will to establish a new regime of virtue, but in reality he started by trying to permanently crowd out the remnants of the postwar class compromise. For public consumption, he named this strategy (with the help of sociologist Anthony Giddens and in a joint venture with Bill Clinton) the Third Way.[6] With the help of his spin master Peter Mandelson, he transformed the New

---

[5] For the history of these reforms see Kelsey (1995).

[6] The 'Third Way' was originally a term used by reform-minded Marxist economists in the sixties and seventies, meaning there could and should be an alternative to both capitalism and (really existing) socialism. Today, it represents a new direction in (capitalist) economic policy 'between those who said government was the enemy and those who said government was the solution – an information-age government that must be smaller, must be less bureaucratic, must be fiscally disciplined, and focused on being a catalyst for new ideas'. President Bill Clinton, *Address on Social Security*, 9 February 1998, on the White House website. The elaborated version, of course, is Giddens (1998). Wendy Wheeler sums up the critical definitions of the 'Third Way' as follows: 'The third way means the celebration of globalised capital alongside prudent management of the economy, with some added investment in education and training. In other words, global capital has triumphed and the only sensible response from government is to accept the fact and to do what can be done to equip people to be more "competitive" players in its game. This is government as facilitator, as efficient manager.' (Wheeler, 1999, p. 14).

Labour Party into a streamlined decision making machine run strictly from above, with no influence left for the trade unions and rank and file members. Even sympathetic observers of 'New Labour' politics, like Lord Dahrendorf, soon noted that 'the politics of the Third Way are not about an open society or about liberty. It does contain a strangely authoritarian strain, and this not only in practice'.[7]

But then, one could argue, was this not precisely what was intended? Does the political therapy plan of the Third Way not actually prescribe the weakening of party structures and rank and file participation in leadership decision making and the corresponding emphasis on 'leadership' and political communication? So the New Labour leadership successfully subordinated, in the words of Thomas Meyer:

> Everything else including the party's discourse, the role of the party and even the role of the parliamentary party…to the rule of the perceived necessities of successful media communication of the party leader's image and his symbolic project…The image of the leader hero, the selection of the issues and the design of the way they are presented to the media, the disciplining of the party and all its actors beneath the strategic apex have not only created a new way to conduct politics but also a new type of relation between the social democratic party, its members, its leadership and its relation with society as a whole. Therefore, it cannot be seen as a change in marketing and communications only, it is rather a substantially new type – defining the role of the party in the process of formulating and implementing policies. It is basically nothing less than a new type of media democracy (Meyer, 1999, p. 4).[8]

In other words, Blair's *Third Way* was, among other things, the attempt to realign the British parliamentary system after the American model. There, elections are not about divisive issues and class-oriented party programmes, but about individuals who present themselves to a 'middle class' public as trustworthy and morally impeccable leaders, using and playing the media for this purpose. There is no doubt that this was the model that the top New Labour strategists had in mind when they created their 'party of a new type'.[9]

The New Labour project was studied carefully by Gerhard Schröder and the German social democrats. They were especially interested in the way New Labour was using the media and they copied some of their concepts. So they presented themselves to the German voters, carefully directed by their own group of media

---

[7] *New Statesman*, 6 September 1999.

[8] For the entire complex history of New Labour in Britain see Anderson and Mann (1997).

[9] The individual who was mostly responsible for this shift in the self-image and political strategy of New Labour was undoubtedly Peter Mandelson (Mann, 1996). It should also be noted that the change in thinking about political economy was put in place under the leadership of John Smith. based on policy papers by Gordon Brown and John Eatwell, both 'classical' 68ers. What Blair added was just tinkering (Anderson and Mann, 1997, p. 73).

managers and spin masters, as the 'Neue Mitte' ('New Centre'). Nonetheless, a complete adaptation of the Mandelson strategy – i.e. the reduction of the SPD to a mere electoral 'pledge group' for the 'modern leader' Schröder – was out of the question. In Germany as well as in France, the social democratic parties including their internal structures of functionaries are still anchored in their respective national societies. Here even the most charismatic and internationally well-respected leaders must acknowledge their dependence on the party and represent the concerns of its key constituencies. In the long run, attempts to completely ignore the party platform, or to reformulate it by simply making declarations to sympathetic media, may very well backfire. At the next party conference the changes may be denounced and voted down. And even in Britain, where the New Labour leadership certainly forced the greatest changes upon the internal organization of the Labour Party towards a socially undefined nationalist mass party, the possibility of a future democratic 'backlash' by the incapacitated rank and file cannot yet be ruled out.

The Socio-Cultural Base of 'Third Wayism'

When one discusses 'modernized' social democracy, one question inevitably comes up: How are these changes to be interpreted? Do they represent something like treason to the cause, or are they to be seen as shrewd tactical adaptations to win power back for the left in an age of neoliberal/conservative hegemony? The final political truth here will reveal itself in practice; the truth for the political scientist today lies beyond moral-political considerations.

Blair and Schröder are as much political actors as they are the offspring of profound historical changes in postwar Western society. The student and youth protests of the late 1960s symbolized such changes, when a morally and culturally frustrated new generation directly challenged the corporative structures that had defined the 1950s. But then these structures were already in a crisis. Although they provided broad economic security, their organization was informally authoritarian, and effectively 'collectivist' with regard to individual life styles and attitudes. Despite their formal foundation in democracy and individual freedom, the postwar societies in the West rested body and soul (functionally and philosophically) on traditional mentalities of status, patriarchal custom, seniority, and voluntary recognition of acquired and assumed authority. They were utterly conformist.[10] At the same time, however, they significantly broadened the base for a prosperous and stakeholding 'middle class', including certain sections of the unionized working class.

---

[10] For the United States, for example, this stifling conformism was thematized by David Riesman, *The Lonely Crowd*, New Haven 1950.

The immediate postwar generation owed their life chances to this constellation. At the same time, they challenged its structures and mentalities, because it was still dominated by a prewar ruling elite. Their activists attacked them under a variety of banners, including 'socialism' Some even rallied under the banner of Marxism-Leninism, but this was an unimportant minority, whose subjective 'avant garde' consciousness never reflected reality. Much more important was the widely popular 'anti-authoritarian' identification. More than anything else, it was this sentiment that united even those who had little natural inclination or desire to see themselves as part of a specific 'movement'.

The anti-authoritarianism of the 68ers was generally directed in equal measure at authorities in both the West and East, at states grounded in both capitalism and 'actually existing socialism', at middle class universities as well as in working class trade unions and leftist political parties. The young leftists of the time rebelled against authoritarian oppression of sexual minorities and other socially marginalized groups. Centuries old religious and moral values were deemed ridiculous; self conscious 'identities' for these 'underprivileged' groups were actively sponsored. The 68ers fought against 'repressive tolerance' and other subtle techniques of oppression. Unmasking the connections between 'sexuality and dominance', they denounced patriarchal structures discriminatory to women within the family, work place and everyday life. Trying to overcome national and regional provincialism, they began embracing the cultures of southern European peoples traditionally looked down upon by 'civilized' Germany.

What interested most 68ers least of all were the economic structures and mechanisms of their own countries. Although there was a rhetorical anti-capitalism evident in not only the many leftist sectarian groupings, but also in the youth organizations of the major parties, this was more provocative posturing than reasoned critique. Economic conditions under the control of capital were experienced as the most trivial of evils. After all, at this time there was neither considerable unemployment nor a recruitment freeze in public service, and the universities. In fact, the education system was expanding. Although some former 68ers may not want to admit it: even with its most radical extremists, the student rebellion ultimately represented less a polemical response to capitalism as such than an impatient chafing under the bridle of parental and institutional control. At issue was 'personal development' and 'emancipation', not economic justice and class solidarity – at least not with the working class in their own country. The rallying cry was 'revolution', but there were bitter fights about what exactly was to be revolutionized: society or the individual?[11] After all, the most readily accepted of all the slogans circulating at the time was 'The personal is political'.

---

[11] A good example for the self-absorbed eccentricity and theoretical megalomania of some of the much admired 'revolutionaries' at the time is Krahl (1971).

In West Germany, the self-liberation of the postwar student generation from the cultural yoke of their parents' Nazi heritage definitely helped with the liberalization and democratization of the entire country, it was not limited to academic institutions. For many, hierarchies and bureaucracies lost their ability to intimidate; for others, they lost their god-given constancy and authority. At last, rules and meaningless customs could be called into question. Gender roles were reevaluated, and cultural traditions reappraised. The intellectual world was opened to a new dimension. University curricula covered substantially expanded areas and aspects in the traditional disciplines; new fields of research and even new disciplines were introduced.[12] Although these developments would have to be defended against nationalistic and conservative attacks in the future, they also served, whether the activists at the time intended so or not, to erode the traditional demarcation line between 'left' and 'right'. To the 68ers and the generation of activists that followed, 'left' politics were no longer associated with the actual class interests of the working man and woman 'within' society, but instead with the individual's liberation and emancipation 'from' state and society.

A whole generation of German Social Democrat and Green politicians came of age in an environment where the primacy of class antagonism was no longer an issue for them because they were social climbers who used the left parties not so much for representing their class but for helping their individual careers. It was not uncommon for them to move directly from youth and student organizations into responsible positions within the state bureaucracy, political parties, NGOs, education system or parliament. Few were shaped by lengthy experience in the work world of private enterprise. Their causes included women's liberation, the environment, disarmament, solidarity with the Third World, multiculturalism (social integration of foreigners) and European integration. Amongst themselves, they still made an effort to voice the rhetoric of radical anti-capitalism, but its first purpose was simply to rally the cohort for their march through the establishment's institutions.

So, from a sociological point of view, 'modernized' social democracy represents not so much a betrayal of its ascribed class interests as an adequate reflection of a change in the membership composition of the party and of their new leaders' class interests. In other words: No matter what their former rhetoric was like, in real life they represent a new meritocratic middle class of social climbers who experienced their advancement in life as a result of their competence and 'hard work'. In demographic terms, it was primarily a result of the expansion of higher education in the sixties and seventies. Today, the revolutionary children of

---

[12] Some of the new academic fields of research that became fashionable in the sixties were, for example, *Bildungsökonomie* (Political Economy of Education), Political Psychology, and, of course, Culture Studies.

the sixties have become the new ruling class of 'modernized' capitalism,[13] and as such they advocate a sort of a partyless democracy, run by a strong leader with the help of a well-educated meritocratic elite. For the masses, who do not take much interest in parliamentary politics anyway, there is populist fodder to be disseminated in the coolest possible fashion by friendly media, which constantly enlighten the public about the only 'modern' role model for running public institutions from the national government down to the local nursery.

This role model is of course the private corporation. For this is the actual meaning of 'modern' today, not just in the context of Social Democracy, but in all political camps: behaviour of governments or other organizations is 'modern', i.e. acceptable and progressive, as long as it is modelled on the behaviour of profit-making corporations. Private corporations are seen as agents of cultural modernization and job creation, especially when it comes to innovative developments in connection with computers and the internet. Governments and their 'bureaucracies' are, on the contrary, held to be wasteful and ponderous, obsessed with procedures instead of driven by outcomes!

There is little in the experienced history of 68ers anywhere in the Western world which would not be compatible with this view, considering the fact that most of their anti–capitalism was always directed against the capitalist *state*, not against private enterprise. And they always stood for the self-actualization of the individual. It was their rebellion which had effectively challenged the postwar corporate welfare state and thereby paved the way for a new cultural attractiveness of an exciting, unbureaucratic, inspiring capitalism in which genuine talent and hard work were being rewarded with social and economic advancement, but eliminating the personal costs one had to pay in the old days for joining the elites as a social climber: stifling rules of behaviour, a deferential attitude towards old money, boring conversations and a suffocating dress code. Now they are free to feel at ease among themselves and still be regarded as elite. They are social democrats because the conservative slot was already taken and they genuinely represent a new elite.

The Risks of the Third Way

With this 'professionalized' Left, there is an increasing probability that not only today's growing number of marginalized and disadvantaged, but also the wide mass of working people will no longer find their interests represented by them. Many already consider the 'modernized' Social Democratic establishment as indistinguishable from the 'ruling class'. As a result, we see increasing political

---

[13] This argument is the core of Tom Nairn's brilliant analysis of Britain under New Labour (Nairn, 2000).

frustration, voter apathy and a turning to populist right-wing parties in many European countries. When union-organized workers express resistance to neoliberal reforms, it is not uncommon for 'educated' Social Democrats and Greens to disdainfully denounce them with airs of progressive cosmopolitanism. For example, when the German retail salespersons' union spoke out in favour of maintaining regulated store hours, many Social Democrats and Green Party functionaries joined in the chorus of the business propagandists by enthusiastically recalling the 'emancipating character' of the unregulated store hours encountered while visiting the United States.

In France this 'battle of two lines' is already underway. There was a sharp debate within French intellectual circles following the strike of government employees in the fall of 1996. While some deemed this new outbreak of social protest as 'prehistoric', others supported the workers struggling to maintain their standard of living. The latter group's influence remains strong enough to shape the political agenda set by the Socialist and Green parties in power. Naturally, as they are part of the ruling coalition, the French Communists also have a role to play in this constellation of powers. As the only leftist party that has a substantial following among the working poor and the unemployed, they still exert a check on any neoliberal drift by the Socialists and Greens.

The German left has yet to cross this fork in the road. The spontaneous, but disingenuous solidarity of SPD and Green leaders with striking coal miners in the Ruhr and Saarland in 1998 demonstrated how unprepared the party elites were for such unexpected 'old-fashioned' class conflict. At the moment, the left has obviously no intention to take advantage of, let alone sponsor, such protest 'from below' and use it to counter the neoliberal programme.

The central question relates to how the role of the state is valued. The greater part of the left still defines 'democracy' and 'emancipation' in terms of freedom 'from' the state, particularly those who have the economic wherewithal to afford a weak state. Also far from unified is the position vis-à-vis the processes of globalization (and Europeanization) of economics, politics and culture. While most of the leaders see in these developments an intellectual and cultural enrichment of life (and, often related, greater professional opportunities), a growing segment of traditional Social Democratic voters feel directly threatened by such trends. With fewer qualifications, such as limited secondary language abilities, they foresee losing out in an increasingly competitive international job market. With compensatory offers and opportunities not forthcoming, they turn to the security of the classic nation state to protect their social status and human dignity.

Satisfying the diverse interests of their voters currently comprised of established and satiated 68ers, civil servants, salaried workers as well as the working poor, the unemployed and pensioned, will pose a great future challenge, not only to the SPD-led government in Germany, but to all the left-of-centre governments that have been in power in Europe. If they want to convince their present voters that they should stay with them rather than vote for populist right-wing parties in future elections, their leaders will have to do some hard thinking. The German Social Democrats won the 1998 elections on the strength of the still prevalent popular belief that they were the 'party of social justice'. Unless they can convincingly prove in the near future that this slogan was not just some unsubstantiated spin, they may soon lose a great portion of their voters to right-wing parties or to abstention.

References

Amin, S. (2000), 'The Political Economy of the 20th Century', *Monthly Review*, Vol. 52(2), pp. 3–16.

Anderson, P. and Mann, N. (1997), *Safety First. The Making of New Labour*, Granta, London.

Baier, L. (1990), *Volk ohne Zeit. Essay über das eilige Vaterland*, Wagenbach, Berlin.

Friedman, T. (1999), *The Lexus and the Olive Tree: Understanding Globalization*, Farrar, Straus and Giroux, New York.

Goldhagen, D.J. (1997), *Hitler's Willing Executioners. Foreword to the German Edition*, Knopf, New York.

Hirsch, J. and Roth, R. (1986), *Das neue Gesicht des Kapitalismus. Vom Fordismus zum Postfordismus*, VSA, Hamburg.

Hofschen, H.G. (1989), 'Kontinuität und Wandel: Die SPD seit 1982', in J. von Freyberg et. al., *Geschichte der deutschen Sozialdemokratie*, Pahl-Rugenstein, Köln, pp. 523–52.

Jessop, B. (1993), 'Towards a Schumperian Workfare State? Preliminary Remarks on Post-Fordist Political Economy', *Studies in Political Economy*, Vol. 40, pp. 7–39.

Kelsey, J. (1995), *The New Zealand Experiment: A World Model for Structural Adjustment*, Pluto Press, Auckland.

Krahl, H.-J. (1971), *Konstitution und Klassenkampf. Zur historischen Dialektik von bürgerlicher Emanzipation und proletarischer Revolution*, Neue Kritik, Frankfurt/M.

Maaz, H.J. (1995), *Behind the Wall: The Inner Life of Communist East Germany*, Norton, New York.

Mann, N. (1996), 'Top Spinner: Notes Towards an Unauthorized Biography of Peter Mandelson', *New Statesman & Society*, 8 March 1996.

Meyer, T. (1999), 'The Third Way, Some Crossroads', *Forum: Scholars for European Social Democracy*, Working Papers I.

Nairn, T. (2000), 'Ukania under Blair', *New Left Review*, Vol. 1, pp. 69–103.

Perger, W.A. (1998), 'Linkes Europa. Sozialdemokraten haben die Mehrheit. Haben sie auch die Macht?', *Die ZEIT*, 15 October 1998.

Riesman, D. (1950), *The Lonely Crowd*, Yale U. Press, New Haven.

Schmidt, I. (1999), 'Vom keynesianischen Wohlfahrtsstaat zur neokeynesianischen Stabilisierung des Kapitalismus', *Sozialismus*, Vol. 10, pp. 9–16.

Semler, C. (2000), 'Secrets and Lies in Germany', *Le Monde Diplomatique* (English Edition), April 2000.

Soros, G. (1995), *Soros on Soros: Staying Ahead of the Curve*, J. Wiley, New York.

Wehr, A. (1998), 'Innovationen für Deutschland – Die SPD auf dem Weg zurück zur Macht', in F. Unger, A. Wehr and K. Schönwälder (1998), *New Democrats, New Labour, Neue Sozialdemokraten*, Elefanten Press, Berlin, pp. 127–77.

Wheeler, W. (1999), *A New Modernity*, cited from Guardian Weekly, August 26, 1999, London.

Chapter 8

Beyond the Politics of Nostalgia

Warren Magnusson

It's called *parité* [France's new law 'obliging the country's political parties to fill fifty percent of the candidacies in virtually every race with women'] – literally, parity – and it's about political power, and the women who thought it up know now that the smartest thing they did was to call it *parité*, because *parité* sounds so French and friendly and enlightened, like a citizen's right to free samples at a perfume store.

What made *parité* suddenly so attractive to the [Socialist] Party strategists, embarrassed in Europe and alarmed by the extent to which they had lost women like [Francoise] Gaspard, and even lost women who might be voting for *them*, was the fact that, whatever else happened to the idea of *parité* in France, it was not likely to get tossed into the trash can of American ideas that the French reject – ideas having to do with affirmative action and multiculturalism and communitarianism and all the other isms of an invasion that spell the beginning of the end of France. The French sociologist, Eric Fassin…says you can understand the entire evolution of the *parité* argument as an attempt not to sound American (Kramer, 2000, p. 112 and p. 114).

'The Third Way' is like *parité*. Much of the term's appeal comes from the fact that it is not American. For Britons especially, it marks a reversal of the American turn implicit in Margaret Thatcher's policies. It signals a move that is supposed to bring the Isles back into Europe, and take Europe on a path different from the American Way. The path is not towards socialism, but there can be little doubt that socialist aspirations have motivated the search for something other than a naked liberalism. In the United States, where socialists long ago learned not to speak the 's'-word publicly, the spiritual partners of the European exponents of the Third Way have described themselves as 'communitarians'. This is the code word for a socialism that dares not speak its name, a socialism that has surrendered all but a few of its original aspirations. In Europe, the Third Way has a broader appeal, because it promises liberation from America itself. Parity in fact is the aspiration: Parity with America. The hope, in effect, is to make a different but no less powerful modernity real, a modernity other than the one on offer in the USA. To achieve that would be to reverse the results of the twentieth century, to free the Old World from the New, and to demonstrate the moral and cultural (if not the military and economic) superiority of Europe to the United States. This project has a certain appeal to

Canadians (and perhaps also to Australians, New Zealanders, and other inhabitants of European settler societies). In adopting the Third Way ourselves we might at last redeem our own mission to be a better, more open, more civilized – thus, more European? – version of the USA. Such at least are the unacknowledged aspirations of the 'Third Way'.

The acknowledged aspiration is of course to refurbish social democracy – or what the Americans call 'liberalism' – in light of the experiences of the last thirty years. Old-style socialism, in all its variants (West European, East European, and Third World), seems to have gone off the political agenda. Thus, there has been an opportunity to rethink the original aspirations of the people who were drawn to the socialist cause so many generations ago. Words like democracy and community have been revived and linked firmly to notions about individual freedom. There has been an effort to rethink cultural difference, and to re-embed socialist aspirations within a broader tradition of civic republicanism. Nevertheless, Third Way thinking has generally set itself against the liveliest critical tradition of our time, the one usually described as post-modernism or post-structuralism. In doing so, the Third Way has repeated an earlier pattern. The social democrats of the 1950s, '60s, and '70s also set themselves against the liveliest critical traditions of their own time, including existentialism, Frankfurt School critical theory, humanist and structuralist neo-Marxism, and various forms of Gramscian analysis. Exponents of the Third Way join with others in labelling post-modernists and post-structuralists as nihilists, akin to the anarchists of the 1890s, the surrealists of the 1920s, and the existentialists of the 1950s. Third Way thinking certainly repudiates the Marxisms of the 1970s (much as earlier forms of revisionism had repudiated the Marxisms of the 1930s or the 1890s), but it also differentiates itself from forms of critical thinking that appear to undercut clear 'political' commitments. The aim of Third Way thinkers and leaders is not only to pose an alternative to Thatcher, Reagan, and the American Way, but also to establish an intellectually and politically credible alternative to forms of critique that lead not to a rearticulation of old political projects but to something altogether different.

It is by no means clear what this altogether different politics might be, but it is clear that the critical intellectuals who most excite the young are not the ones who have been involved in articulating the Third Way. Witness the recent exchange between Judith Butler, Ernesto Laclau, and Slavoj Zizek (2000). These people are touchstone intellectual figures, whose work resonates among the young. They situate themselves in relation to Lacan, Foucault, Derrida, and Deleuze: hence, in relation to a critical tradition that Third Way theorists would prefer us to forget. Butler, Laclau, and Zizek are not uncommitted or disengaged politically: on the contrary. Nor do they see themselves as people outside 'the left': again, on the contrary, they lay claim to the legacy of the left, and seek to show how to think and act politically *now*. Thus, to the extent that there is a struggle for intellectual hegemony on the left, the Third Way faces a challenge not only from old school Marxists and socialists, but also from new school post-structuralists. In the long run, the latter will be the more formidable opponents, for not only have they captured the imagination of the new generation of young, critical intellectuals, but they have posed (and continue to pose) a series of problems that have yet to be taken seriously by Third Way intellectuals and practitioners.

In this chapter, I offer a way of thinking about those problems. It is not the only way, but it is a way that takes seriously the most common complaint about post-structuralist theory, namely that it approaches politics so obliquely that it leaves us with no sense about what we are to do or how we are to think politically. Complaints about 'nihilism' or about the 'obscurity' of the theorists concerned – although more often heard – are actually secondary to this complaint. It is not that people cannot read the work in question if they try hard enough; it is that their reading leads them to no definite politics, or at least to no politics that others on the left can identify. What I seek to do here is to bring some insights from post-structuralist theory into direct relation with the problem that Third Way theorists pose for themselves, namely the problem of articulating a politics appropriate for an era in which neither socialism nor the nation state appears to provide an adequate frame for progressive action. I want to suggest that the traditional linkage between socialism and the nation state depends on a particular conception of politics, a conception motivated by nostalgia for the Greek *polis*. Communitarianism, civic republicanism, and the Third Way all embody this nostalgia. They are not unique. Indeed, I want to suggest that the politics of nostalgia is the dominant form of contemporary politics, a form that is keyed into images of the *polis* on the one hand and the sovereign on the other. A central task for us now is to think *through* this form towards other alternatives. But, first, let me say a few things about the way *we here now* conceive of our current situation.

Thinking the Present

According to many commentators, we live in an age of neoliberalism or neoconservatism. The point of labelling it so is to highlight the revival of nineteenth century liberalism and conservatism. After decades of ideological retreat – roughly from the 1890s to the 1960s – liberals and conservatives seem to have been winning on every front, so that the main political tension in many places is not between a pro-capitalist liberal-conservatism and a phalanx of socialisms, but rather between a militant economic liberalism and an equally militant social conservatism (often rooted in religious or ethno-nationalist sentiment). Of course, politics was rarely what socialists hoped it would be. It seldom had the focus on class issues that would have facilitated working class unity and enabled socialist gains. Nevertheless, thirty years ago it was easier than it is now to imagine that politics had the essential form that socialists expected. For Canadians on the left at that time, Western Europe was the very model for a politics to be achieved, one that put issues of class at the centre, restrained religious, ethnic, and regional tensions, and enabled the nation state to put the economy to work for the benefit of everyone. Europeans might be startled to realize that they were so perceived – especially since Europe had just emerged from the most devastating and barbaric war in its history. Nonetheless, there was a time when the politics of Britain, France, or West Germany had – from a Canadian perspective, at least – a certain purity and simplicity: an unambiguous struggle between left and right and, what's more, a struggle that the left sometimes won. The European model had much charm in relation to the American Way, especially for people who had cultural as well as ideological reasons for wanting to establish something different from the United States.

In this context, the articulation of a Third Way that seems so close in spirit to George W. Bush's 'compassionate conservatism' seems less like a political achievement than a capitulation to an overly familiar pattern. But, if the Third Way is a capitulation, to what is it capitulating? It seems simplistic to say 'the American Way'. In searching for deeper explanations, we tend to revert to terms that were given to us generations ago. On one view, we are faced with the triumph of a particular way of thinking: one that asserts the superiority of the market as a mechanism for unplanned coordination of large-scale human activities, reasserts the connection between economic freedom and other forms of freedom, and denies the possibility (or even the desirability) of eliminating most forms of social privilege. On the other view, we are confronted simply with the triumph of capitalism: that is, of a particular mode of production, economic system, set of social relations, or ensemble of material practices. In the end, these two approaches to explaining the present – we would have called them 'idealist' or 'materialist' a few years ago – begin to look remarkably similar. Capitalism is liberalism, and *vice versa*; and so, it is as easy to account for the ensemble from one starting point as the other. What is new in the current commentaries is a sense that the ensemble we confront – however we might describe it and whatever account we might give of its origins – is so well entrenched, so deeply inscribed in everyday realities, so much a part of common sense understandings of the way the world has to be, that nothing else can really be entertained. One can rage against the machine or establish perverse and destructive alternatives in little parts of the world, but in the end there is only one possibility for a tolerably humane existence: capitalist liberalism. To an increasing extent, this view is shared by commentators on the left and right, and it helps to motivate the search for a Third Way. The aim is not to create something altogether different, but rather to inflect capitalist liberalism in a way that will bring socialist aspirations into it, rather than set them outside as an enemy to be defeated. What gives hope to many proponents of the Third Way is precisely the fact that dismays socialist critics: namely, that politicians on the right have been forced to give ground and make their own peace with socialist aspirations. Hence, 'compassionate conservatism' can be taken as a sign of victory.

The trouble with these ways of understanding the present is not that they are simply wrong: on the contrary, one can develop quite a plausible account of things along any one of these lines. The real difficulty is that to do so is to fall back into what we might call 'the Hegelian trap'. To think like a Hegelian is to imagine that all of history has a pattern intelligible to us here and now, to suppose that this history – and hence our present moment – has a certain unity to it, and, most of all, to think that our 'knowledge' of that unitary pattern will enable us to respond more rationally to the challenges of the present. So, the diagnosis comes first, then the action. The intellectual's particular responsibility is to get us to understand the broader pattern, and hence to recognize that the malign symptoms we perceive are the result of diseases or processes that are more fundamental and widespread. To engage with the fundamentals is to deal seriously with the world, and not to be diverted by trivialities or by our wild imaginings about what might be important and what might be achieved. Thus, we are led back to an intense effort at diagnosis, an effort motivated by a concern to know the whole, and hence to have a ground from which to act holistically. This effort is nowhere more apparent than in the work of ideologists on the left and right, not least the ideologists of the Third Way. Nonetheless, it is the weight of 'common sense' that is most decisive, for 'common sense' gives us a picture of the whole and a guide to aspiration and action that is relatively resistant to ideological critique. Common sense is a sort of everyday Hegelianism.

Of course, there is another understanding of things that is always already there, alongside this everyday Hegelianism. It is the understanding that reminds us that unexpected things always happen, that our understanding of things is always inadequate and incomplete, that much of what happens conforms to no intelligible pattern, that things are always different from day to day and place to place. We know all this. We know that the events of 1989 were not anticipated, and probably could not have been anticipated in any detail. We also know that the same could be said of the events of 1968, 1933, or 1917. These are events that changed the world, or so we are told. Historians work to knit them into coherent narratives that make sense of our present, and tell us who we are and where we are going. And yet, though we present these events to ourselves as intelligible and perhaps even inevitable results of particular circumstances, we also know that, from the point of view of the participants, they were largely if not entirely unpredictable. The idea that *we* could be different, that we could somehow come to an understanding of the whole of which we are part and act accordingly is a strange conceit. It is a conceit implicit not only in the rhetoric of the Third Way, but also in other attempts to designate the present as this or that. It is no accident, of course, that the present depicted in the literature is almost always some variant of the everyday reality of intellectuals in Boston, Berlin, Los Angeles, or London. But, this parochialism is just a symptom of a more general practice, in which we put aside our own understanding of contingency, complexity, and uncertainty in favour of some simple representation of present day reality.

One of the most interesting ideas recently advanced by sociologists is that the present is an era of 'advanced' liberalism, not one of neoliberalism or neoconservatism. This argument is adumbrated in different ways in two remarkable books: Nikolas Rose's *Powers of Freedom* (1999) and Mitchell Dean's *Governmentality* (1999). The thought that they develop (in a more sophisticated way than I can indicate here) is that the ideas and practices we associate with neoliberalism are actually part of a larger 'assemblage'. Practices like contracting out, performance based audits, and risk management are part of this assemblage. So too are practices like 'responsibilization': i.e., getting the individual or the 'community' to take responsibility for his/her/its fate. One can say of the various elements in this assemblage that they are all related to a particular strategy of governing, a strategy that follows on from earlier liberal strategies of government. Those strategies involved governing 'at a distance'. To organize the state in this way was not just a matter of separating the governors from the governed: that had always happened. Such a strategy also involved treating the governed as self-directing people whose conduct was subject to influence, but not to direct determination. The discovery of liberalism was that people could be educated, encouraged, and otherwise stimulated to be more productive and self reliant. Force and restraint had their place, but only in the background. Indeed, to a large extent the restraining rules were ones that people could be taught to impose on themselves and one another. As J.S. Mill made clear, liberty was a matter of *self-government*. According to Rose and Dean, advanced liberalism brings the strategy of governing at a distance – governing *through* the freedom of the individual and the freedom of the individual community – to a new level of sophistication. Moreover, the strategy is deployed as much by the left as by the right, as much by agencies outside the state (corporations and 'non-profits') as within it, as much by activists and intellectuals promoting social welfare as by companies seeking profits: in short, by any and all individuals and organizations who seek to govern through freedom.

To see the present in this way is to notice the family resemblances between the plans, strategies, and tactics being developed in 'autonomous' organizations like universities or charitable trusts, and the ones being adumbrated at the same time in profit-making companies and government departments. It is also to see the resemblances between things happening in Europe and America (under both right-wing and left-wing governments) and expectations about 'good governance' articulated internationally from above (the IMF, World Bank, G-8, WTO) and below (democracy movements in Nigeria, Indonesia, et cetera). It is to take note of a certain syndrome, a certain governmentality, a certain range of techniques and practices that have come to seem rational, necessary, modern, and democratic. To attribute this syndrome entirely to the triumph of capitalism, the spread of right-wing ideas, or the influence of American culture is too simplistic. There are shifts and changes today that have more than one source, more than one implication, and more than one colouring in terms of ideological origin or social objectives. For instance, it is not immediately evident that the effort to encourage people to take more responsibility for their sexual activity is either perverse or oppressive. Nor is it clear that the effort has much to do with the needs of corporate capital, or indeed even with the concerns of the religious right. It may in fact be about what it says: controlling the spread of sexually transmitted diseases like AIDS. Nevertheless, there is a family resemblance between efforts to make people responsible for their sexual activity, to encourage them to take responsibility for their physical fitness, to get them to be life-long learners and life-long employment seekers, to make each and every employee accountable for his or her success on the job, to displace responsibility for policing from the state to neighbourhood communities, to get everyone to have a retirement plan, and so on.

The sort of analysis that Rose, Dean, and other students of 'governmentality' offer is not meant to provide a 'Hegelian' account of the present (although it may do so despite its own theoretical arguments to the contrary). Advanced liberalism, supposedly, is not to be understood as the latest in a historical sequence of liberalisms, produced by an over-arching logic that can be related back to deeper causes. Nor is the analysis of advanced liberalism meant to tell us what to do about it, or how to respond to it. Governmentality theorists are good Foucaultians, who deny the logic of looking for totalistic explanations. And yet, there is a motivating absence or 'lack' in their work, as there is in Foucault's. The king whose head has yet to be cut off, the state that is no longer at the centre, the narrative that has been displaced by a multitude of stories, the unified history that can never be written, the unifying politics that can only oppress or deceive us, the understanding that (in a reversal of the flight of Hegel's owl of Minerva and Benjamin's angel of history) will at last allow us to see forward: all are at the centre of what is presented. 'Advanced liberalism' is the assemblage that substitutes for the missing totality, and as such it motivates the politics that lurks behind analyses of governmentality. This is a politics that avoids the Manichean representations of neoliberalism (the ones that tell us that the freeing up of markets is freedom itself or, on the contrary, that market mechanisms are synonymous with capitalist domination) in favour of a Foucaultian insistence on the danger of all that we do. Moreover, it is a politics marked by a sense that the present is qualitatively different from the past and hence that it is to be understood in terms of 'advance' rather than reversion (as in the idea that contemporary liberalism involves a rearticulation of Victorian ideas).

The 'constitutive lack' of governmentality theory (the absent presence that motivates it), like the constitutive lack of post-structuralist thought more generally, is the sovereign. The absent sovereign is the one who strategizes, and more importantly the one who governs. This absent presence makes talk of government, governance, and governmentality intelligible by marking an imaginary relation between governors and governed. That relation implies a time and a space. If the king – or in modern parlance, 'the government' – is the one who is supposed to govern, the state is the territory and historical presence within which the relation of governing appears. Sovereignty is the alpha and omega of government: both the origin and the end. Government is supposed to be a necessity because people are inherently sovereign, as individuals: that is, they are capable of autonomous action that may disrupt the lives of others or interfere with plans to organize others in particular ways. Sovereign individuals are reduced to order by a sovereign government. A sovereign government needs definite boundaries within which it can rule. Moreover, it needs continuity over time, a capacity to pass over from one generation to the next. The modern nation state gives a certain form to sovereignty, although this particular form is not essential to sovereignty itself. The project of sovereignty can be worked out in other ways. Advanced liberalism may be one of them, if we conceive of it as a form in which the rules that enable both sovereign individuals and sovereign communities to exist in a kind of harmony are internalized by the communities and individuals concerned and mutually enforced. Adam Smith's hidden hand is the hand of sovereignty. It need not appear as a king or a government, nor indeed as a state or a system of public law, to be effective in the ordering of things and people.

Post-structuralist theory (which informs the literature on governmentality and hence on advanced liberalism) is motivated by a recognition that the assumed presence of the sovereign is actually an absence, an absence that is no less effective for being an absence. Political scientists think of sovereignty in terms of the state. Sociologists and cultural theorists try to describe what lies behind the state and what constitutes it as such. Economists claim to discern a natural order within which states must subsist. Psychoanalysts, sociobiologists and philosophical anthropologists say that they probe deeper still and uncover the order that orders economic, political, social and cultural orders. All these analytical efforts point at some 'form' that underpins the present ordering of things and people. How that form is to be understood is in many ways less important than the fact that it is perceived *as* a form: as an absent presence that somehow constitutes what is as it is. Post-structuralist critiques draw our attention to the fact that this presence comes into being (or is identified as an absence that has to be filled) as a result of our efforts to fill a perceived lack. In assuming that there has to be a *there* there (to paraphrase Gertrude Stein) we produce the lack that we try to overcome by positing a 'reality' that will henceforth be the necessary ground for thinking and action.

Unfortunately, this process of reality-production has usually been described by post-structuralists in psycho-linguistic terms: thus, in terms that draw our attention away from the *political* anxieties that motivate us. Psychoanalysis and linguistics, like the social and natural sciences more generally, involve a retreat from politics. The science or understanding that they posit is depoliticized, and the reality that they ask us to understand is supposedly something other – deeper, more profound – than merely political reality. The latter then appears as superficial and ultimately rather uninteresting. None of the leading poststructuralist thinkers have made 'politics' a particular study, even though political anxieties have motivated much of what they have written and – perhaps more obviously – have motivated most of the readings of their work. As a result, people who are looking for an explicitly political analysis in post-structuralist theory often come away disappointed. All they see is the claim that the ground on which we build our institutions – be it the ground of 'human nature' or 'individual rights' or 'social solidarity' or 'material needs' or whatever – is not the solid foundation we would like it to be, but rather the effect of our own desperate efforts to fill a lack. It is by no means evident how people should respond when they recognize that this is what they are doing.

But that, of course, is the point. Although post-structuralist theory tends to evade the political in one way (by talking about almost everything *but* what is normally called politics), in another way it puts the political front and centre. It reads putatively 'foundational' structures like language, psychology, economics, and history as political productions to be understood in terms hitherto reserved for analysing plays of power in politics, government, and diplomacy. Matters once assigned to science or philosophy thus appear within a broader field of political analysis. There is a triple move implicit in this shift. What is literally sovereign, namely the state and the domain of the political centred on the state, is treated initially as an effect of foundational structures of an historical, economic, or psycho-linguistic type. Those foundational structures are then interpreted as political productions subject to change and open to plays of power. Thus, politics is presented as an activity that produces the foundations that underpin the state. It follows that politics as the sub-foundational 'grounds' politics as normally conceived. But, as the post-structuralists are at pains to say, things also work the other way around. Indeed, to think in terms of sub-structures and super-structures, depths and surfaces, is to revert to a Hegelian mode of analysis. So, the third move in post-structuralist theory is to treat the various domains of politics – politics in the state, politics in the household, the politics of mental illness, the politics of taste – as if they were on the same surface. To look at things in this way is to refuse (or at least suspend judgement about) claims to the effect that *this* (capitalism, patriarchy, the state system, consumer culture, modernity itself) is the basis for *that* (bourgeois/white-male domination, great power politics, environmental degradation, et cetera). Instead, one assumes that politics in all domains is both important and dangerous, and treats with great suspicion any claim to the effect that politics in *this* domain is more important because it lays the foundations for politics elsewhere. One is even less impressed by the claim that such and such a domain is important simply because it is *called* politics at the moment.

Governmentality studies are exemplary of the post-structuralist approach in the sense that they present matters normally conceived as effects of government decision, as appearing in fields of political struggle that cut across (without encompassing) the domains of private business, voluntary initiative, social service, professional organization, and so on. Governmentality and politics go together, but they are not coterminus with the state's field of action. Nor is there an architectonic structure or template for governmentality and politics. There are many governmentalities and many politics. At best, there is a certain homology between politics in one domain or level of existence and another. The politics that one discovers in government (in the ordinary sense) is analogous to the politics one discovers in personal life, and that politics is in turn analogous to the politics of the self and the politics of representation (of the world, the other, or the self: to oneself and others). Politics appears and reappears in these different domains, but the politics in one domain or at one level is not the cause of politics elsewhere. Homology there may be, but not causation (at least not causation as heretofore understood). Although the political is primal, it lacks any definite form, it has no particular origin, and it fails to structure things in a definite way. There is an openness or uncertainty to it, which stands in sharp contrast to the traditional image of the sovereign. The presence of politics and the lack of a sovereign are two dimensions of the same phenomenon.

The most simplistic reading of this lack of a sovereign is in terms of the death of the nation state. Everyone knows that states are still with us, but many people sense that states can no longer deliver on the promise of social democracy, or even on the more limited promises of liberalism. What is the point of a state if does not enable people to achieve their most important political objectives? Should not our politics be in search of a new political form? Or, do we have no alternative but to recreate the form that we seem to have lost? The drive in the latter direction is strong, but the felt lack of an appropriate *political form* haunts even post-structuralist musings (see, for instance, Derrida, 1994, 1997).

The Sovereign Politics of Nostalgia

Third Way politics is a bid for what the Gramscians call 'hegemony': that is, (to use Laclau's terms) for a certain discursive articulation that brings differences into a relation that makes the particular appear universal. On the Gramscian account, a way of being in the world (and hence of thinking about the world) becomes hegemonic at the point at which it begins to seem natural and any other way of being in the world comes to seem unnatural. Thus, by 1991, many Russians were saying that they just wanted their country to be a 'normal' country: by which they meant one that was organized on the same principles as the ones in Western Europe and North America. Such thinking is a sign of hegemony: the hegemony of capitalist liberalism. Third Way politics is evidently a bid for hegemony within this hegemony, an effort to make a certain way of thinking about capitalist liberalism seem natural and necessary. If the bid succeeds, the George W. Bushes of the world will have to go on describing themselves as 'compassionate conservatives' in order to communicate with a mass public. And, socialists will have to describe themselves as radical democrats or civic republicans.

A politics that orients itself towards hegemony is a politics that re-enacts the quest for sovereignty. Whatever is hegemonic is in effect sovereign. We no longer expect the sovereign to be a person, but we do expect that there will be an order, a set of rules and expectations, or a way of being in the world that will set the norm (not only in the sense of setting an example, but also in the sense of enforcing the norm as a norm). A serious politics is a politics oriented towards sovereignty in this sense: that is, it is oriented towards changing, challenging, reorienting, protecting, or in any case doing something in relation to the ensemble that sets the norm. Socialist politics seemed like a serious politics throughout the twentieth century because it challenged the norm-setting ensemble at the centre of Western civilization (and hence at the centre of the modern world). Once it ceased to pose a serious challenge, it ceased to appear like a serious politics. This happened in two stages: first, the destruction of the socialist movement in the United States and its externalization as a threat to 'the Free World'; and, second, the destruction of socialist regimes in the Soviet Union and elsewhere and the reintegration of the countries concerned into a global economy/society/polity led by the United States. Third Way politics is an attempt to make the politics of the left serious again by giving it goals consistent with the hegemony of a capitalist liberalism that has defeated the socialist challenge. It is a politics that remains under the spell of sovereignty.

To identify hegemony with sovereignty and to connect politics with the quest for hegemony/sovereignty (as I have done here), is to gesture at a pattern of thought and action that is so familiar to us that we scarcely notice it. In the textbook accounts (as well as in popular imagination), politics and government are associated with the state. The state in turn is conceived as that which provides for law and order. Its branches are the legislature, the executive, and the judiciary. It generates new laws as required; it enforces whatever laws have been established; it adjudicates particular cases. Thus, the state is the ground and completion of civil society (as Hegel argued). A serious politics is necessarily oriented towards the state because the state *is* the juridical order. If there is something that lies behind that juridical order, something that needs to be changed (as socialists have always argued), that something must be the ultimate object of a serious politics. Nevertheless, such a serious politics must pass through the state, since the state is what secures the thing that lies behind. So, in the classical Marxist view, socialist politics had to be society-centred for purposes of popular mobilization, but state-centred in terms of its medium term objectives, in order that it could break up the obstacles in the way of the revolution it sought at the level of society. Ultimately, the state itself would become redundant, but in the medium term it had to be at the centre. The revisionist or social democratic view was not much different in its state-centricity, except that it abandoned the hope of overcoming the state as it abandoned the hope of a complete revolution. The Third Way follows on from this thinking.

Hobbes posed the problem of sovereignty/hegemony in a way that has troubled everyone since. His argument (to put it simply) was that people were *naturally* sovereign *as individuals*, and that this natural sovereignty put them at odds with one another in a way that made civilization impossible. The only way out of the dilemma was for people to surrender their sovereignty to a ruler who would give them back such freedom as was consistent with the maintenance of the ruler's artificial sovereignty over them. This idea – that civic freedom depended on the surrender of natural sovereignty to an absolute ruler – was scarcely congenial to those who had come to regard sovereignty as the ultimate value. For liberals, individual sovereignty was not just the natural condition of humanity (as Hobbes believed); it was also the proximate aim of any appropriate effort at civilization. Individual sovereignty – or what the liberals called 'freedom' – was the ground and completion of civilization itself. To insist, as Hobbes did, that individual sovereignty was inconsistent with civilization was deeply troubling. Subsequent liberal thought has been largely concerned with showing that Hobbes was wrong: demonstrating that sovereign individuals could generate a civilized order without surrendering their sovereignty. Such an order has been called a 'free society,' which is to say a society characterized by (and founded upon) the principle of 'self-government' (or autonomy, as Kant would have it). Self-government is a principle that is supposed to extend from top to bottom and from side to side. Individuals are to be self-governing, groups are to be self-governing, communities are to be self-governing, nations are to be self-governing, the world is to be self-governing. The problem, of course, is that it is not immediately evident how all these modes of self-government are to be reconciled with one another. There are many disagreements among liberals about how this objective is to be achieved, but a broad consensus has emerged since Hobbes's time.

We all know what that consensus is. The idea is that people should be allowed, as far as possible, to order their own lives as they please. The power of the state should be deployed to restrain people from interfering with one another in inappropriate ways. Moreover, it should be used to encourage if not to require people to take responsibility for themselves and to behave responsibly towards others (that is, in ways that respect and encourage other people's 'freedom'). These responsible/free/self-governing individuals will themselves be the ones who, together, will control the state and deploy its powers. Self-government is to be extended to the level of the state through a political process that is necessarily liberal (in the sense that it allows for the orderly but free exchange of ideas) and democratic (in the sense that is inclusive of everyone who is to be governed). So, the circle is closed by establishing a state that is organized on the principle of self-government and deploys its powers in a way that protects and enhances (if not actually produces) the self-governing individuals necessary for self-government at the level of the state. A homologous order of self-government, running from the individual on up is the liberal ideal. Socialism has always presented itself as a *fulfilment* of liberalism: that is, as a social order that eliminates the obstacles to genuine freedom or self-government. The proof of this – according to Marxist theoreticians – is that socialist order would not need the state, in the end, because the relation between self-governing individuals would be such that coercive power would become redundant. This, of course, is the anarchist dream. It has its classically liberal counterpart in the ideal of the minimal state, expressed by thinkers like Hayek.

It should be evident that the idealized order of liberalism or socialism is an order of *sovereignty*: not in the sense of a sovereignty *over* individuals but in the sense of a sovereignty that individuals exercise over themselves: self-sovereignty or self-government. Liberty and democracy are two aspects of this ideal of self-sovereignty. Equality and justice are normally conceived in terms that only make sense in relation to this ideal of self-sovereignty. *Pacem* Hegel, the role of the state in relation to this ideal is quite contingent. One might imagine the nation state as essential, as a sort of mediated order necessary to make sovereignty real at any level. On the other hand, anarchists, free-market liberals, communitarian socialists and others have always been sceptical about the necessity of the nation state. Ideas of federalism, confederalism, and the community of nations have long been about. It is quite possible to conceive of an order of sovereignty in which the nation state plays a comparatively minor role. It remains to be seen how practical that might be. Nonetheless, it is significant that the most imaginative of contemporary liberal thinkers are reviving notions of civic republicanism, federalism, and treaty-bound alliances to enable thinking about new political possibilities. Obviously, the European Union is one of the most significant of those new possibilities.

It should also be evident that the order of sovereignty drags a certain conception of politics in its wake. Politics, at its most serious, is about the creation, adaptation, improvement, preservation, and/or transformation of whatever order of sovereignty is established. For the order of sovereignty to be an order of self-sovereignty, the politics that produces, reproduces, or changes it must be itself a politics of self-sovereignty. Such a politics is more popularly described as a politics of freedom or a liberal politics or a democratic politics. It normally refers back to an imagined experience of self-government that is more authentic than the one in which we are presently engaged. In Western thought, the Athenian *polis* is the major point of reference. It represents the point of origin for practices of politics, freedom, and democracy: that is, for practices of self-sovereignty. Other experiences may be invoked: tribal assemblies and village meetings; clubs, societies, and corporations of various sorts; the practices of the early Roman republic or the medieval Italian city states; the early American republic; and so on. What links these experiences together and makes them a source of inspiration is that they appear to be instances of self-government. It is not just that they seem to be characterized by free and democratic relations between the individuals involved. It is also that these bodies or practices seem to allow the people concerned to set some if not all of the conditions of their own existence through a process of deliberation, decision, and collective action. This process appears to be one of government, but in a profound sense. Such government is not just superficial; it is constitutive or foundational. It is a way of producing the form of life that the people want.

To conceive of politics as a process whereby a way of life is produced, reproduced, tended or transformed is to think of it in terms that centre it on the moment of hegemony or sovereignty. It is by politics that we seek to fill that moment, and so govern ourselves. Unfortunately, sovereignty/hegemony always seems to recede from our grasp. It is constantly displaced by processes that we only dimly understand and that we cannot control. So, the moment of 'sovereignty' that we achieve through practices of self-government or practices of politics (are they not ultimately the same?) never seems quite real. Sovereignty is the grail that justifies our quest, but it constantly recedes from our grasp.

One way of thinking about a politics keyed to sovereignty is in terms of a motivating nostalgia. We are nostalgic for the Greek polis, the Roman republic, the New England town meeting, the tribal village, the small town, or some other imagined community in which the people were supposed to have been self-governing. But, we are also nostalgic for a time when our institutions of government actually seemed effective: when they actually seemed capable of determining some, if not all of the important conditions of our lives. Many people on the left see the Keynesian welfare state in these terms: not as something that was ever perfect, but something that always promised and partially delivered a certain control over the capitalist economy and a certain network of public services that enabled a watered down socialism. For a person to have guaranteed housing, guaranteed education, a guaranteed job, guaranteed health care, guaranteed transport, guaranteed recreation facilities, guaranteed social services and a guaranteed pension was no small thing. To organize a whole country in a way that secured these objectives was a substantial achievement. Now it seems that the strategies that enabled governments to create welfare states (by managing economies in a way that stabilized employment, secured new jobs, and left a substantial surplus for public services) no longer work. The reasons for this are complex, and perhaps it might have been otherwise, but it seems that the horse of capitalism is already out of the barn of the nation state. There is no obvious way of putting the horse back in the barn. If it is to be managed at all, we will have to use new strategies. Hence, the seductive appeal of 'advanced liberal' strategies of government like responsibilization (that is, requiring people to take responsibility for their own wastes, their own health, their own education, and so on and extending this requirement for responsible behaviour to the corporate sector), ethicization (that is, encouraging people to think of their responsibilities in ethical terms and requiring organizations to develop and maintain their own codes of ethics), auditing and accounting, publicization (of performance results), privatization (of immediate responsibility for particular tasks of activities), and so on. If the old strategies of government do not work, perhaps the new ones will. Perhaps the latter are more appropriate to a world in which people have become accustomed to live as individuals with a wide range of choices and in which economic, social and cultural activity spreads across national borders.

There is a certain appeal in such responses, but note the way that they are motivated by our own nostalgia. We are nostalgic for a government that is really effective, effective in a way that the state 'used to be'. Note also that we are nostalgic for a time – in our imagination usually prior to the time at which we had an effective state – when people could really participate as equals in the process of government. We have 'lost' the state as a locus of effective government, and we have lost the *polis* (or some sort of *polis* surrogate) as a locus of democratic politics. We are pointed forward to a time in which we can bring government and politics, state and *polis* back together: a time that we were already supposed to have had by virtue of 'liberal democracy,' the form that the state was supposed to have taken as a result of the triumph of liberal-democratic politics. So, what we seek is a revival or adaptation of something that we were supposed to have had but never really did. Our nostalgia for this way of life that we imagine we ought to have had drives us on towards a new and perhaps better version of the same thing. *La republique est morte. Vive la republique.*

This nostalgic vision enables us to represent reality in a particular way, and filter out things that do not fit. The massacre in Rwanda, drug wars in Colombia, communal riots in Indonesia, criminal gangs in Kosovo, aerial warfare against Iraq, the corruption of the Los Angeles Police Department: phenomena like these flit through our imaginations, but we do not really know how to relate them to the vision that is emerging. The world that we read of in the newspapers or see on television and the imagined global community – liberal, democratic, orderly, tolerant – do not really mesh, and no one can really conceive of a process that would make the latter triumphant. There is no imaginable politics that could deliver on the sovereigntist vision, which is of a world 'fit for sovereigns'. What the analysts of advanced liberalism have helped us to see is that current strategies of governance are keyed into the idea of governing 'at a distance' and hence 'through freedom'. What needs to be added is that this is a strategy of governing *through sovereignty*: that is, through the sovereignty of the individual, the community, and on 'up'. 'Sovereignty' and 'freedom' are the same things: they are but different names for autonomy. The liberal/socialist quest is still for an order that makes sovereignty/freedom manifest at all levels, in all domains, in all cultures of the world. Many, many heads and hearts will have to be broken if this objective is to be achieved.

Beyond Nostalgia

The question at the heart of post-structuralist critique is this: are there any other possibilities? In other words, is there any other way for us to relate to the quest? Or, are we just fated to behave in this way? Note that the quest that motivates these questions is not the one for a world in which we all become true believers in Christ, or learn to follow the precepts of the Koran, or key our hearts to the insights that come from yogic meditation. Religious or quasi-religious quests are already subject to effective liberal critique, at least in so far as they are used to justify political or governmental arrangements. The quest at issue is the liberal/socialist/humanist quest for a world ordered on the principle of self-sovereignty. It is at issue precisely because it is so compelling. It is hard for a thoughtful person not to identify with this quest in some degree. And that is not a bad thing in itself. But, it is dangerous. None of us is free from the tendency to clothe ourselves in the righteousness of this quest, and applaud the bombs dropping on the religious fundamentalists, ethno-nationalists, war lords, drug dealers, peasant insurgents, underclass low lifes, and the other bad guys who populate our Hollywoodized imaginations. Nor do we find it that difficult to forget all the things that we need to forget in our aim to convince ourselves that we are making 'progress'.

Is there then any other way of being political than to situate oneself within this quest and say, 'Go here, not there!'? Perhaps. What emerges from post-structuralist critique is not a diagnosis that gives us a clear sense of who we are and where we should be going. At best, we come to recognize that all constructions of 'reality' are effects of our own desires, mediated by political struggles that occur in many different domains, in accordance with many different logics. We can take from physics and biology reminders about non-linearity in causation, the inherent unpredictability of 'chaotic' systems, the relationality of time and space, the impact of the analyst on the object of the analysis, and so on. This may help us to recognize that scientific objectivity is not a matter of making dogmatic assertions about 'reality', but of being modest, careful, and skeptical in our judgements (compare Haraway, 1997). In that spirit, we may be able to see that the liberal/socialist/humanist quest for sovereignty or freedom as a form for human life is just about as dubious as all the other quests in which humans have been engaged from time to time. It needs to be subjected to the same searching criticism that we have applied to religious fundamentalism or ethno-nationalism. As we apply that criticism to *ourselves*, we may well discover ways of being political that are not so dependent on dogmatic assertion.

It would be wrong to suggest that post-structuralist theory takes us beyond the politics of nostalgia. On the contrary: it too is affected by insistent longings for a sovereign who could order otherwise, a politics that could *be* sovereign, and a freedom that could be as political as it is personal. Such longings appear in speculations about radical democracy, civic republicanism, agonistic politics, and so on. The same longings haunt most of the work of post-structuralist theorists. A nostalgic politics is one that keeps bringing us back to these longings, and hence to images of ancient Athens or the early American republic or the Paris Commune. The ostensibly radical politics of contemporary social movements is as nostalgic in this respect as the more mainstream politics of the Third Way. No doubt it helps us to see that the dream of freedom will not be realized in the form of the liberal-democratic nation state. But, it is more helpful to see that the dream itself is a dream of sovereignty and that sovereignty involves a forceful imposition of our own imaginings upon the world. A different way of being political is to treat our own dreams as sceptically as everyone else's. Perhaps then we will be less inclined to let our nostalgia govern us.

Beyond the Politics of Nostalgia					197

References

Butler, J., Laclau E. and Slavoj, Z. (2000), *Contingency, Hegemony, Universality: Contemporary Dialogues on the Left*, Verso, London.

Dean, M. (1999), *Governmentality: Power and Rule in Modern Society*, SAGE, London.

Derrida, J. (1994), *Specters of Marx: The State of the Debt, the Work of Mourning, and the New International*, Routledge, New York.

Derrida, J. (1997), *The Politics of Friendship* [trans. George Collins], Verso, London.

Haraway, D.J. (1997), *Modest_Witness@Second_Millennium.FemaleMan©_Meets_Onco-Mouse™: Feminism and Technoscience*, Routledge, New York.

Kramer, J. (2000), 'Liberty, Equality, Sorority: French Women Demand their Share', *The New Yorker*, May 29.

Rose, N. (1999), *Powers of Freedom: Reframing Political Thought*, Cambridge University Press, Cambridge.

PART IV

THIRD WAY POLITICS IN PRACTICE – NEW POLITICAL SPACES FOR DEMOCRATIC RENEWAL?

Chapter 9

Urban Governance Restructuring: a Template for New Progressive Politics or the Endrun of Neoliberal Urbanism?[1]

Roger Keil

Introduction: The Third Way Ain't No Urban Street

At the turn of the millennium, the western world was talking about a Third Way. Yet, the ascendance of New Left/New Labour and talk about various 'Third Ways' in national governments in Western countries presents us with a dilemma. This move away from more conservative governments in the 1980s to a new brand of social democracy during the 1990s occurred at a time when many big cities, traditionally the stronghold of official and unofficial progressive politics, fell into the hands of rather aggressive conservative, neoconservative, or neoliberal governments. Neoliberal urbanism is a wider phenomenon that can be studied in cities all over western societies. In some cities, the ascendance of right-wing urbanism coincided with the restructuring of governance systems that provided the background for exemplary struggles over issues of local democracy, urban citizenship, and social justice. The official neoliberalism espoused by the entrepreneurial governments of large cities is, of course, counteracted by ever more sophisticated and potentially radical urban movements, which have begun to redefine the urban as a meaningful site for the forging of new alliances, for new political strategies and new substantive concerns. But many of these movements have left the pathway of left-wing urban politics. If there is neoliberal urbanism and progressive urbanism, there are also new emerging coalitions and constellations that we may call the urban Third Way. But let us first consider why the Third Way has bypassed the city.

---

[1] Previous versions of this chapter were published in *Alternatives*, 25(2), 2000 and Albert Scharenberg (2000) (ed.), *Berlin: Global City oder Konkursmasse*, Karl Dietz Verlag, Berlin. It should also be noted that the argument presented here was developed before 9/11, which changed the context of urban politics once again, particularly in New York City.

Third Way and New Labour politics are mostly discussed in the traditional framework of national and international politics. It is the contention of this paper that globalization has brought with it a rescaling of governance in significant new ways. Notwithstanding the insistence of many authors that the nation state continues to be the main arena of societalization even in a global age, a great deal of those material and discursive processes we call globalization occur through channels outside the policy arena of national politics (Panitch, 1994; Hirsch, 1995; Altvater and Mahnkopf, 1996; Panitch and Leys, 1999). Cities, and particularly large core cities of the global economy, play a major role in providing the political, economic, social and cultural conduits of globalization. Cities are important sites of the formation of post-national states (Keil, 1998a).

The shift of urban governments to the right is very important in this context as urban politics regulates many of the contentious issues of globalizing societies: migration and settlement; police and social control; social services; environmental regulation; schools and education, et cetera. To a certain degree, cities have become the political place where the dirty work of globalization is being done. Evidence for this development is available in many literatures. One salient example in the scholarly debate has been the work of Loïc Wacquant who has studied the new ghettoization dynamics and authoritarian policies in North American and European cities. In a much publicized article in *Le Monde Diplomatique* in early 1999, Wacquant maintains that '[the] state retreats from the economic arena and emphasizes itself the necessity of reducing its social policy role and to simultaneously strengthening the apparatus of repression' (Wacquant, 1999, p. 1). Not surprisingly, while advertised internationally by conservative American research institutes, the recipes for social control espoused by the state focus on the urban dimension of the control and on the capacities of the local state to intervene in social matters. New York City under Mayor Rudolph Giuliani gained some notoriety in sweeping the streets clean of homeless people, drug addicts and other undesired elements. The so-called 'broken windows' theory and policies of 'zero tolerance' and 'three strikes, you're out' directed at petty criminals in particular have a decidedly urban dimension. The discursive reconstruction of urban politics into an arsenal of authoritarian measures to regulate social problems is paralleled by a broad media attack on the poor, the homeless, the marginal, the alternatives and their political advocates. While there are periodic rituals of public solidarity in cities with homeless people and children in poverty, the overall tone of public discourse on the urban 'Other' has become noticeably more rough throughout the 1990s. Again, cities, often correctly hailed as the multicultural, multi-class, multi-sexual orientation strongholds of globalized postmodern society, are also at times the focal point of reactionary politics. A case in point has been the unprecedented campaign of the Toronto Press against the radical poverty advocacy organization *Ontario Coalition Against Poverty* (*OCAP*) and its charismatic leader John Clarke. While all Toronto papers have chastised OCAP and Clarke for their confrontational, direct action approach to anti-poverty politics for some time, the demonstrative squatting of a downtown park in the summer of 1999 brought out particularly violent reactions by pundits across the city. One neighbourhood paper made Clarke the subject of a front page article with the headline 'Poverty Pimp'. In an inside article short on information about the surge in homelessness and poverty in Tory Toronto but long on red-baiting, misrepresentations and badmouthing, OCAP and Clarke are accused of exploiting the homeless for the purpose of a radical Marxist agenda (McLeod, 1999, p. 5).[2]

When a version of the 'Third Way' became national policy in the UK under Prime Minister Blair, in Germany under Chancellor Schröder, and in the USA during President Clinton's time in office, urban politics in some European and North American cities moved into the opposite direction: the installation of decidedly more conservative municipal governments. In the past, urban governments in Europe were often considered strongholds of social democratic or communist parties; in the US, mayors tended to be Democratic and often minority; in Canada, urban politics has also been associated with periods of radical reform such as the early tenure of the Montreal Citizens Movement or the bourgeois left-liberalism of Toronto in the 1970s. In fact, if any strategy of the Thatcher government – perhaps apart from crushing the unions during the miners' strike – will be remembered clearly and universally, it is the Tories' remorseless attack on red city halls, particularly the dismantling of the Greater London Council under Ken Livingstone. Today, we cannot be so sure that *local* necessarily means *progressive* politics. In fact, many urban political climates have shifted so far to the right that they appear more conservative than state, provincial, or *Land*-governments around them. The same can be said about their relationship to national or federal governments. Often (like in Frankfurt under Mayors Wallmann and Brück, 1977–89) conservative municipal governments have served as the idea givers and laboratories for conservative state and federal governments, which were to follow.

In all cases, the shift towards more conservative government has had a basis in the socio-spatial restructuring of urban regions and in globalization of urban economic and social relations. There have been spatial shifts of industries and population from the centre to the periphery of cities; with gentrification and 'yuppification', there has been a marked exchange of certain groups of inner city populations, which has led to a shift in political agendas and political participation. Global capital, if we assume for a moment that such a thing exists, has noticed that it needs to get involved in urban politics as it takes root in the dramatically

---

[2] Another publication, the weekly *Toronto Eye* magazine, broke the ranks of the united press front in Toronto, and documented many instances of the 'war on John Clarke', whom they considered 'the most unpopular man in Toronto' in the summer of 1999 (see *Eye*, 9/19/1999).

restructured downtowns and edge cities of western urban areas; and global capital has usually noticed that its interests are best served under conservative urban governments whose policies and ideologies of deregulation, tax-cutting, fiscal restraint, social control and workfare appear to harmonize perfectly with their own agenda of downsizing, globalization, and lean corporate governance.

Conservative Urbanism: Burning Down the House

During the winter of 1998–99, a bizarre spectacle occurred on websites and email listserves across North America. Mike Davis and his second volume of a projected Los Angeles trilogy, *Ecology of Fear*, published earlier in 1998, became the focus of a vicious campaign, mostly orchestrated by right-wing commentators, pundits and scholars. Davis, the celebrated author of *City of Quartz*, arguably the most influential book on cities in the 1990s, became subject to a barrage of accusations that ranged from shoddy scholarship to outright falsification of facts (Davis, 1990, 1998). While Davis had little opportunity to defend himself or explain some of the issues involved in the debate on his person and his work, there seemed to be an unending capacity on the part of some of his detractors to make him into the symbol of everything that was wrong with progressive urban scholarship. While this is not the place to fully revisit the Davis debate, a few noteworthy lessons can be learned from it and can be insightful in the context of this chapter.[3] The aggressive right-wing reaction to the radical analysis put forward in Davis' book bore witness to two related shifts in urban realities. On one hand, it demonstrated the new found self-confidence of the new right which had taken over many city halls and municipal governments from more progressive political regimes since the 1970s; on the other hand, it marked a backlash on the academic front: in urban studies generally, where neo-Marxist and neo-Weberian progressives had made inroads since the 1960s, a conservative tone took hold over the past few years which buttressed the real politics of urban conservatism with theoretical justifications. Let us look at these developments in turn.

Hostile Takeovers: The Urban Experience

In a review of the debate on *Ecology of Fear*, Robert Beauregard argues that as part of the shift from democratic liberalism to neoconservatism from the 1960s to the 1990s in the United States overall

---

[3] See the September 1999 issue of *Capitalism, Nature, Socialism* for a review symposium on *Ecology of Fear*.

many conservatives have become pro-urban. They have discovered a way to combine their moral disapproval of the poor and minorities, on which their initial anti-urbanism was based, and their persistent interest in economic growth with a new appreciation of city life (Beauregard, 1999, pp. 40–41).

Beauregard makes the case that the nasty controversy around Davis' book

concerned how conservatives in particular and less so liberals and progressives are repositioning themselves on the political terrain of the cities. That conservatives should even care, given their post-World War II dismissal of things urban is a significant part of this story (Beauregard, 1999, p. 41).

Now, he says,

[n]eo-conservative mayors, Republican and Democrat, are much more common. They include Rudy Giuliani in New York City, John O. Norquist in Milwaukee, Stephen Goldsmith in Indianapolis, Susan Golding in San Diego, and Bret Schundler in Jersey City (NJ) among others (Beauregard, 1999, p. 42).

Los Angeles in the 1990s faced a choice between 'an urban republic and republican urbanism'. The riot-induced shift from the liberal, Democratic Bradley coalition to the paradoxical 'populist elitism' of Republican millionaire Richard Riordan in 1993 marked a watershed in the city's political development. While Bradley's 20-year reign had grown out of an uneasy combination of grassroots protest politics (environment, race), labour and global capital, Riordan's populist ways can barely hide his country club political home and right-wing agenda. Making government increasingly work and look like a private corporation has been the goal of many entrepreneurial municipal leaders, yet in Riordan, this shift becomes personified. In the waning years of his second term, there is little doubt that Riordan has reduced much of the political in urban politics to the capacity of his leadership to raise campaign contributions. From his struggle for the new City Charter and against suburban secessionism to the staffing of the Los Angeles School Board, there has been serious interference of big money (and its predictable political agenda) with matters of democratic decision making (Keil, 1993, 1998b).

The American experience of Republican mayors and neoliberal Democrats monkeying their policies is also reflected in European and Canadian developments. In Frankfurt, for example, Christian Democrat Walter Wallmann catapulted the city in 1977 out of its crisis ridden postwar status as the nation's ugly duckling and made it somewhat of a success story of postmodern urbanity during the 12 years of his conservative party's reign. In the 1989 elections the Christian Democrats (CDU) were removed from office by the voters who would not follow them into the netherworld of blunt racism, when the party embraced anti-immigrant election slogans. The ensuing 'red/green coalition' of Social Democrats and Greens started with reformist enthusiasm but with a weak coalition agreement that allowed the continuation of Frankfurt's world city growth but gave some more or less symbolic handouts in return to the Left's traditional constituencies of social and ecological reform. In hindsight, the red/green government, which for all intents and purposes ended with the election of conservative Petra Roth as Mayor of Frankfurt in 1995, can be read as a case study in the dismantling of a progressive urban project in German cities. While in economic matters, there has been ample continuity from the Wallmann years, through the red/green project to the current social democratic and Christian democratic 'grand coalition',[4] the biggest change was the introduction of fiscally conservative cutbacks and lean government under Mayor von Schöler and Chancellor of the Exchequer Tom Koenigs. All but a few progressive policy features introduced under pressure from social movement constituencies in 1989 were abandoned. As the local social democrats had already sidelined the classical social justice constituency in the party, the so-called '*Beton-Fraktion*' or concrete faction – a reference to its base in working class, often construction worker, milieus – the most significant, and in some ways surprising, loser of the turn to the right under 'red/green' was the environment. An ambitiously designed Green Belt project, which at times looked like the core urban planning feature of the new government, was abandoned before it could bear fruit. Other grand schemes of ecological reform were pushed onto the back burner as the economy and the budget became the main concern (Ronneberger and Keil, 1993, pp. 19–50).

In Canada's metropolis Toronto, the classical liberal urbanism devised by a coalition of 'red Tories', environmentalists, labour and left liberals, has suffered extreme setbacks during the 1980s and 1990s. First a dull and ineffective administration of June Rowlands muddled through the catastrophic recession in the early 1990s and then suburban appliance salesman and showster Mel Lastman, a former North York mayor, was elected mayor of all of Toronto in 1997. He effectively introduced suburban standards of policy making to Canada's largest metropolis. The government of moderate social democrat and social welfare advocate Barbara Hall from 1994–97 can, in hindsight, only be considered an interlude in a conservative project to bring Toronto to its neoliberal senses (Keil, 1998c, pp. 151–67).

These examples bear witness not just to a substantive move to the right on almost all issues, they also have experienced procedural changes unimaginable at the beginning of the decade when the world was buzzing with the hopeful talk of civil society and democracy. In all cities, the governing process has talked the talk of governance and walked the walk of decisionism. A few democratization and

---

[4] Klaus Ronneberger pointed out to me in a personal conversation that the 'grand coalition' was perhaps the specific German form of conservative hegemony in German cities during the 1990s. Next to Frankfurt, the Berlin example is important here.

social justice gains notwithstanding, urban government in all three cities appears less open to political influence from citizen groups and social movement fragments. As the call for tax cuts and service cutbacks started to stand in for urban discourse in cities around the western world, these three cities did not stand back. In addition, it appears particularly troubling that the call for more police action in these cities (which accompany and complement 'market liberalization') come at a time when police forces in New York and Los Angeles are under intense public scrutiny for corruption and racism, while Toronto's police union has attempted to influence the political process by bullying politicians and citizens who have been critical of the police in the past.

Delegitimizing Critical Urbanism: The Academic Experience

The shift in the real world of urban politics from the left to the right has been accompanied by an even more profound attack on the foundations of critical urban scholarship which had characterized the earlier decades.[5] One or two generations of radical scholars in sociology, geography, and political economy had grown up to view the urban question as central to social theory and political action in the capitalist West. The 'urbanization' of Marxism in particular had been triggered by the pathbreaking work in the 1960s and 1970s of Europeans Manuel Castells (1972, 1978), and David Harvey (1973, 1982) (both of them influenced, in different ways, by the spatial and urban theory of Henri Lefebvre).[6] While quite diverse in their respective approaches to the urban problematique, these authors shared a common interest in 'the wild city' (Castells), which had been the most visible site of boom and doom of post-World War II western capitalism (Fordism). Eruptions of rebellions, rent strikes, transit fare struggles, urban social movements, and counter cultures blanketed the western world in the 1960s and 1970s like a wildfire from the Watts ghetto in Los Angeles to the west bank of Paris. These events, which often took place in close vicinity to the alleged success stories of post-World War II urbanism – inner city redevelopment sites and peripheral

---

[5] This section builds on Keil and Lehrer (1999).

[6] From the point of view of the urban question, Henri Lefebvre's (1968, 1970) work in the late 1960s, strongly influenced by the upheavals of May '68, were most important. While these publications had a great impact on the French and German discourses (*La revolution urbaine* was published in German), it had only limited impact in the English speaking world, where writers who built on this work such as David Harvey, Mark Gottdiener, and Edward Soja were the exceptions. Among Lefebvre's many publications, the following probably had the most decisive influence on the English language urbanist debate: Lefebvre (1979, 1991, 1996). For an excellent current review of the influence of Lefebvre's thinking on urban studies see Neil Brenner, 'The urban question as a scale question: reflections on Henri Lefebvre, urban theory and the politics of scale in the late 1990s', forthcoming in *International Journal of Urban and Regional Research*.

housing estates – became the backdrop for a radical urbanist practice throughout the next two decades.

When the urban crisis transformed itself into regeneration during the boom of the 1980s, two kinds of discourses took hold. A culturalist discourse of images and signs replaced much of the articulation of social and political concerns that had previously been in the centre of radical urbanism. And an economic-geographical debate, largely based on the realist middle range philosophy of the regulation school, replaced the topos of *la revolution urbaine* with paradigms of regional capacity building, urban governance and reflexivity (Harvey, 1989; Soja, 1989; Scott, 1988). But things took an interesting turn after that. While the world of urban studies was busy debunking the myths of waterfront redevelopment, malls and cultural palaces through discourse analysis and semiotic exercises, and while it was rebuilding its links to hegemonic projects through ideas of endogenous regional economic growth and urban renaissance, Mike Davis planted the *City of Quartz* into the centre of the debate. This book enabled students of urbanism to develop new categories of critique, but to stay in the trajectory opened up by neo-Marxist and neo-Weberian urban research since the 1960s. Davis' contribution was an act of liberation of thought and practice because it touched on the major urban themes of the nineties: carceral cities, urban ecology, right-wing populism, middle class environmentalism and environmental justice, global urbanization, the immigrant city, urban histories, large scale projects, urban governance, et cetera.

The attack on *Ecology of Fear* goes to the heart of the legitimacy of the kind of fundamental urban critique *City of Quartz* had proposed for Los Angeles and elsewhere. Radical urban praxis that exceeds the comanagement dispute resolution philosophy of the 1990s is now being delegitimized the way rap music has become synonymous in the mainstream media with preaching violence and socio-ethical decay. The significance of the attack on his work as fundamental urban critique lies in its contextualization in the liberal-conservative shift change: it affects all of critical urban research in that it questions the very right of scholars and activists to expose 'their' city, or other cities, to a fundamental critique (Beauregard, 1999, p. 43). At the same token, the universalist claims of progressive urbanism – considering the urban as a space of liberation – comes under attack. The Fordist-Keynesianist idea of a middle class society had its urban equivalent in progressive urbanism's post-World War II traditions. This claim for the city as a space of possible liberation has given way to the image of the city with 're-naturalized' differences of social status, life chances, and citizenship. The neoliberal urban project revels in the new inequalities that are sometimes clouded in romantic rhetoric of urban diversity.

While the project of the academic right seems to sail full steam ahead, the left engages mostly in rearguard skirmishes for the sake of saving its traditional mantra of progressive urbanity which Beauregard has characterized as follows:

Liberal and progressive critics of the city have traditionally condemned rapid growth, speculation, and profit-driven real estate development, while celebrating an urban way of life that is diverse, tolerant, and stimulating. Their urbanism has been anchored in praise for an industrial working class, support for the poor, and castigation of the middle class for fleeing to the suburbs. Now it also includes scorn for the 'new' urban middle class (Beauregard, 1999, p. 43).

Academics who socio-economically often belong to the group of gentrifiers and downtowners and epochally to the boomer generation, have a hard time dealing with the contradictions this position has entailed for their own politics and research. Risking the danger of over-simplification, let me suggest that there are mainly two camps in progressive urban intellectual and academic circles today. While quite distinct, they are not mutually exclusive and often inform or reinforce each other. One camp is what I would call the 'critics' and the other one I call, somewhat awkwardly, the 'changers'.

The 'critics' include most prominently erstwhile representatives of the neo-Marxist revolution which shook our understanding of cities 30 years ago. In various countries, the critical school has had its own incarnation.[7]

The 'changers' are emphasizing the possibilities the urban offers for social liberation. This alternative current has been a more action- and policy-oriented strand of analysts who have worked with concepts such as democratization, civil society, citizenship, social and environmental justice and so forth. In the camp of the changers, there has been some innovative work on the local state, and the potential of urban politics in their specific location between the state and civil society (Keil, 1998, pp. 616–46). The reintroduction of the concept of 'civil society' into a perspective on planning and progressive urban change is part of this tendency (Douglass and Friedmann, 1998). Much work has also been done following the battle cry of Henri Lefebvre to claim back the right to the city and a thousand little empowerments have taken place in cities all over the world and have been recorded and theorized accordingly.[8]

Perhaps the most visible and effective figure to integrate these two strands of

---

[7] In Germany, a very strong radical current has occupied the space Mike Davis has carved out (Sambale, 1999). Intellectuals grouped together in the Space Lab project and urban trendsetters in the *Innenstadtaktion* have been the most visible representatives of the new urban critique in that country. See, for example, Ronnenberger/Lanz/Jahn (1999). In Canada, little urban writing has been as unequivocally radical in style and contents as the ones mentioned but some work on homelessness, poverty and social services has begun to make references to the 'critical' school. In the US, writers like David Harvey, Neil Smith, and Peter Marcuse can be counted as members of the 'critical' school.

[8] Theorists and practitioners of urban politics have followed Lefebvre's call in many ways. Perhaps the best current collection of reports on such efforts is INURA 1998. For a perspective on alternative planning histories see Sandercock (1998).

radical urban thinking has been David Harvey, who calls for a living utopianism of process and the creation of possible urban worlds. While he persistently sticks to a radical urban critique, Harvey extends his argument to the positive reinforcement of existing real urban struggles such as the one for a living wage (Harvey, 1996; INURA, 1998, pp. 26–39).

The Left and the City: Disappearing Constituencies and Loss of Vision

It is quite possible to argue that the left has historically built much of its identity and meaning around the struggle of urban populations for economic justice and political democracy. The city used to be 'naturally' the locus of left-wing politics. Anything from social democratic politics (including both municipal socialism and more mainstream approaches) to revolutionary movements and urban rebellion, general strikes and armed struggle have populated the history of urban Leftism. Particularly, the New Left has, since the 1960s, built many of its myths around urban struggles of all kinds. The fight for People's Park in Berkeley the early 60s, Paris in May 1968, the demonstrations during the Chicago Democratic Convention in 1968, squatters in Berlin in 1980, youth revolt in Zurich in 1980, the militant movement against neofascists in Frankfurt in the early 1980s, particularly the demonstrations following the killing of demonstrator Günter Sare by Frankfurt police in September 1985, the Greater London Council in the early 1980s, the Toronto general strike of 1996.

Not accidentally, often the left has been strong in local politics before they could gain influence in national or regional politics. The German Greens' strength throughout local government in the 1980s and 1990s is a case in point. So are Santa Monica, California and Burlington, Vermont, as well as other progressive cities in the USA. Liverpool and London are famous examples of municipal socialism; Bologna was the showcase of communist local government in Italy. More recently, progressives have drawn solace in difficult times from radicals and environmentalists in power in southern cities such as Porto Alegre and Curitiba in Brazil.

Equally, the moment of the 'commune' has been a founding myth of the modern revolutionary movement ever since the workers were left to fend for themselves and to defend Paris by themselves in the Commune of 1871. While recognizing the chaotic quality of the concept 'commune', it is remarkable that cities as diverse as Berlin (1953/1989), Los Angeles (1965/1992), and Toronto (1992/1996) have all seen events in the postwar years which could somehow be classified as 'communes' in their own right. The relationship of the left to events as diverse as an urban uprising and a democratic revolution has not been unambiguous and there are no linear traditions that could be evoked. Yet, it is necessary to mention that these events, at least partially, nurtured the visions and myths through which the left has created its agenda.

All this seems history now. The left of the 1990s has no urban vision while the liberal middle revels in bourgeois utopias of all manner and the right merges vision with power into a new urban reality. The universalist Lefebvrian claim of the right to the city has been pushed aside or altered into fragmentary political projects. While this is not always and necessarily a bad thing – it has brought us many new urban experiments and resistances – it is a far cry from the revolutionary upheaval of earlier decades which purported to take the *whole* city *now*.

In addition, finally, the basis of urban social movements (USMs), long considered a prime locale of New Left politics, has been undermined in the three decades since Castells taught us that the city consisted of the spaces of collective consumption. Privatization of collective service, privatization of public and social housing, deindustrialization and inner city decay, decollectivization of lifestyles in the 'risk society' of today's cities, and many more factors have led to a deconstitution of the conditions where USMs can thrive. Also, often ideologically conservative groups have appropriated the ground of the USMs. This development has been most visible and pervasive in the many NIMBY (not-in-my-back-yard) activities in urban neighbourhoods which have often served to propel social segregation and spatial inequities. In some cases – for instance the revolt of the Northern fringe of Frankfurt in the early 1990s (Keil and Ronneberger, 1999), the mobilization of exurban conservatives against attempts to find a metropolitan waste disposal solution for Toronto in the mid-1990s and the secessionist posturing of the San Fernando Valley and San Pedro/Wilmington in Los Angeles – concerted middle class action with complex political liabilities and loyalties has created an entirely new type of social movement activity neither easily classifiable as left or right.

As a group, the mostly visionless urban leftists of the boomer generation, whose continued presence in the political arena is fuelled by various past local experiences stands in the way of both: the left's renewal of a radical or progressive vision and the complete success of the right's project of hegemonic urbanism. Much has been written about the role of the middle classes in city politics. In a nutshell, there has been a contradictory development which, on one hand, saw some segments of the middle classes disappear or dwindle in the face of urban restructuring while, on the other hand, some segments – the so-called 'new' middle classes – could gain ground in cities (Smith, 1996). The first dynamic is poignantly expressed by Harold Meyerson in the following description of Los Angeles at the end of the millennium:

Over the past 20 years, Los Angeles – once the model of postwar mass prosperity, where the backyard swimming pool became an ornament of middle-class life – has now become the model of the post-mass-prosperity metropolis. Of the 300,000 new jobs created in the county since 1993, the *L.A.Times* reports, more than 150,000 of them pay under $25,000 a year. Since 1991, the number of local jobs paying between $40,000 and $60,000 annually has actually declined by 97,000. Concurrently, L.A. has the lowest percentage of jobs offering medical coverage to its workers, – just 59 percent — of any American city, and one of the lowest percentages of homeowners. In short, the bottom hasn't fallen out of the L.A. economy, but the middle certainly has – and already in the nascent campaign for mayor, a surprising number of the candidates are pushing plans on how to bring that middle back (Meyerson, 1999, pp. 24–32).

The other dynamic, the emergence of new middle class segments is a counternarrative, heard sometimes in objection to the thesis of the vanishing middle class and sometimes in agreement with it. The bottom line of the argument seems to be that traditional working class and middle class occupations (and social milieus) do indeed disappear from cities as industries close and downsizing occurs; at the same time, however, new, and often younger segments of middle class people move to and gentrify inner city areas and occupy key positions in the burgeoning high tech and information based industries which tend to link their corporate culture to urban life. The consequences of this shift are as predictable as significant: The new middle classes become the mercenaries of cultural 'urbanity' and the supporters of a political project which allows the neoconservatives to retain selectively *anti*-public policy when desired (when, for instance, it comes to privatization of government services and the cutting of social programmes) and *pro*-public policy when needed (when, for example, it comes to policing the margin). Hence urban politics in the hands of the new middle classes become class politics in the crudest sense as it 'centres on an affluent middle class deeply implicated in growing corporate and financial services, high-end retailing and entertainment, downtown living, and robust housing markets' (Beauregard, 1999, p. 42; Smith, 1996). Beauregard concludes that left liberals and progressives, due to their traditional allegiances and political priorities, are now left 'with an urbanity that privileges groups that are disappearing and morally problematic, while marginalizing groups that are politically powerful and ascendant' (Beauregard, 1999, p. 43).

Which Way Third Way?

The result of the struggles over the meaning of the city will largely depend on whether the middle classes will be tempted to give in to the neoliberal and conservative agendas represented by politicians like Giuliani, Riordan, and Lastman, or if they are willing to and can be pressured to by radical urbanists to explore new coalitions with the challenger groups to neoliberal urbanism. A possible urban version of the Third Way, then, faces a crossroads between different options.

It is impossible to delineate clearly the choices ahead, as there might be quite diverging developments across various urban areas. Yet, it is possible to speculate about a few possible scenarios towards which we might be headed. I suggest differentiating three pathways in a landscape of 'possible urban worlds' – to borrow a term by David Harvey (Harvey, 1996). This landscape can be determined by the reality of recent and current events and by extrapolating some trajectories that are not entirely developed at this time. For the purposes of this discussion, I call these three pathways neoliberal urbanism, progressive urbanism, and 'Third Way' urbanism. These three fields are potentially overlapping and sometimes interdependent in their discursive construction in the political arena. In fact, most substantive issues of urban politics are addressed by competing factions in relation to each other's traditional policies and political preferences. Immigration and settlement policies, for example, are relational outcomes of often contentious political processes in which the nativism and bigotry of one political camp might be tampered or alternatively worsened by anti-racist and cosmopolitan positions in another camp.

Urban politics in large globalized cities are best viewed as a set of political arenas – such as the globalization of the local economy, immigration and settlement, identity and community, cultural politics, spatiality, class struggle, social welfare, urban ecology, and possibly others. These arenas are different from the classical policy areas of local politics in that they are shifting rapidly as globalization occurs. In fact, they are both the conditions for and the products of globalized urbanization. The three pathways outlined below relate in distinct ways to these political arenas as they develop.

With these caveats in mind, let us look, then, at the scenarios as if they were distinct projects: (1) the neoliberal project; (2) the progressive project, and (3) the Third Way project.

(1) The Neoliberal Project

The neoliberal project is characterized by the combination of two kinds of politics: the neoliberal economic agenda of deregulation, deficit cutting, and downsizing of urban government and the application of a series of policing measures for social control (Isin, 1998, pp. 169–92; Isin and Wolfson, 1999; Ronneberger et al., 1999). The neoliberal project combines the freeing of urban economies to the world market with the most conservative social, and often anti-immigrant, and always anti-marginal policies politically possible. Being both destructive of existing local economies and conservative of traditional hierarchical, patriarchal and exploitative structures (often clad in a populist ideology of folksy place-specificity) is the defining strategy of the neoliberals. They imagine a city with a commercialized and malled streetlife, lean urban government, suburbanized inner cities (cf. Times Square in New York City), lean urban government, home ownership over rental housing, low residential property taxes, private instead of collective consumption, law and order, invisible poverty and homelessness, controlled public spaces and managed segregation on various scales. Among the liberal and right-wing visions and cherished concepts of urbanism at the end of the millennium are

PRIVATOPIAS, most visibly in gated communities; COMMUNITOPIAS, or new urbanism; MILITARITOPIAS; the carceral or surveillance city; DOLLARTOPIA, the new consumption spaces, spectacles; and ENVIROTOPIA, the status quo sustainable city (admittedly a contradiction in terms).

(2)   The Progressive Project

The progressive project is in many ways the counterimage of the neoliberal one. Driven into a largely defensive stance by the aggressive neoliberal agenda of the last 15 years, urban progressives rarely have a comprehensive vision to offer when it comes to urban futures. In fact, many urban activists and intellectuals on the Left are outright critical of any attempt to create an overall vision due to fears of the undemocratic character of blueprints and masterplans. In his book *The Progressive City*, Pierre Clavel stated:

> The main features of progressive politics as practiced in these cities[9] included attacks on the legitimacy of absentee-owned and concentrated private power on the one hand, and on nonrepresentative city councils and city bureaucracies on the other. These attacks led to programs emphasizing public planning as an alternative to private power, and to grassroots citizen participation as an alternative to council-dominated representation. In most respects, these new programs produced a flood of institutional inventions (Clavel, 1987, p. 1).

Clavel goes on to mention three important features of these cities: First, in times of rampant privatization when local governments 'sold out' to or collapsed in the face of capital interests everywhere, these cities actually established what Clavel calls 'substantive' governments. Second, while governments in the 1980s moved to the right almost everywhere, these cities championed the poor and working people. Third, planning was recast as a link between a vital grassroots citizens movement and the desires of progressive political leaders to formulate redistributive politics. Historically, at least in the United States, the emergence of progressive cities occurred in the wake of the decline of growth politics. Industrial employment stopped growing; the demography of the inner cities changed dramatically; and while transfer payments of central governments to cities continued, the composition of local ruling coalitions changed also; in addition, the fiscal crisis of the state and gentrification of inner city neighbourhoods meant that while fewer services were available to the urban poor, the selective and exclusive investment of gentrifiers displaced inner city residents and called redistributive politics into question; and finally, the neighbourhood movement came into its own

---

[9] Clavel looked at Hartford, Cleveland, Berkeley, Santa Monica and Burlington.

as a countermovement. The reaction to these tendencies defined the progressive position in cities and ultimately the position of progressive cities.

Little of this dynamic seems to be alive today, despite the continued presence of progressive governments in various, mostly smaller, cities in North America and Europe. Instead, the dynamics of progressive urbanism has once again moved into the realm of civil society organizing and unofficial politics. Among the tangible features of the progressive urban project are the emergence of 'living wage' and other new labour movement strategies that are decidedly local and urban (Harvey, 1996; Standke, 1999). Other areas in which the progressive project has succeeded in claiming a piece of the urban discourse are the environmental justice problematic, citizenship struggles, progressive identity movements, community economic development, the reconciliation of urban and suburban politics, as well as homeless and poverty advocacy. We can also count among progressive urban policies the democratic budgeting processes under way in Brazil in cities governed by the Workers Party (PT). Yet, rarely do these campaigns and policies gel into a comprehensive progressive urban project or radical alternative. Even the Left seems to have given up on the idea of a universal urbanity as a project of liberation and seems to have saved itself on individual islands of issue specific urbanism.

(3) The Third Way Project

Let us, therefore, return to the beginning and to the question of whether the Third Way necessarily needs to bypass the city or whether there is the possibility of movement from the rightist centre to the leftist middle? The key to answering this question lies within the urban middle classes, who seem to have barricaded themselves politically and socially against progressive and marginal groups in urban society. But there are real and imagined collaborations of progressive-marginal and bourgeois-liberal camps in the city that can lead to new territorial and political compromises in cities. Such a collaboration could result in a new progressive urban hegemony against the neoliberal project. The consequences of this hegemony would be beneficial to these cities. The Third Way project is slightly different from the first two projects as it is both a product of independent social democratic, liberal and moderate environmental urban politics and a contested terrain located in a field of tension between neoliberal and progressive projects. This project is characterized by compromises of the growth machine with competing or alternative forces in cities. Most prominently, ecological modernization (sustainability and smart growth), entrepreneurialism, cultural modernization, and modest feminist politics are its hallmarks. Urban design is often seen as a means through which to devise social solutions (Lehrer and Milgrom, 1996). While not as conservative as the neoliberal project on social issues, identity is still used by Third Way proponents to draw a mostly traditional urban society. The difference is now that the Third Way will accept social difference and integrate it into the vision of social engineering through urban design. Ecological modernization, sustainability and new urbanism are the fields of dreams of boomer middle classes (this comes with an acceptance of the suburbanization of the city both in the suburbs and in the inner city (gentrification, spectacularization); it also comes with the market as the sole ruler of urban affairs and with a shift from the collectivity of earlier projects of *Stadtbürgertum* to the individuality and self-centredness of market-based activity of the suburban consumer middle classes).

In addition to providing the channels through which previous progressive welfare regimes are transformed into authoritarian workfare regimes, urban politics governs and regulates the processes through which the built environment, the spatiality of globalization, is being developed. It is necessary to remember that the social democratic model as well as the neoliberal model, which succeeded it came with a specific built form. The attention of those who concern themselves with urban matters must now be on the question of whether the Third Way comes with a distinctive built environment.

Housing provision, for example, under social democratic Fordism, usually had some aspect of urban mass social housing and also single family dwellings in suburban environments. The concrete form and process through which the mix of these two forms was achieved differed across national borders. The neoliberal Reagan-Thatcher era brought an aggressive attack against this social democratic model. The most well known instance of this attack was the economic, moral and aesthetic critique of tower blocks and council housing in the UK, which were identified by the Thatcher Tories as a prime symbol of 'socialist failure'. From an urbanist point of view, we will need to examine what suggestions Third Way politics makes for urban form and design. Table 9.1 represents the three scenarios:

Table 9.1. Three Scenarios for Urban Politics

The neoliberal project	The progressive project	The Third Way project
• law and order city	• living wage and new labour strength	• ecological modernization
• no homeless	• environmental justice	• urban design as a social solution
• commercialized streetlife	• citizenship struggles	• identity as conservatism
• suburbanization of the inner city	• identity as liberation	• seceding from responsibility
• lean urban government	• city and suburbs	• making cities entrepreneurial
• controlled public space	• metropolitan strike	• spectacularization
• segregation as politics		

Contesting Urbanity: Revolt and Reform in Cities

The focus in today's large cities must be on the creation of newer, more flexible, accountable and civil society-based forms of governance which help global cities self-regulate their affairs without enclosing them in questionable new forms of municipal administration and government. The urban right has no recipes for this. If these newer complex forms of governance are to be found, it must be in the tradition of the progressive city which in itself is a response to the complexity of its constituencies. Cities are the multicultural, diverse, complex frontiers of modern societies. They are also a constant hearth of societal innovation and social revolt. While the current Third Way may be interpreted as an attempt to pull together the existing society at the centre, urban governance in large western cities demands a different set of solutions: the creation of a new social future in lived diversity. This task is clearly different from the classical – assimilationist and hierarchical – integration provided by the nation state. Urban governance is an important scale of societal regulation overall. There is no reason to cede this arena to the neoliberal right. If old and new progressive forces can forge alliances of middle class and marginalized urban populations, there is hope for another shift change in urban politics. If the Third Way can be outlined from these traditions, there is the possibility of winning the city back for its people. What the Third Way can bring back into the debate, is an insistence on a 'negotiated universalism' of democratization, of social justice and urban ecology. If the urban middle classes in western cities can be forced into accepting this alternative road, there may be hope for an urban (that is pragmatic) utopianism beyond the globalizing project of neoliberal urbanity.

References

Altvater, E. and Mahnkopf, B. (1996), *Grenzen der Globalisierung. Ökonomie, Ökologie und Politik in der Weltgesellschaft*, Verlag Westfälisches Dampfboot, Münster.

Beauregard, R. (1999), 'The Politics of Urbanism: Mike Davis and the Neo-conservatives', *Capitalism, Nature, Socialism*, Vol. 10(3), Issue 39, p. 40.

Castells, M. (1972), *La Question urbaine*, Maspero, Paris, [engl. *The Urban Question: A Marxist Approach*, 1977, MIT Press, Cambridge, Mass].

Castells, M. (1978), *City Class and Power*, St. Martin's Press, New York.

Clavel, P. (1987), *The Progressive City*, New Brunswick: Rutgers University Press.

Davis, M. (1990), *City of Quartz Excavating the Future in Los Angeles*, Verso, London.

Davis, M. (1998), *Ecology of Fear: Los Angeles and the Imagination of Disaster*, Metropolitan, New York.

Douglass, M. and Friedmann, J. (eds) (1998), *Cities For Citizens: Planning and the Rise of Civil Society in a Global Age*, John Wiley, Chichester, Sussex.

Harvey, D. (1973), *Social Justice and the City*, Johns Hopkins University Press, Baltimore.

Harvey, D. (1982), *Limits to Capital*, Basil Blackwell, Oxford.

Harvey, D. (1989), *The Condition of Postmodernity: An Enquiry Into the Origins of Cultural Change*, Basil Blackwell, Oxford.

Harvey, D. (1996), *Justice, Nature and the Geography of Difference*, Blackwell, Cambridge, USA and Oxford, UK.

Harvey, D. (1998), 'Globalization and the Body', *INURA* (eds.), Birkhäuser, Basel, pp. 26–39.

Hirsch, J. (1995), *Der nationale Wettbewerbsstaat, Demokratie und Politik im globalisierten Kapitalismus*, ID Vlg., Amsterdam/Berlin.

INURA (eds.) (1998), *Possible Urban Worlds: Urban Strategies at the End of the 20th Century*, Birkhäuser, Basel, Boston, Berlin.

Isin, E. (1998), 'Governing Toronto Without Government: Liberalism and Neoliberalism', *Studies in Political Economy*, Vol. 56, Summer, pp. 169–92.

Isin, E. and Wolfson, J. (1999), 'The Making of the Toronto Megacity: An Introduction', Working Paper No. 21, *Urban Studies Programme*, York University, Toronto, Canada.

Keil, R. (1993), *Weltstadt – Stadt der Welt: Internationalisierung und lokale Politik in Los Angeles*, Westfälisches Dampfboot, Münster.

Keil, R. (1998a), 'Globalization Makes States: Perspectives of Local Governance in the Age of the World City', *Review of International Political Economy*, Vol. 5(4), Winter, pp. 616–46.

Keil, R. (1998b), *Los Angeles: Globalization, Urbanization and Social Struggles*, John Wiley and Sons, Chichester, Sussex.

Keil, R. (1998c), 'Toronto in the 1990s: Dissociated Governance?', *Studies in Political Economy*, No. 56, Summer, pp. 151–67.

Keil, R. and Lehrer, U. (1999), 'L.A. Story: Visions of Los Angeles' Other Futures', *Capitalism, Nature, Socialism*, September, pp. 45–52.

Keil, R. and Ronneberger, K. (1999), 'The Globalization of Frankfurt am Main: Core, Periphery and Social Conflict', in P. Marcuse and R. van Kempen (eds), *Globalizing Cities*, Blackwell, Oxford.

Lefebvre, H. (1968), *Le droit a la ville*, Editions Anthropos: Paris.

Lefebvre, H. (1970), *La revolution urbaine*, Gallimard, Paris.

Lefebvre, H. (1979), *The Survival of Capitalism* [translated by Frank Bryant from the French original: *Survie du Capitalisme*], Allison and Busby, London.

Lefebvre, H. (1991), *The Production of* Space [translated by Donald Nicholson-Smith from the French original: *Production de l'espace*], Blackwell: Oxford, UK and Cambridge, Mass.

Lefebvre, H. (1996), *Writings on Cities* [selected, translated and introduced by Eleonore Kofman and Elizabeth Lebas], Blackwell, Oxford.

Lehrer, U. and Milgrom, R. (1996), 'New (Sub) Urbanism: Countersprawl or Repackaging the Product?', *Capitalism, Nature, Socialism*, Vol. 7(2), Issue 26 (June), pp. 49–64.

McLeod, J. (1999), 'Portrait of a Poverty Pimp', *Toronto Free Press*, August 17–30, p. 5.

Meyerson, H. (1999), 'Cattle Call: the Race to Succeed Richard Riordan – and to Shape the Future of Los Angeles – Has Already Begun', *L.A. Weekly*, August 20–26, pp. 24–32.

Panitch, L. (1994), 'Globalization and the State', in R. Miliband and L. Panitch (eds.), *Socialist Register 1994: Between Globalism and Nationalism*, Merlin, London.

Panitch, L. and Leys, C. (eds.) (1999), *Socialist Register 1999, Global Capitalism Versus Democracy*, Merlin, London.

Ronneberger, K. and Keil, R. (1993), 'Riding the Tiger of Modernization: Reform Politics in Frankfurt', *Capitalism, Nature, Socialism*, Vol. 4(2), pp. 19–50.

Ronneberger, K., Lanz, S. and Jahn, W. (1999), *Die Stadt als Beute*, Dietz Verlag, Bonn.

Sambale, J. (1999), '*The Ecology of Fear* Meets German Angst', *Capitalism, Nature, Socialism*, Vol. 10(3), Issue 39, September, pp. 63–68.

Sandercock, L. (1998), *Towards Cosmopolis*, John Wiley, Chichester, Sussex.

Scott, A.J. (1988), *Metropolis: From the Division of Labor to Urban Form*, University of California Press, Berkeley and Los Angeles.

Smith, N. (1996), *The New Urban Frontier*, Routledge, London.

Soja, E.W. (1989), *Postmodern Geographies: The Reassertion of Space in Critical Social Theory*, Verso, London.

Standke, O. (1999), 'Progressives Economic Development im postfordistischen Los Angeles: Die Renaissance des Labor/Community Organizing und ihr Einfluss auf die Glokalisierung nach 1992', unpublished Diploma Thesis, Department of Sociology, Free University Berlin.

Wacquant, L. (1999), 'Die Armen bekämpfen', *Le Monde Diplomatique*, April 12, p. 1.

Chapter 10

Federalism and the Third Way: Possibilities for Post-parliamentary Democratic Governance

Thomas O. Hueglin

Without it, the eventual resolution of such devastating conflicts as in Northern Ireland or the Middle East seems unthinkable. In countries like Spain and South Africa, it has accompanied the process of democratization. In Mexico, it is the hope of a democratic opposition. It may have prevented the break-up of Belgium. Canada might not exist without it. For the process of European integration, it provides a hotly debated yardstick of institutional development. Cosmopolitan democracy in a globalizing world will require some measure of it.

At the same time, it has been invoked as a licence for selfish parochialism. In southern Germany and upper Italy, it lends its name to a right-wing agenda of fiscal desolidarization combined with xenophobic attitudes towards foreigners, immigrants or migrant workers. In Carinthia, it has provided a regional platform for the national rise of right-wing populism in Austria. And for the micro-nationalist sentiments in Quebec and Catalonia, the self-governing autonomies it establishes are never enough.

I am talking about federalism. Historically focused on the centralized territorial nation state, a mostly Jacobin left has for the most part either neglected federalism as a potentially emancipatory category of politics, or it has regarded it with suspicion as a conservative retreat to feudal conditions of localized tyranny. This chapter offers suggestions why a new left should reconsider its reluctant attitude towards the politics of federalism. It also advances the hypothesis that in neglecting federalism, it leaves the field to a right-wing agenda that is already in the process of restructuring political space.

What's Left of the Left

I suppose that I should briefly identify what I think the left is – or what is left of it. Left for me continues to mean struggle: for political structures that allow meaningful participation of citizens in the making of decisions affecting them; for righteousness in a distribution of justice that does not stop at the letter of the law but extends an appropriate measure of public compassion to all individuals and groups of citizens; and for a degree of material equality that is the unalienable prerequisite for both other goals. I therefore have no problems if left is redefined as a struggle for radical democracy (Mouffe, 1992) as long as it is well understood that class struggle still is very much a part of it, at the material front between a small minority making most of the decisions, and a majority whose life chances are very much dependent on these decisions, for instance, or at the ideological front between those who think that a political system is legitimate if its performative activities lead to market-efficient outputs, and those who generally cannot afford to give up the idea that political legitimacy must be based on participatory input.

Taking these identifications as a yardstick, I do not see much left of the left. In one of his first major speeches as German Chancellor-elect, for instance, the leader of one of the largest and oldest social democratic parties, Gerhard Schröder, fully subscribed to the neoliberal creed that democratic politics has to succumb to the economic necessities of our time. In an age of flexible production and globalized economic relations, he held forth, nobody can expect to spend a life time in the one job s/he has been trained for. It did not even occur to him to explain – leave alone question – why or how this was a policy statement resulting from a democratic process of decision making, why or how it was inevitable, or what the consequences and/or alternatives might be. There *are* no alternatives because we live in what arguably is the most ideologically totalizing period in human history – quite possibly the end of history indeed.

It is symptomatic both for that period, and for the sorry state of conformist political science that accompanies it with many learned footnotes, that the obvious has been stated most clearly by the pen of one courageous investigative journalist, Linda McQuaig, who, in the words of Canada's most powerful newspaper mogul, Conrad Black, on national radio, should be horsewhipped for it:

> Thus, in the global economy, there is only one valid position, and it is the position traditionally known as 'right-wing.' But now it's been stripped of that 'right-wing' label, since there is no 'left-wing' any more to distinguish it from. This position is now called 'pragmatic,' 'realistic,' in line with the 'realities' of the global marketplace. What used to be clearly understood to favor the rich – policies that the rich have been pushing aggressively since time immemorial – are now presented as pragmatic and in everyone's interest (McQuaig, 1999, p. 28).

Leo Panitch has always insisted that social democracy, even when it deserved that name, was a march of folly, that the forces of capital were never willing to share power with organized labour except when pushed by persistent struggle, which was successful only under the most exceptional conditions of postwar economic growth and full employment (1986). James O'Connor had made a similar argument earlier (1973), pointing out that the attempt at accommodating both social and economic interests through public spending, as if it were a positive sum game, could only lead to fiscal disaster. Economic interests had to find a way of curbing the commitment to social equality, and they found it by bullying governments into giving away the mechanisms of domestic fiscal and monetary control.

If the Third Way really was a middle way, the history of the last fifty years probably would only repeat itself. But it isn't. Supported by strong social democratic parties, the old left at least had, during the years of the postwar settlement, a chance of being dealt a favourable hand. The cards now appear almost entirely stacked in favour of business interests. Even suggestions aiming at minimal controls of what Susan Strange has aptly called casino capitalism (1986), like the Tobin tax, are now forwarded by 'enlightened reactionaries' (Polanyi, 1944) rather than social democrats. If history is going to repeat itself, it will likely be the history of the last 150 years. The painful lessons of market liberalism at the nation state level will have to be relearned on a global scale.

Why Federalism Can Make a Difference

In order to avoid misunderstandings: The concept of federalism advanced here has little if anything to do with the modern practice of the federal state. Insofar as that state has been constructed from Madisonian principles of federalism, the traditional suspicions of the left appear appropriate indeed. In the words of Michael Harrington, those principles constitute 'one of the greatest defences of human manipulation in the name of political theory' in order 'to frustrate majorities' (Harrington, 1990, p. 5, p. 67). It need not be reiterated at length that there is a venerable political economy tradition that has analysed and interpreted that kind and tradition of federalism as the spatial expression of conflict among fractions of particular classes, as an arena for struggles within a spatially and functionally fractured business class, or more generally as a structural device of blocking class-based politics altogether (Simeon and Robinson, 1990, pp. 14–15). That kind of federalism, in other words, provides pluralized access points to the political process only for some, while excluding others, arguably the vast majority.

The concept of federalism underlying this chapter and argument draws from a different tradition of federalism aiming at a politics of inclusion that is frustrated by parliamentary majority rule under conditions of integration and fragmentation in multilevel settings of governance. It rejects as a liberal myth the idea of a homogeneous sovereign people of individuals governing themselves democratically by majority rule. It identifies as the subject of democratic politics a plurality of life worlds that includes, following James O'Connor again, regionally and locally based 'community control movements, labour groups, radical and revolutionary organizations, and other social forces with everything to lose and nothing to gain' as well as 'small scale' or 'competitive sector' capital (O'Connor, 1973, pp. 214–15). As a concept of 'diverse federalism' (Tully, 1995), it aims at the empowerment of such groups and movements in a structurally and spatially organized 'politics of diversity' (Young, 1990). Its democratic objective is organized balance between particular rights of autonomous self-governance and a universal need for social solidarity. Its organizing principle is not a constitutional division of powers but an ongoing discourse of negotiated agreement.

I am offering three lines of thought why a democratic left should be interested in this kind of federalist project: The first one has to do with political geography. It has become fashionable in recent years to talk about debordered space, de-territorialized politics and denationalization (Kohler-Koch, 1998). I prefer to talk about the rearticulation of political space, whereby the conventional borderlines between domestic and international politics, but also between state and society, appear redrawn in a complex relationship of mutual interdependence among regions, organized interests, nation states and transnational regulatory agencies (Hueglin, 1999a). This does not just amount to a structural redrawing of borders and boundaries in the name of efficiency. It entails a massive relocation of power. The question is from whom and to whom. Perhaps that is still unclear but David Harvey has given a fairly clear indication about the general direction:

> One of the principal tasks of the capitalist state is to locate power in the spaces which the bourgeoisie controls, and disempower those spaces which oppositional movements have the greatest potentiality to command (Harvey, 1989, p. 237).

The point here is not to engage in a – however necessary – debate whether the capitalist state, by divesting itself of all kinds of powers, which are either given up to autonomous international organizations, or handed down to public, semi-private and private actors at the subnational level, does not in fact strengthen its relative autonomy (Wolf, 1999) vis-à-vis those oppositional forces and movements traditionally operating at the nation state level, and endowed with less mobility than the dereified circuits of finance and speculative capital. It is to draw attention to the fact that the relocation game is very much a power game over space.

As such a game, it cries for democratically controlled rules about who gets to decide what and where in a complex multilevel setting of governance. In principle, at least, federalism is just that. In its traditional aversion to federalism as a clever structural device of balkanizing the popular will (Lowi, 1984), the left may have neglected spatial aspects of the power struggle – except perhaps in Canada where there is a long and venerable tradition of spatial political economy. The neoliberal rearticulation of political space in a globalizing world is thriving in that void.

The second line of thought has to do with political sociology. For a considerable amount of time now, Michael Greven has conjured up a pessimistic scenario of a politicized world without *citoyens* (1997). The choice of *citoyens* instead of citizens intends to give expression to the widely observed phenomenon that individuals, while engaging in a wide variety of policy-specific activities, policy communities or networks, may no longer feel any significant degree of responsibility for the polity as a whole. The gap between the reach of individualized moral responsibility and the structuration of large political organizations has become so enormous that individual behaviour no longer appears linked to the common good. Consequences are decreasing electoral participation, a membership decline in large civic organizations including political parties and unions, fragmented policy fanaticism, and a seesaw of quickly changing political fashions driven by political opportunism and the populist mass media.

To put it somewhat differently: Because they are no longer at home in comprehensible structures of responsible government, individuals no longer feel constrained by the kind of Kantian imperative according to which they would only do what they also might expect from others. Normative individualism (see Føllesdal, 1998) gives way to rampant individual liberalism. Individuals become footloose citizens in a world of transient commitments and fragmented solidarity. Without such a commitment and solidarity, however, it becomes easy for the members of a 'modernization coalition' (Kohler-Koch, 1996) driving the process of regional and global market integration to hold entire societies hostage to an agenda from which they stand to benefit the most: deficit reduction, price stability and capital mobility at the expense of full employment, social security and community.

While the description of symptoms is as impressive as it is depressing, it begs for a more convincing explanation: Why do individuals appear to give up their rights and commitments as *citoyens* so easily? Is agency giving way to some sort of structuralist fatalism? One possible answer points to the distancing gap between individual reach and the ever more complex structures of multilevel governance. According to Anthony Giddens' structuration theory, human beings are knowledgeable social actors 'fashioning and fashioned by structural properties, within which diverse forms of power are incorporated' (Giddens, 1984, p. 220). This would mean that human behaviour currently appears to be fashioned by structures discouraging the active involvement of *citoyens*. This should not come as a surprise since the structural properties safeguarding price stability and free trade have not been fashioned by those recursively exposed to the consequences. Individual social actors have not been asked whether they want to live under the rules of the World Trade Organization or a European Central Bank, and if they had been asked, they would not have been able to give a knowledgeable answer. Once in place, however, these structural properties begin to fashion individual behaviour nevertheless.

The question is then very much which structural properties or institutions are likely to fashion social actors as *citoyens*. These would obviously have to reduce the gap between the reach of individualized moral responsibility and the structuration of large political organizations, combining, as Montesquieu once suggested, the virtue of small republics with the stability of a large commonwealth

(1748, Book VI, chapter 2). In principle again, federalism offers the concept for such a structuration. It gives form to the idea that diverse powers can be accountable to different groups of citizens. It fosters active citizenship by linking particular concerns to particular structures of governance. It leaves to the large structures general concerns that affect all in the same way. To make knowledgeable decisions about these appears more likely within the reach of average citizens than to judge, say, what the effects of a multilateral agreement on investment will be on their individual life chances. This is a matter of subsidiarity, the allocation of powers to the most appropriate level of governance, which cannot be decided once and for all by a constitutional document but only by a perpetual democratic discourse (Hueglin, 1994a; Føllesdal, 1998).

The third line of thought has to do with political culture. In an article widely quoted in Germany, Peter Graf Kielmansegg has argued that a parliamentary system of democracy is not a viable option for the European Union because Europe lacks the very preconditions that make majority rule acceptable: a resilient collective identity based on the commonality of communication, experience and history (Kielmansegg, 1996). Obviously, the same argument can be made even more forcefully for any kind of world government based on popular representation and majority rule. It may further and increasingly apply to territorial nation states as well. On the one hand, these are becoming more culturally fragmented due to an accelerating dynamic of migration and the rise of identity politics in its wake (Hudson and Réno, 2000; Schmidtke, 1996). And on the other hand, when the congruence of political, economic and cultural spaces is broken up by processes of uneven denationalization (Albert, 1998; Zuern, 1992), national parliaments lose their capacity as forums for the communicative exchange of common experiences.

One might even go one step further and argue that national parliaments have never had this capacity except for rare and rather deplorable instances of nationalism and ideological alienation. When the world of medieval pluralism broke up in the aftermath of Renaissance and Reformation, it was replaced by the rule of absolutist princes. These were in turn overthrown by a series of bourgeois revolutions from the seventeenth to the nineteenth century. The fiction of the absolutist prince was replaced by the fiction of the sovereign people. To be sure, parliamentary majority rule may have given better approximate expression to this fiction than any other system to date, but it never gave away governance to real majorities, to the working class even when there was not the shadow of a doubt that there was one, or to women even after they had been allowed to become citizens. And it almost always defied the rights of self-determination for cultural minorities and peripheral regions.

The time simply may have come to move beyond the short-lived history of parliamentary democracy and its mixed record. But what can take its place or at least complement it? It is quite curious to remember that the politicization without *citoyens* argument has been made similarly before, by Samuel Huntington, some twenty five years ago, as an attack on what he saw as the hedonistic counter-culture of the 1960s, and as the dawning of a new age of fragmentation that might occasion the rise of new and unpleasant forms of neoauthoritative government (Huntington, 1974). Such governance has been established in the meantime (Aznar, 1994), albeit at the transnational level, with central bankers and trade officials as the new absolutist princes who do not derive their authority from divine law, of course, but instead from a new economic constitutionalism (Campanella, 1995; Gill, 1992), whose stipulations on price stability and terms of credit and trade are removed from public accountability. This constitutionalism primarily serves the interests of transnational capital valorization. It can hardly be seen as a defensive reaction to societal hedonism. If citizens now lose faith in collective and responsible political action, dissipating instead into fragmented policy communities, this is so because the neoauthoritative forms of governance appear beyond their reach. Politicized individualization, it would seem, is not the cause for the rise of neoauthoritative government, it is the consequence of a widening gap between individual reach and political structuration.

In fact, the fragmentation of societal interests is reinforced by the new structures of governance. In the 'new power play' between parliaments as 'territorially fixed' actors and transnational economic actors representing the interests of 'capital, finance and trade' (Beck, 1999, p. 11), the policy making capacity of the former tends to become confined to 'highly reactive, uncoordinated and non-interventionist' strategies (Howlett, Netherton and Ramesh, 1999, p. 289). Such strategies, while seemingly neutral and aimed at a 'spaceless economy', nevertheless produce 'spatially specific effects' (Brodie, 1990, p. 72). My assumption is that the alienation of *citoyens* from the overall polity occurs in these differentiated spatial contexts, at the local-regional level, but also within social movements and communities of class, gender and cultural identity, which are likewise affected unevenly by these strategies. Political space, in other words, is taking on a more fragmented societal dimension within and beyond traditional territorial boundaries as well.

The problem is the incongruence between these differentiated socio-spatial contexts and the structural fixation of national and international politics on assumptions of social homogeneity and policy neutrality. The concept of federalism at least allows one to begin thinking about restructuring political space in such a way as to give a plurality of life worlds access to the political process. Pessimists like to point out that structural renewal beyond the political forms of representative democracy of the eighteenth and nineteenth centuries is not an option seriously entertained by those empowered with political responsibility (Greven, 1997, p. 249). For a new left deserving that name, that is exactly the point. In the next section, I will try to show that federalism has indeed been a – however neglected – tradition of the old left.

Recourse to a Left Tradition of Federalism

The left aversion to federalism has two main origins. One is federalism's *'semblance* of feudal distinctions'. In Germany, for instance, as Marx explained, the absolute monarchy first encouraged trade and industry for its own national glory, and then tried to weaken the rising powers of the bourgeoisie by decentralizing the access to power (1847, p. 328). The other is federalism's emphasis on restructuration rather than the revolutionary overthrow of social relations, an agenda which Marx and Engels identified with the interests of the petty bourgeoisie, and, as a form of 'conservative, or bourgeois, socialism', with a desire of preserving 'the existing state of society minus its revolutionary and disintegrating elements' (1848, p. 513).

Nevertheless, a mostly neglected left tradition of federalism can be discerned in the Proudhonian tradition of socialist federalism (1), among British guild socialists and state pluralists (2), in the notion of cultural communities of character explored by Austro-Marxists (3), and as a hidden agenda in postmodern conceptualizations of just society (4).

(1) Proudhonian Tradition of Socialist Federalism

Marx's main object of scorn was the French socialist-anarchist Pierre-Joseph Proudhon. One can only marvel at the vituperative viciousness of Marx's attack on Proudhon which, in many ways, foreshadowed the factionalism and *ad hominem* derision that – except under the fake conditions of *really existing socialism* – would weaken the common cause of the left for all times to come.

But Marx was right, of course, in that the petty bourgeoisie, wherever it had a chance to stabilize and grow, did absorb the proletariat's revolutionary energies, and in that the structures of federal decentralization, wherever they only pluralized power among the usual suspects, made social change even less probable than under Jacobin conditions of centralization. Proudhon, I would submit, had a Machiavellian sense of what most people really want – if a jump in time is permitted: an L-shaped bungalow and a swimming pool.[1] He did not give much thought to whether that constituted a form of alienation from the true self, instead focusing on how the problem of power and control could be reconciled with a world of bungalows and swimming pools. His main idea was that of an agro-industrial federation (1863), which first of all needs to be distinguished from the modern federal state which has been very much designed as a territorial power compromise among ruling elites. Thomas Hobbes could have been writing about

---

[1] Machiavelli was not just a realist in his analysis of power. Of the people he said that only a small minority want to be free to rule, while the large majority just wants to live in security (*Discorsi* I. XVI).

the United States of America before and after 1865, in his scathing attack on 'compounded government' which

> would no whit advantage the liberty of the subject. For as long as [the different branches of such government] all agree, each single citizen is as much subject as he can possibly be: but if they disagree, the state returns to a civil war... (Hobbes, 1642, VII. 4).

By comparison, Proudhon's vision of federalism entails more than just divided governance. In the combination of territorial federalism and socio-economic mutualism, he envisioned a regime, albeit with rather fuzzy contours, of territorial as well as functional communities entering into multiple contractual, or better, treaty relationships. The difference between these and the Rousseauian or Hobbesian social contract is that they are not based on a fictitious act of alienation, but instead establish a concrete and ongoing process of negotiated agreements. Moreover, the federal pact does not establish constitutional supremacy for central government. The negotiating partners always retain more powers than they agree to delegate to the next higher level. And finally, functional or producer groups are tied into the territorial scheme by a system of corporate or council representation (Roemheld, 1990; Voyenne, 1973).

It is really too bad that Marx, once he had made up his mind about the intellectual deficiencies of Monsieur Proudhon, did not take a second look at Proudhon's federalism. Perhaps his assessment of the similarly organized Paris Commune, which he saw merely as 'the rising of a city under exceptional conditions' and by no means as a socialist revolution (quoted in Bottomore, 1983, p. 359) would have been different. And it would have been at least more difficult for Lenin to draw the conclusion that only 'centralism from above' was to be rejected, not centralism as such (quoted in Vernon, 1979, p. xlvii). Centralism, of course, is always centralism from above.

The historical disdain of Marx and the traditional left for federalism is unfortunate for another reason as well. During the 1930s, the Proudhonian tradition of federalism was given sharper contours by an internationalist group of thinkers who eventually began to refer to themselves as 'integral federalists' (Voyenne, 1981; Roemheld, 1990; Kinsky, 1995). At various times, it included Alexandre Marc, a Marxist Russian Jew who had renounced Soviet-style communism, Denis de Rougemont, a Swiss, who would later become one of the most thoughtful spokespersons for a united and federal Europe (Tassin, 1992), and the Jewish philosopher Martin Buber, who would later warn the newly formed state of Israel of the dangers inherent in state-centred territorialism (1950). Members of the group later were active in various European resistance movements (Lipgens, 1968). They were joined by other European federalists such as the Italian Altiero Spinelli, who had drafted a manifesto for a 'free and united Europe' in 1940 while still imprisoned by Mussolini (Spinelli, 1972; see also Bobbio, 1972), and the Belgian

Henri Brugmans, later one of the leaders of the short-lived *Union Europénne des Fédéralistes* founded 1946 in Paris (Brugmans, 1965).

Underlying integral federalism is a social philosophy rejecting both individual liberalism and collectivism, and based on *la pluri-appartenance de l'homme*, the assumption that individuals belong to various groups and communities. Integral federalism advocates the radical federalization of all political systems and mass organizations, recognition of urban neighbourhoods, regions and socio-cultural groups as autonomous entities, and the replacement of the welfare state system with a minimum guaranteed social wage. In the Proudhonian tradition, this does not mean the selfish encapsulation of local and/or social community tyrannies. Integral federalism is very much understood as a system of mutual solidarity, as a regime of negotiated balance between particular desires and universal needs. In the words of Alexandre Marc: 'Power should be everywhere, even at the centre' (Kinsky, 1995, p. 7).

There was, in other words, a genuine effort among radical federalists, during the last years of World War II and the immediate postwar period, to deconstruct the centralized territorial nation state and its dangerous liaison with the powers of capital. For a gasping moment, until that liaison was given legitimacy again in the name of cold war efforts at defending the free world against the perceived perils of Soviet expansionism, a broad alliance for social and political renewal under the federalist banner seemed possible. In Germany, for instance, Alexander Mitscherlich's admonishment that democratic liberation from the twin monster state and capitalist economy could only come through organized group life (1947), was echoed by those representatives of the German *Staatslehre* who argued that all social life was federal by nature, and that the German constitution of 1949 was all but a travesty of federalism (Jerusalem, 1949; Hesse, 1962). Had the European left abandoned its Jacobin predilections at this critical historical conjuncture, a progressive alliance for the democratic restructuring of the European political space at least might have been an option.

(2) British Guild Socialists and State Pluralists

Centralism, democratic or otherwise, very much came to be rejected by guild socialists and state pluralists in early twentieth century Britain as well (Nicholls 1994). These advocates of what might be called the original British 'Third Way' between market liberalism and central planning, most prominently G.D.H. Cole and Harold J. Laski (Hirst, 1994), took their cues not so much from Proudhon as from Otto von Gierke, the nineteenth century German champion of associational or fellowship law, who had rediscovered the *Politica* of Johannes Althusius as the first modern theory of societal federalism (Hueglin, 1999b).

Cole believed that 'power must be dispersed into specific functional domains and controlled primarily by those involved in those domains' (Hirst, 1994, p. 105). Indeed, functional representation was one of the 'most distinctive doctrines' of

British guild socialism (Black, 1984, pp. 222–23). As especially elaborated in his *Guild Socialism Restated* (1920), Cole's structural ideas of representation aimed at a bicameral legislative system in which parliament would continue to represent people as consumers, and a Guild Congress would represent people as producers. As Althusius and Gierke before him, Cole rejected the modern notion of state sovereignty, advocating instead a regime of co-sovereignty among state and functional communities (Black, 1984, p. 223; see Olson, 1965, pp. 114–16).

Laski held that the 'notion of a single sovereign power' is a 'myth that modern states inherited from early-modern royal autocracies' (Hirst, 1994, p. 28). At least during his 'pluralist period' (Dyson, 1980, p. 194), he conceived organized social life as a matrix of spatial and functional structurations in which neither one was to be superior to the other. In his *A Grammar of Politics*, he insisted that only such a plural structuration of society could 'provide for a constant interchange of opinion and ideas between the centre and the circumference of government' (1925, p. 385). In other words, he rejected a statist tradition built upon constitutional certainty, espousing instead a constructivist vision of politics committed to a process of communicative action.

Laski's commitment to state pluralism faded under the influence of Fabianism with its emphasis on social democratic reform, gradualism and state permeation, occasioned by the Labour Party's brief access to government power in 1924 (see Dyson, 1980, p. 194). Guild socialism, on the other hand, according to Hirst (1994, pp. 101–11), failed because it was unable to capture the imagination of the Labour movement, which by then had been fully mainstreamed into a regime of centralized industrial relations. If that regime appears to be falling apart now, under conditions of globalization and uneven denationalization, with powers indeed more and more dispersed into the functional domains of specialized policy communities, a case can be made to bring this original 'Third Way' back to life.

*(3)   The Notion of Cultural Communities of Character Explored by Austro-
       Marxists*

Another group very much concerned about a Third Way of organizing democratic politics were the so-called Austro-Marxists, notably Karl Renner and Otto Bauer (Bottomore and Goode, 1978). One of the concerns of this group was the adaptation of socialist theory to the realities of the multinational Habsburg Empire. Bauer defined 'nations' as 'communities of character' which would continue to exist in a socialist society precisely because they are held together by a commitment transcending the conditions of material reproduction. Bauer also offered an explanation as to why capitalism cannot tolerate the autonomous existence of such communities. They stand in the way of universalized wage relations. In order to secure these, capitalism must insist on an atomized society of individuals held in check by a centralized state. Referring to Gierke again, Bauer pointed to an epochal transformation, beginning already with the age of absolutism and carried to its logical conclusion under liberalism: Intermediate social organizations (such as nations or cultural minorities, for example) would be henceforth recognized only as local manifestations of the state or as individuals themselves (Bauer, 1924, p. 135, pp. 276–78).

Both Renner and Bauer envisaged the eventual replacement of the centralized territorial nation state with a multi-national federal state or nationality state. In that state, each nationality that so desired would be free to administer its own cultural activities. It would be permitted to tax its members accordingly and/or receive public funding from the central government. Moreover, membership in these nationalities would to be voluntary or corporate, as in churches or political parties, and it would not be tied to living in a particular territory. Linking cultural to personal autonomy, individuals would be free to move and carry their membership with them. These memberships would be recorded in national registers. For electoral purposes, nationalities would serve as constituencies, and those registered as members of a particular nationality would accordingly vote for a number of its candidates proportional to its size (Friedrich, 1975, pp. 228–30; Walzer, 1983, p. 44).

Again, if one of the current problems for a democratic left is the reconciliation of the *citoyen* with 'identity politics', a 'genuinely political problem that is increasingly gaining importance in the course of a noticeable ethnicist transformation of politics (Greven, 1997, p. 242), the ideas of some kind of non-territorial or cultural federalism should be given more serious consideration. Such non-territorial federalism entails more than granting autonomy and representative status to a limited number of spatially dispersed cultural groups. As an attempt at resolving social conflict with territorial means, the historical success of federalism has always been tenuous at best. In a mobilized world of risk and opportunity, David Elkins has argued, non-territorial communities of shared interest and/or values, while unlikely to replace territorial communities altogether, 'will supplant the territorial communities and will gain in number and significance' (Elkins, 1995, esp. pp. 148–92). Non-territorial or societal federalism entails the idea to provide these communities with formal access to the representative legislative process of democratic politics.

(4)   A Hidden Agenda in Postmodern Conceptualizations of Just Society

Membership combined with rights becomes citizenship. The *citoyen* is the active or participatory citizen. After the end of Soviet-style communism, as Chantal Mouffe has argued, the agenda for the left can only be radical and plural democracy. The goal is to 'restore the idea of politics as the realm where we can recognize ourselves as participants in a community'. This sounds promising even though there is of course no reason whatsoever why the demise of one corrupted socialist formation should rule out further search for radical alternatives to liberal democracy, or why 'the creation of a common political identity can no longer be conceived in terms of *class*' at all (Mouffe, 1992, pp. 1–5), especially when there is so much emphasis on deessentialized plurality. But class is not the only category ruled out by this new postmodern orthodoxy. Another is federalism.

Introducing the various contributions to her book, Mouffe devotes a brief paragraph to a chapter by Etienne Tassin on the prospects of Europe as a political community (1992, p. 8). In that paragraph, she characterizes Tassin's central idea as the necessary dissociation of citizenship from nationality but she entirely omits to mention that, according to Tassin, only a federal European order can establish a European community beyond the nation state. It is hard to imagine that she did not catch it since Tassin uses the terms federal and confederal some forty five times in a text of twenty two pages.

This omission is symptomatic for the Victorian attitude of a self-styled postmodern, post-Marxist or whatever-post left towards the f-word. In his widely influential first publication on cosmopolitan democracy, David Held (1992, p. 33) has admitted, in almost clandestine fashion in a footnote, that he substituted 'cosmopolitan' for 'federal' because the latter term was somehow too controversial in the context of the European integration debate.[2] And Iris M. Young (1990) has given an account of diverse politics and justice in her ideal of a multicultural city that almost literally yet unknowingly reproduces the idea of the *cité fédéraliste* developed by Proudhon and the French school of integral federalism.

There also seems to be a fashionable tendency to invoke the historical authority of John Neville Figgis, the spiritual godfather of British state pluralism, when searching for a Third Way in between the selfishness of individuals or groups and the sovereign state as the provider of a redistributive and conflict-mediating public order (Keane, 1988, p. 1 and p. 15; Hirst and Thompson, 1996, p. 193). Little is said, however, as to how this *in between* might be organized. Figgis, on the other hand, an ardent admirer of Gierke once again, was quite clear about it, placing his hope in the growth of the kind of federalism that had already existed once, before the rise and organizational success of the omnipotent state (1916, p. 17). And he was by no means content suggesting ways in which an associational world of civil society might be empowered as a separate institutional sphere with its own distinct communicative logic, mediating between the sphere of politics with its logic of accountable power control, and the market sphere with its contractual logic (Cohen and Arato, 1992; see Hueglin, 1994b). The mediation of pluralized autonomy, according to Figgis, had to follow the one and only political

---

[2] Elsewhere (1995, pp. 229–31), Held elaborates on a democratic cosmopolitan order as located somewhere between federalism and confederalism. Apart from Immanuel Kant, his source of inspiration apparently is a conversation with Johan Galtung. The absence of any substantive self-exposure to the burgeoning field of federalism studies in theory and practice only underscores the main thesis of this chapter that a more serious dialogue between federalism and democratic discourse is badly needed.

logic of representative accountability. The British House of Commons, he advanced, had received its name not in reference to the mass of common people but as the representative assembly of a 'community of the communities' (1913, p. 80).

Finally, there has been a proliferation of thought devoted to the idea of enhancing the representative and performative character of democracy through the inclusion of associative group structures. In particular, an entire volume has been compiled with responses to the discussion of secondary associations and their role in democratic governance by Cohen and Rogers (Wright, 1995). Most respondents in the volume, however, remain skeptical both about the radical democratic quality of such associative structures when they appear as a state-crafted project of engineering an efficient barrier against the mischievous facetiousness of grassroots movements, and about the viability of such a grand restructuring scheme when it seems so much at odds with the dominant liberal tradition and practice of disjointed group competition in the market place. Again, there is in the entire volume not a single word about the tradition and practice of federalism as just that, a structured effort at the coordination of group interests on the basis of mutual agreement. To be sure, such agreement may have been practised in the modern federal state only as a compromise among spatially distinct factions of ruling elites. But the point is exactly to ask whether the federal form cannot be extended in a more radically democratic way.

It is time, I would submit, to discuss the merits of federalism for a new left project of radical and plural democracy.

Federal Options for a New Left

Whatever suggestions follow, they have to be prefaced by caution. Franz Neumann once wrote that there is no value inherent in the federal principle as such (1967, p. 220). As all other auxiliary forms of social organization, it can be used and abused. In North America, where federalism constitutes the normalcy of political life, critics like the late William Riker could point to the American south where federalism has been instrumental, for more than a century, in retaining parochial societies based on racism and segregation (1964). In turn, federal enthusiasts would be quick in pointing out that it was federalism in Canada which allowed, at the provincial level in Saskatchewan during the 1940s, the first conceptualization and implementation of a social democratic welfare state scheme tailored to the specific needs of farmers and urban workers. It pushed subsequent federal governments into the same direction. The fact that, at least until now, some degree of social democracy has been able to establish itself in North America, originating in a social gospel movement, transformed into a radical and cooperative prairie movement, and finally into the New Democratic Party of Canada, is in no small measure owed to Canadian federalism (Conway, 1983).

I would in fact go one step further, by offering a somewhat bold macrohistorical observation – which is meant to encourage further contemplation and research rather than claim established certitude: The rise of prairie radicalism in the Canadian West was a regionally specific response to the socially devastating effects of the Great Depression combined with the intransigence and inflexibility of statist politics at the national level. The brief endorsement of radical federalism in Europe during the same period of time was a response to the statist catastrophes of two world wars. There seems to be considerable evidence across cultures and times that people have a tendency of turning to some sort of federal organization in times of crisis. The first known federal covenant was concluded among the Jewish tribes of Israel when they faced an existential crisis after their exodus from Egypt (Elazar, 1994). The Biblical origins of federalist thought became a major source of inspiration for persecuted Protestant minorities after the Reformation. A plethora of pamphlets and treatises called for organized and 'confederated' resistance (Laski, 1924, esp. p. 99; Salmon, 1975). It is from these sources that Althusius developed his theory of federalism. Moreover, this recourse to federalism is not just a Western or European phenomenon. Faced with a crisis of intertribal warfare, North America's native peoples had already developed federal forms of self-governance before they came into contact with the Europeans. The Great Law of the Iroquois or Haudenosauenee, for instance, shows striking similarities to the Althusian model (Hueglin, 1993).

To say that federalism can be a particularly adequate form of social organization is one thing. It is quite another to constitute that form as a realm, as Mouffe demands, where we can recognize ourselves as participants in a community. As even the cursory review of federal traditions in the previous section ought to have indicated, the possibilities are as varied as the problems daunting. In this chapter, I will have to restrict myself to a discussion of three aspects central to all federalist projects: plural forms of representation (1), the adequacy of power distribution (2), and common universal standards of socio-economic behaviour that need to frame the autonomy of community life (3). And even at that, it will not be possible to do more than provide some initial sketches of the structural and procedural contours such a federal form might take.

(1) Plural Forms of Representation

The difference between pluralism and federalism is this: Plural systems derive legitimacy from the assumption that different interests have access to, and compete for influence upon, one government representing the general will. Federal systems derive legitimacy from the assumption that different interests have access to plurality of governments which in turn compete for influence upon the formulation of the general will. The modern federal state has given constitutional expression to this pluralization of governance only in part. It has divided the powers of governing among two or three levels of government, and it has established a regime of dual or bicameral representation at the national level, once on the basis of population (lower house, parliament), and once on the basis of region (upper house, senate). In the name of radical or plural democracy, this regime ought to be expanded by means of radical federalization in two ways.

First, the duality of spatial representation at the national level ought to be extended to the regional and local level as well. One of the institutional hallmarks of federalism is that unmitigated majority rule is constrained at the national or federal level of government by the existence of upper legislative chambers representing regional jurisdictions.[3] This representative constraint is typically lacking at the level of subnational, regional and local government. In most federations, subnational legislatures are monocameral. In the United States, they are bicameral (except for Nebraska), but state senators are elected from different popular districts and not from distinct jurisdictions. Radical federalization means that states or provinces ought to become bicameral as well, with upper houses equally and fairly representing cities and rural municipalities. But bicameral federalization also ought to be extended to the local level. Recognizing neighbourhoods as constituencies with equal rights of representation in bicameral city councils would go a long way of addressing the principle of fair representation in increasingly multicultural urban settings, for instance.

A particularly difficult question of institutional design is the formal inclusion of non-territorial communities into a federal scheme of representation. The idea of functional representation is inevitably seen as opening up a pandora's box of concerns about admission criteria, formal status and manageability (Anderson, 1979). Yet it is entirely possible to conceptualize ways of organizing a system of mixed bicameralism whereby citizens have the choice of voting for spatial as well as social representatives (compare Schmitter, 1995). The seats in second legislative chambers could be divided, for instance, allowing organized interests to compete for half of the seats. They could be funded in the same way political parties are. A 5 per cent threshold of received votes could prevent unmanageable and ineffective proliferation. It would also likely lead to coalitions among communities with similar interests, among labour organizations, environmental groups, Blacks, native peoples, Jews, women's organizations and those of gays and lesbians, business organizations, consumer groups, and so on. Their combined veto power over lower chamber legislation could be based on qualified majority rule.

There is simply no reason why such an institutional design had to be less

---

[3] For the purpose of this discussion, I will leave out to what extent these upper chambers hold co-equal powers. For a detailed overview of comparative federalism, see Watts (1999). I will also abstain, at this point, to reenter the debate whether institutional federalism just serves the purpose of frustrating majority rule or does indeed represent the interests of different spatial constituencies. How such representation can be achieved more democratically will be discussed below, in the section on non-territorial representation.

efficient than the murky world of special interest politics or policy networks. There is also no reason to assume that such a system would impose an undue participatory burden on citizens. There is a rich associational life in modern representative democracies that is kept in motion by tireless, often voluntary and frustrated leaders. Their frustration precisely stems from a lack of formal recognition that relegates their work to the unequal vagaries and inefficiencies of pressure group politics. As outlandish as these suggestions may sound, taking federalism seriously as a system of pluralized governance clearly requires rethinking the two- or three-storeyed federal state in terms of a more complex or 'cybernetic model' (Riklin, quoted in Hafen, 1994, p. 123) of adequate political structuration.

There is another and more serious concern, and especially so for the democratic left. The right will always pull in the one direction of the free market, commodification and accumulation. By comparison, the left will always pull in many more directions (Bahro, Mandel and von Oertzen, 1980). It is always easier to agree on how to defend the status quo than to develop strategies on how to change it. Typically, the right also has more resources and can play multilevel games more easily (Putnam, 1988). So what if a federalized playing field of small communities fell into the hands of a right-wing agenda? Is it not true that the loudest cries for more federalism come from regional voices that are increasingly parochial and xenophobic, from Umberto Bossi's *Lega* in upper Italy, or from Jörg Haider's Austrian Freedom Party with its home base in Carinthia? There is no easy answer.

The call for radical and plural democracy requires faith: If supplied with adequate structures, human beings will be compelled to do the right thing – which is of course the left thing. Structures, even if adequate, need to be filled with real life and action. Most regional right-wing movements are based on populism. The formal inclusion of a wide variety of local and functional communities into federalized regional governance would broaden and diversify the basis for reasonable discourse. It would make the success of such populism more difficult if not impossible. My suspicion would be that by abandoning the plurality of small structures and communities, the left has made it easy for the right to occupy that space.

(2) The Adequacy of Power Distribution

Adequate structuration alone is not enough, though. It has to be complemented by an adequate distribution of powers. Historically, federal states have typically been constituted as a compromise between national economic modernizers and regional cultural traditionalists, Yankeeland and Dixieland, Prussia and Bavaria, English Canada and Quebec, liberal and Catholic Switzerland. As a consequence, a general pattern of power distribution evolved, centralizing trade and commerce at the national level while leaving culture, education and social policy at the subnational level.

Soon this became a problem for modernizing and mobile societies. Federal trade and commerce policies created or reinforced patterns of uneven regional development. Overburdened with social policy problems, regional governments became dependent on federal transfers. Fiscal revenue was increasingly spent by governments that did not have the capacity to raise it. Fiscal distribution and transfer schemes became the main preoccupation of federal systems (Watts, 1999, pp. 43–55). The original separation of powers became blurred by political interlocking – as in the German system (Scharpf, 1988), by the wild growth of a mostly conditional federal grants system – as in the United States (Wilson and DiIulio, 1998, pp. 69–75), or by a complex web of intergovernmental fiscal transfer and tax sharing arrangements – as in Canada (Barker, 1998). The main result has not so much been inefficiency, as the new output efficiency democrats allege (Scharpf, 1998; Greven, 1998), but a breakdown of accountability. Citizens can no longer recognize who is responsible for what.

From the perspective of democracy, therefore, it is time to rethink radically the distribution of powers in federal, or generally, plural and multilevel systems of governance. Maybe it is too simple a suggestion for a left trying to reinvent itself: that it could be a very radical act of democratization indeed to engage in the humble task of sorting out anew who should do what in an complex world of integration and fragmentation. And again, I would submit that the task for the left would be to re-occupy space that has been abandoned. In the European Union, for instance, a reshuffling of powers has already begun, in the name of subsidiarity, but it appears for the most part trapped in a neoliberal discourse about cost efficiency combined with national self-interest (Sbragia, 1997). At the international level, a Multinational Agreement on Investment with far-reaching consequences for the distribution of powers almost went into effect unnoticed, had it not been for a last minute civic consciousness raising campaign led by some forty non-government organizations which resulted in the French withdrawal from the negotiations (Council of Canadians, 1998).

The problem with such actions is that they are not part of the political system. Spot checks by concerned citizen groups more resemble the medieval right of resistance than democracy. Democracy requires constitutional security about the limits of responsible government, and in multilevel settings of governance this means a principled division of powers. This is not an issue for which ready-made answers exist. The European subsidiarity debate, for instance, has opened up a new discourse (Diez, 1996; Føllesdal, 1998) that is as yet open ended at best, or already captured by national market interests at worst. I will venture to make one suggestion about how subsidiarity as an invitation to rethink the allocation of powers in multilevel systems of governance can be taken up. It goes back to the aforementioned theory of federalism by Althusius who, at the beginning of the modern age very much sought to transform the traditional right of resistance into a constitutionally secured mode of pluralized governance.

Althusius' understanding of subsidiarity centred on the old sentence of Roman Law according to which *quod omnes tangit, ab omnibus approbari debet* (what touches all must be approved by all; 1614, p. IV.20 passim). In his interpretation this meant that a particular community would retain veto power (operationalized by a consent requirement) and self-regulatory autonomy in matters affecting it in a particular or unequal way, whereas common decisions (allowing majority voting) were possible in matters pertaining to all communities equally or in the same way.

On the basis of this conceptualization it is possible to argue that social policy, health care, welfare et cetera – which affect everyone and every community equally – ought to be centralized responsibilities based on universal programmes. The constituent members of a federation, on the other hand, should be given 'responsibility for the productivity agenda' (Rivlin, 1995, p. 199), including regulatory powers over terms of trade as well as capital investment and productive location commitment because these are matters affecting particular communities very unevenly. It is not difficult to envisage the consequences for political deliberation and policy making.

At the local level, for instance, municipalities suffer from the displacement of small business (which employs most people and offers real market choice) by large retail corporations in a free rental market. They might opt for a split market, controlled for small business, and free for corporate business, resulting in a fairer balance of economic opportunity as well as consumer choice. At the regional level, legislation might be introduced entailing that infrastructural and tax incentives for productive investment had to be paid back if the business decides to pack up and leave – perhaps by a regional Tobin tax of sorts. As long as the nation state continued to provide an important rallying point for civic identity, its principal role would be to act as a mediator between local and regional interests internally, and to represent these interests in the international arena. There, necessary institutions like the World Bank and IMF would have to become federalized and governed by mutual agreement among regional councils.

In comparison to the traditional scheme of power division in federal systems, in other words, the radical act would be to put federalism back on its feet. I do not think that this is idealistic or utopian at all. Nor would it be economically inefficient, or constitute a return to the closed organic communities of the Middle Ages. If all the rhetoric about a second industrial divide, the rise of virtual communities and policy networks holds any water at all, citizens will be able to make intelligent choices about local *and* world markets. In other words, this is not an argument against free trade. It is one about a reallocation of the powers of determining what should be free in free trade.

(3) Common Universal Standards of Socio-economic Behaviour

As a community of communities with power everywhere, 'even at the centre', such a pluralized system of federalism requires agreement on universal social rights and standards of common economic conduct including environmental protection. Maybe *this is* idealistic. But it is the kind of idealism without which even the most traditional scheme of representative democracy cannot be sustained.

The idea of a universal charter of social and economic rights is not new. It can be traced back to British Chartism, which was a 'a movement for civil rights, not bread' (Harrington, 1990, p. 6). It was endorsed, in principle, even though substantively watered down later on, by the architects of the European Single Market (Dinan, 1999, pp. 423–28). The idea of some form of guaranteed minimum income has been a persistent theme in conceptualizations of welfare in federal systems (Hirst, 1994; Geay, 1996). It even found its way into the recommendations on economic development by a Canadian Royal Commission, as a 'Universal Income Security Program' to offset the negative effects of trade liberalization on 'equity, security, opportunity, responsibility and sharing' (*Report*, 1985, pp. 537–38, pp. 794–95). In an age of globalized financial transactions, however, it ought to be coupled with a chartered protection of savings and pensions, prohibiting the losses incurred from financial speculation to be passed on to individual citizens or the collective saving plans of entire social communities. Such a provision probably would do more in the way of curbing the excesses of 'casino capitalism' (Strange, 1986) than as an appeal to self-binding regulations (Reinicke, 1998; Hueglin, 1999c). The idea of sanctions to enforce minimum standards of environmental, labour and human rights protection, through the imposition of social tariffs also is not new (Cohen, 1992).

Most federal systems also have recognized the need for fiscal equalization of spatial inequities.[4] The Canadian Charter of Rights and Freedoms affirms that all provinces must be able 'to provide reasonably comparable levels of public services at reasonably comparable levels of taxation' (Section 36.2). The German Basic Law stipulates the 'equitability of living conditions' as the underlying principle of fiscal equalization (Article 106.3). The principle behind these stipulations should find much wider application. Framed as an unconditional general commitment, fiscal equalization would allow different communities to pursue a wide range of policy options – albeit subject to the usual constraints arising from individual rights and due process provisions. It is also conceivable extending equalization entitlements to social communities as constituted under the provisions for mixed bicameralism. Providing Black communities in the United States with a right to equalized funds for self-organized education, for instance, might make a lot more sense than did bussing their children into hostile environments.

---

[4] Among the major federations, the United States is the only one without a commitment to a 'generalized equalization scheme' (Watts, 1999, p. 54). Americans tend to react angrily when their federal system is exposed as a case of fiscal exceptionalism. Rightly, they will point to the equalizing effects of the federal grants system. 'Effects', however, are not the same as 'commitment'.

The elements of a universal charter of social and economic rights, in other words, exist to varying degrees in theory and practice. They are endorsed in principle, by socialists and social democrats as well as 'enlightened reactionaries'. The prospects for such a universal charter are dim nevertheless. The thrust of the WTO and the – for now aborted – MAI is exactly to skirt the issue (Howlett, Netherton and Ramesh, 1999, p. 136), and to further constrain nation state governments (Robinson, 1995). Given the broad support across ideological boundaries, it is difficult to see this state of affairs as a transnational capitalist conspiracy alone. Rather, I would suggest, it is once again a consequence of the inadequate structuration of public space and discourse. Chartist Bronterre O'Brien understood this very well when he exclaimed: 'Thus your poverty is the result not the cause of your being unrepresented' (quoted in Bowles and Gintis, 1987, p. 9).

Universal norms and standards furthermore do not sit well with the 'growing incredulity toward foundational meta-narratives' (White, 1994, p. 117) associated with postmodernism, feminism, identity politics, social movements and the politics of diversity in general. Yet few would deny that at least some general rules of universal solidarity are needed, not only in order to protect the weaker from the stronger, but also in order to provide a balance between the common and the particular. I would argue that skepticism or outright rejection are not so much directed at universal norms and standards *per se* as they are directed at the defining processes leading to their establishment. My suggestion would be that the institution of a universal charter of social and economic rights can be federalized itself, as a charter of charters. The meaning of social solidarity is different for industrial and developing societies, Christians and Muslims, agrarian and urban populations. Regional and community charters would spell out particular principles of social and economic justice. Much in the sense of framework legislation, a universal charter would have to establish general principles on the basis of mutual agreement among a variety of different communities. These principles would in turn frame the variety and flexibility of particular charter provisions.

Such flexibility might even help to save existing trade regimes such as the WTO where fundamental differences between the United States and the European Union openly clash over principles of health and food safety (Dinan, 1999, pp. 548–51). With regard to hormone-treated beef or genetically modified organisms, for instance, the American principle is *innocent until proven guilty*. The European principle is *suspect until proven innocent*. Within the European Union, similar differences exist between Britain and continental Europe over environmental regulation (Sbragia, 1997). The insistence on regulation according to universal standards might blow trade regimes apart in the end. The acceptance of difference might deuniversalize trade in some areas but save the general commitment – not even to speak of the possibility that the formal inclusion of a wider plurality of spatial and social constituencies in the process of negotiation might change altogether the discourse about what is right and what is wrong.

One essential prerequisite for a pluralized world of organized justice is the open ended access to information and communication. The current rave of merger mania in the multinational entertainment and information industry (*The Economist*, January 15th, 2000, pp. 22–24) does not bode well for a diversified discourse on right and wrong. Former US presidential adviser Zbigniew Brzezinski already coined the expression for a new world discourse: 'tittytainment', a combination of 'entertainment' and 'tits' that would keep the masses happy in a world beyond their control (Martin and Schumann, 1997, p. 13). There is of course no point demanding that CNN and Microsoft should have to confine their activities to any other than a global community. These are communication highways that do provide information about what is global, and they also can facilitate the efforts of small communities to get their messages out. But a federalized scheme of information and communication needs to insist on far more radical limits to the monopolization of media ownership.

Media subsidiaries in different countries could be made accountable to independent and indigenous supervisory boards. A tax could be imposed on media profits resulting from transborder activities. Collected revenue could be used to subsidize the independence of information sources unable to attract financing from business advertising. In fact, the commitment to providing equitable public services in federal systems could simply be extended to include the provision of equitable sources of information, community newspapers, television channels and so on. As a corollary, of course, the secrecy of deliberations in intergovernmental relations, trade tribunals and all other forms of political deliberation at all levels of governance would have to be replaced with open door policies and full disclosure (see Robinson, 1995, p. 375).

Conclusion: Medieval Anarchy or Federal Plurality?

The brave new world of integration and fragmentation has already been likened to the medieval world of anarchy (Bull, 1977). Then as now, governance was pluralized among a multitude of smaller and larger communities, local fiefdoms, city republics, principalities, kingdoms and the Empire. Stability rested on the Emperor's ability to organize consent. When he failed, the power of the sword replaced politics. Solidarity existed *within* communities such as city republics, but rarely *among* them. When the thin bond of Christian universality was torn by the individualizing effects of Renaissance and Reformation, civil society was thrown into an abyss of religious and territorial wars. The rise of the Westphalian order eventually restored stability at least *within* the centralized territorial nation state, but rarely *among* these states. The fading of exclusive nation state sovereignty, the rise of multilevel governance in the European Union, and the intensification of distributive struggles in a globalizing world of universalized trade relations, all point to a massive restructuring of political space. Without a new commitment to solidarity, that globalizing world might indeed be on a slippery slope towards a neo-medieval world of intercommunal anarchy, thinly veiled only by occasional crusades against the infidel such as the Gulf War.

The entire idea of organized and balanced governance in pluralized settings is precisely what distinguishes federalism from medieval anarchy. The question is whether it can lead to a more enlightened regime of democratic plurality than either the Middle Ages or the modern state system. Ultimately, this is a question about whether the organization of plurality and consent, diversity and unity, autonomy and solidarity, is possible.

In her elegant critique of Jurgen Habermas and Benjamin Barber, Susan Bickford (1996, pp. 13–18) has pointed out how conceptualizations of consensus are grafted upon modernist notions of social harmony. Barber, she says, insists that in pluralized settings a 'creative consensus' can only be achieved through civic participation. The ultimate democratic goal is a 'common ordering of individual needs and wants into a single vision of the future'. For Habermas, she contends, communicative action is likewise 'oriented to achieving sustaining, and renewing consensus'. And whatever consensus is ultimately reached and agreed upon, it must be based on the 'force of the better argument' alone (all direct quotes from Habermas and Barber). As Bickford concludes, there is in these arguments an underlying normative assumption aiming at purification and elimination of an adversarial and strategic mode of communication.

The point is not whether this is an entirely correct or even fair interpretation of Barber and Habermas (I think it is). But it allows one to rethink the policy making process in federal systems as what might be called a balanced process of open-ended deliberation. Its institutional prerequisites are opportunity structures of pluralized inclusion. Its dynamic is a perpetual and plural process of community building rather than the constitutional fixation on vested territorial interests. Its social fundament is informed open-mindedness. Its ultimate goal is the democratic inhabitation of new political spaces.

I conclude with the opening sentence: This is a think piece. I do not claim that there is a federal solution to all of the world's ills. But I insist that a new, new left serious about radical and plural democracy, and about social and material justice, without which democracy is meaningless, needs to rethink its historically negative attitude about federalism. In a globalizing world of integration and fragmentation, plural communities and multilevel governance, it can either continue to dream a dream of democratic centralism, or it can fight a fight for the democratic empowerment of new spaces. There is no Third Way.

References

Albert, M. (1998), ' Entgrenzung und Formierung neuer politischer Räume', in B. Kohler-Koch (ed.), *Regieren in entgrenzten Räumen*, PVS Sonderheft 29, Westdeutscher Verlag, Opladen, pp. 49–76.

Anderson, C.W. (1979), 'Political Design and the Representation of Interests', in P.C. Schmitter and G. Lehmbruch (eds.), *Trends Toward Corporatist Intermediation*, Sage, Beverly Hills, pp. 271–98.

Aznar, L. (1994), 'Democratic Societies at the Time of Market Authoritarianism', presented paper at the International Poltical Science Association, World Congress 1994, Berlin.

Bahro, R., Mandel E. and von Oertzen, P. (1980), *Was da alles auf uns zukommt*, Olle & Wolter, Berlin.

Barker, P. (1998), 'Disentangling the Federation: Social Policy and Fiscal Federalism', in M. Westmacott and H. Mellon (eds.), *Challenges to Canadian Federalism*, Prentice Hall, Scarborough, pp. 144–56.

Bauer, O. (1924), *Die Nationalitätenfrage und die Sozialdemokratie*, Verlag der Wiener Volksbuchhandlung, Wien.

Beck, U. (1999), *World Risk Society*, Polity Press, Cambridge.

Bickford, S. (1996), *The Dissonance of Democracy: Listening, Conflict, and Citizenship*, Cornell University Press, Ithaca.

Black, A. (1984), *Guilds and Civil Society in European Political Thought from the Twelfth Century to the Present*, Cornell University Press, Ithaca.

Bobbio, N. (1972), 'Il federalismo nel dibattito politico e culturale della resistenza', in S. Pistone (ed.) *L'idea dell' unificazione europea dalla prima alla seconda guerra mondiale*, Einaudi, Torino, pp. 221–36.

Bottomore, T. (ed.) (1983), *A Dictionary of Marxist Thought*, Harvard University Press, Cambridge.

Bottomore, T. and Goode, P. (1978), *Austro-Marxism*, Clarendon Press, Oxford.

Bowles, S. and Gintis, H. (1987), *Democracy and Capitalism*, Basic Books, New York.

Brodie, J. (1990), *The Political Economy of Canadian Regionalism*, Harcourt, Toronto.

Brugmans, H. (1965), *L'Idée européenne, 1918–1965*, De Tempel, Bruges.

Buber, M. (1950), *Zwischen Gesellschaft und Staat, Werke*, Vol. 1, 1962, Kösel, München.

Bull, H. (1977), *The Anarchical Society*, Macmillan, London.

Campanella, M.L. (1995), 'Getting the Core: A Neo-Institutionalist Approach to the EMU', *Government and Opposition*, Vol. 30(3), pp. 347–69.

Cohen, J.L. and Arato, A. (1992), *Civil Society and Political Theory*, MIT Press, Cambridge.

Cohen, M.G. (1992), 'Social Democracy – Illusion or Vision?', *Studies in Political Economy*, Vol. 37, pp. 158–9.

Cole, G.D.H. (1920), *Guild Socialism Re-Stated*, Parsons, London [repr. with an introduction by R. Vernon (1980), Transaction Books, New Brunswick].

Conway, J.F. (1983), *The West: The History of a Region in Confederation*, James Lorimer, Toronto.

Council of Canadians (1998), http://www.canadians.org/index.html, Campaigns – Archive – Multilateral Agreement on Investment – Publications – France's Official Position), September.

Diez, T. (1996), 'Postmoderne und europäische Integration', *Zeitschrift für Internationale Beziehungen*, Vol. 3(2), pp. 255–81.

Dinan, D. (1999), *Ever Closer Union*, Lynne Rienner, Boulder.

Dyson, K. (1980), *The State Tradition in Western Europe*, Martin Robertson, Oxford.

Elazar, D.J. (1994), *Covenant and Polity in Biblical Israel*, Transaction Press, New Jersey.

Elkins, D. (1995), *Beyond Sovereignty: Territory and Political Economy in the Twenty-first Century*, University of Toronto Press, Toronto.

Figgis, J.N. (1913), *Churches in the Modern State*, Russell & Russell, New York [repr. 1973].

Figgis, J.N. (1916), *Studies of Political Thought: From Gerson to Grotius 1414–1625*, Cambridge University Press, Cambridge.

Føllesdal, A. (1998), 'Survey Article: Subsidiarity', *The Journal of Political Philosophy*, Vol. 6(2), pp. 190–218.

Friedrich, C.J. (1975), 'The Politics of Language and Corporate Federalism', in J.G. Savard and R. Vigneault (eds.), *Les Etats Multilingues, problemes et solutions*, Les Presses de l'Universite Laval, Quebec, pp. 227–42.

Geay, M. (1996), 'Interrogations sur le minimum social garanti et l'éonomie fèdèraliste', *L'Europe en Formation*, Vol. 302, pp. 43–76.

Giddens, A. (1984), *The Constitution of Society*, University of California Press, Berkeley.

Gill, S. (1992), 'The Emerging World Order and European Change', *Socialist Register*, Merlin Press, London, pp. 157–96.

Greven, M.Th. (1997), 'Politisierung ohne Citoyens', in A. Klein and R. Schmalz–Bruns (eds.), *Politische Beteiligung und Bürgerengagement in Deutschland*, Bundeszentrale für politische Bildung, Vol. 347, pp. 231–51.

Greven, M.Th. (1998), 'Output–Legitimation', in M. Buckmiller and J. Perels (eds.), *Opposition als Triebkraft der Demokratie*, Offizin-Verlag, Hannover, pp. 477–91.

Hafen, T. (1994), 'Zusammenfassung der Diskussion', in A. Riklin and G. Batliner (eds.), *Subsidiarität*, Nomos, Baden-Baden, pp. 119–32.

Harrington, M. (1990), *Socialism Past & Future*, Penguin, New York.

Harvey, D. (1989), *The Condition of Postmodernity*, Basil Blackwell, Oxford.

Held, D. (1992), 'Democracy: From City-states to a Cosmopolitan Order?', in D. Held (ed.), *Political Studies XL*, Special Issue: Prospects for Democracy, Blackwell, Oxford, pp. 10–39.

Held, D. (1995), *Democracy and the Global Order*, Stanford University Press, Stanford.

Hesse, K. (1962), *Der unitarische Bundesstaat*, C.F. Müller, Karlsruhe.

Hirst, P. (1994), *Associative Democracy*, The University of Massachusetts Press, Amherst.

Hirst, P. and Thompson, G. (1996), *Globalization in Question*, Polity Press, Cambridge.

Hobbes, T. (1983), *De Cive* [Citizen 1642], in H. Warrender (ed.), *De Cive: the English Version Entitled, in the First Edition, Philosophical Rudiments Concerning Government and Society/Thomas Hobbes*, Clarendon Press, Oxford.

Howlett, M., Netherton, A. and Ramesh, M. (1999), *The Political Economy of Canada*, Oxford University Press, Don Mills.

Hudson, R. and Réno, F. (eds.) (2000), *Politics of Identity: Migrants and Minorities in Multicultural States*, St. Martin's Press, New York.

Hueglin, T.O. (1993), 'Exploring Concepts of Treaty Federalism', research report, Royal Commission on Aboriginal Peoples, Government of Canada, Ottawa, CD-Rom.

Hueglin, T.O. (1994a), 'Federalism, Subsidiarity and the European Tradition: Some Clarifications', *Telos*, Vol. 100, pp. 37–55.

Hueglin, T.O. (1994b), 'Johannes Althusius and the Modern Concept of Civil Society', in A. Bibic and G. Graziano (eds.), *Civil Society, Political Society, Democracy*, Slovenian Political Science Association, Ljubljana, pp. 73–93.

The Third Way Transformation of Social Democracy

Hueglin, T.O. (1999a), 'Government, Governance, Governmentality: The European Union as a Universalist Project', in B. Kohler-Koch and R. Eising (eds.), *The Transformation of Governance in the European Union*, Routledge, London, pp. 249–66.

Hueglin, T.O. (1999b), *Early Modern Concepts for a Late Modern World: Althusius on Community and Federalism*, WLU Press, Waterloo.

Hueglin, T.O. (1999c), 'Globalization Without Citizens', in C. Lankowski (ed.), *Governing Beyond the Nation-State*, American Institute for Contemporary German Studies, Washington D.C., pp. 41–64.

Huntington, S. (1974), 'Postindustrial Politics: How Benign Will It Be?', *Comparative Politics*, Vol. 6, pp. 163–91.

Jerusalem, F. (1949), *Die Staatsidee des Föderalismus*, Mohr, Tübingen.

Keane, J. (1988), *Democracy and Civil Society*, Verso, London.

Kielmansegg, Graf P. (1996), 'Integration und Demokratie', in M. Jachtenfuchs and B. Kohler-Koch (eds.), *Europäische Integration*, Leske + Budrich, Opladen, pp. 47–72.

Kinsky, F. (1995), *Federalism: A Global Theory*, Presses d'Europe, Nice.

Kohler-Koch, B. (1996), 'The Evolution of Organized Interests in the EC: Driving Forces, Co-Evolution or New Type of Governance?', in H. Wallace (ed.), *Participation and Policy Making in the European Union*, Oxford University Press, Oxford, pp. 42–68.

Kohler-Koch, B. (ed.) (1998), *Regieren in entgrenzten Räumen*, PVS Sonderheft 29, Westdeutscher Verlag, Opladen.

Laski, H.J. (1930), *A Grammar of Politics*, Allen & Unwin, London, 1925 [repr. 1930].

Laski, H.J. (1972), 'Historical Introduction', in *A Defence of Liberty Against Tyrants*, a translation of the *Vindiciae Contra Tyrannos*, anonymously published under the pseudonym of Junius Brutus in 1579 (New York: Burt Franklin, 1924; repr. 1972), pp. 1–60.

Lipgens, W. (1968), *Europa-Föderationspläne der Widerstandsbewegungen 1940-1945*, Oldenbourg, München.

Lowi, T. (1984), 'Why Is There No Socialism in the United States: A Federal Analysis', *International Political Science Review*, Vol. 5(4), pp. 369–80.

Machiavelli, N. (1977), *Discorsi* [1513–20], in N. Machiavelli (1977), *Il Principe e Discorsi sopra la prima deca di Tito Livio*, Feltrinelli Economica, Milano.

Martin, H.-P. and H. Schumann (1997), *Die Globalisierungsfalle*, Rowohlt, Reinbek.

Marx, K. (1976), 'Moralising Criticism and Critical Morality', Deutsche-Brüsseler-Zeitung No. 92, November 18 (1847), in K. Marx and F. Engels (1976), *Collected Works*, Vol. 6, Lawrence & Wishart, London, pp. 312–40.

Marx, K. and Engels, F. (1976), 'Manifesto of the Communist Party' (1848), in K. Marx and F. Engels, *Collected Works*, Vol. 6, Lawrence & Wishart, London, pp. 477–519.

McQuaig, L. (1999), *The Cult of Impotence*, Penguin, Toronto, 1999.

Mitscherlich, A. (1947), 'Entwicklungsgrundlagen eines freien Sozialismus', in A. Weber et al. (eds.), *Freier Sozialismus*, Lambert Schneider, Heidelberg, pp. 9–35.

Montesquieu, C. (1977), *L'Esprit des Lois* [1748], transl. as The Spirit of Laws, first English transl. by Thomas Nugent [1750], reedited by David W. Carrithers (Berkeley: University of California Press, 1977).

Mouffe, C. (1992), 'Preface: Democratic Politics Today', in C. Mouffe (ed.), *Dimensions of Radical Democracy*, Verso, London, pp. 1–14.

Neumann, F. (1967), *Demokratischer und autoritärer Staat*, Europäische Verlagsanstalt, Frankfurt.

Nicholls, D. (1994), *The Pluralist State*, St. Martin's Press, New York.

O'Connor, J. (1973), *The Fiscal Crisis of the State*, St. Martin's Press, New York.

Olsen, M. (1965), *The Logic of Collective Action: Public Goods and the Theory of Groups*, Harvard University Press, Cambridge.

Panitch, L. (1986), 'The Tripartite Experience', in K. Banting (ed.), *The State and Economic Interests*, University of Toronto Press, Toronto, pp. 37–119.

Polanyi, K. (1944), *The Great Transformation*, Beacon Press, Boston [repr. 1957].

Proudhon, Pierre-Joseph (1863), *Du Principe Federatif et de la Necessite de Reconstituer le Parti de la Revolution* (Paris); abr. English transl. In Richard Vernon (transl. and intr.), *The Principle of Federation by P.-J. Proudhon* (Toronto: University of Toronto Press, 1979).

Putnam, R.D. (1988), 'Diplomacy and domestic politics: the logic of two-level games', *International Organization*, Vol. 42(3), pp. 427–60.

Reinicke, W.H. (1998), *Global Public Policy*, Brookings Institution Press, Washington D.C.

Report (1985), Royal Commission on the Economic Union and Development Prospects for Canada, Vol. 2, Minister of Supply and Services Canada, Ottawa.

Riker, W. (1964), *Federalism: Origin, Operation, Significance*, Little, Brown, Boston.

Rivlin, A. (1995), 'American Federalism: An Economic Perspective', in K. Knop et al. (eds.), *Rethinking Federalism: Citizens, Markets, and Governments in a Changing World*, UBC Press, Vancouver, pp. 196–202.

Robinson, I. (1995), 'Globalization and Democracy', *Dissent*, Summer, pp. 373–80.

Roemheld, L. (1990), *Integral Federalism*, Peter Lang, New York.

Salmon, J.H.M. (1975), *Society in Crisis: France in the Sixteenth Century*, St. Martin's Press, New York.

Sbragia, A. (1997), 'Environmental Policy: The 'Push-Pull' of Policy-Making', in H. Wallace and W. Wallace (eds.), *Policy-Making in the European Union*, Oxford University Press, Oxford, pp. 235–56.

Scharpf, F.W. (1988), 'The Joint-Decision Trap: Lessons from German Federalism and European Integration', *Public Administration*, Vol. 66, pp. 239–78.

Scharpf, F.W. (1998), 'Demokratische Politik in der internationalisierten Demokratie', in M.Th. Greven (ed.), *Demokratie - Eine Kultur des Westens?*, Westdeutscher Verlag, Opladen, pp. 81–103.

Schmitdke, O. (1996), *Politics of Identity*, Pro Universitate, Sinzheim.

Schmitter, Ph.C. (1995), 'The Irony of Modern Democracy and the Viability of Efforts to Reform its Practice', in E.O. Wright (ed.), *Associations and Democracy*, Verso, London, pp. 167–83.

Simeon, R. and Robinson, I. (1990), *State, Society, and the Development of Canadian Federalism*, University of Toronto Press, Toronto.

Spinelli, A. (1972), 'European Union and the Resistance', in G. Ionescu (ed.), *The New Politics of European Integration*, Macmillan, London, 1972, pp. 1–9.

Strange, S. (1986), *Casino Capitalism*, Blackwell, Oxford.

Tassin, E. (1992), 'Europe: A Political Community?', in Ch. Mouffe (ed.), *Dimensions of Radical Democracy: Pluralism, Citizenship, Community*, Verso, London, pp. 169–92.

Tully, J. (1995), *Strange Multiplicity: Constitutionalism in an Age of Diversity*, Cambridge University Press, Cambridge.

Vernon, R. (1979), 'Introduction', *The Principle of Federation by P.-J. Proudhon*, University of Toronto Press, Toronto, pp. xi–xlvii.

Voyenne, B. (1973), *Le Fédéralisme de P.J. Proudhon*, Presses d'Europe, Nice.

Voyenne, B. (1981), *Histoire de l'Idée Fédéraliste: Les Lignées Proudhoniennes*, Presses d'Europe, Nice.

Walzer, M. (1983), *Spheres of Justice: A Defense of Pluralism and Equality*, Basic Books, New York.

Watts, R. (1999), *Comparing Federal Systems*, Institute of Intergovernmental Relations, Kingston.

White, S.K. (1994), *Political Theory and Postmodernism*, Cambridge University Press, Cambridge.

Wilson, J.Q. and J.J. Dilulio (1998), *American Government*, Houghton Mifflin, Boston.

Wolf, K.D. (1999), 'Defending State Autonomy: Intergovernmental Governance in the European Union', in B. Kohler-Koch and R. Eising (eds.), *The Transformation of Governance in the European Union*, Routledge, London, pp. 231–66.

Wright, E.O. (ed.) (1995), *Associations and Democracy*, Verso, London.

Young, I.M. (1990), *Justice and the Politics of Difference*, Princeton University Press, Princeton.

Zürn, M. (1992), 'Jenseits der Staatlichkeit: Uber die Folgen der ungleichzeitigen Denationalisierung', *Leviathan*, pp. 490–513.

Index